Activism For Life

ANGIE ZELTER

Luath Press Limited

EDINBURGH

www.luath.co.uk

First published 2021

ISBN: 978-1-910022-39-9

The author's right to be identified as author of this book
under the Copyright, Designs and Patents Act 1988 has been asserted.

This book is made of materials from well-managed,
FSC®-certified forests and other controlled sources.

Printed and bound
by Ashford Colour Press, Gosport

Typeset in 11 point Sabon
by Main Point Books, Edinburgh

Images © Angie Zelter unless otherwise stated.

ANGIE ZEL1 ι an active campaigner for most of her life. She has designed and participa.... ... nonviolent civil resistance campaigns and founded several innovative and effective campaigns. Her protests have been for a nuclear free world, that shares global resources equitably and sustainably while respecting human rights and the rights of other life forms. As a global citizen she has expressed her solidarity with movements all over the world. This has led to numerous arrests, court appearances and incarceration. Angie has been arrested around 200 times, mostly in the UK, and in Belgium, Canada, France, Germany, Gran Canaria, Holland, Israel/Palestine, Malaysia, Poland and South Korea. She has spent over two years in total in prison awaiting trials on remand or serving sentences. All for nonviolent resistance protests. The author of several books, she is the recipient of the 1997 Sean McBride Peace Prize (for the Seeds of Hope Ploughshares action), the 2001 Right Livelihood Award (on behalf of Trident Ploughshares) and the Hrant Dink Prize in 2014. She continues to actively confront the abuses of corporations, governments and the military.

It has been one of the privileges of my life to be with Angie as she stands up for justice, peace and the environment. She personifies what being an activist means – courage, commitment and a conscience. She's an inspiration to us all.—CAROLINE LUCAS MP.

Angie Zelter's lifelong commitment to her campaigns and PICAT [Public Interest Case Against Trident] legal actions have been a major force towards nuclear disarmament and informing my own conclusion that we should say 'No to Trident.'—COMMANDER ROBERT FORSYTH, ROYAL NAVY (RETIRED)

With decades of experience of local, national and international campaigning on many of the key issues of our time Angie Zelter has distilled an extraordinary amount of determination and learning into an absolute gem of a book.—PROFESSOR PAUL ROGERS

Front cover photo, Lake Padarn by Snowdonia in Wales: Hefin Owen (cc) via Flickr
Back cover photo, Faslane Nuclear Submarine Base: Neil Williamson (cc) via Flickr
Author photo: Charlie Beresford

Windsor and Maidenhead

95800000187281

A prophetic voice from the frontline of nonviolent activism, Angie's book is a riveting account of what it really means to practice the conviction that there is no way to peace, because peace is the way. And though she is probably best-known as a passionate campaigner against nuclear weapons, which is where so many members of the Iona Community have encountered her, her belief that 'human rights, land rights and indigenous peoples' rights are all part of our struggle for a more just, equitable, peaceful and truly democratic world' has taken her to stand with defenders of life on earth in many places and situations. Her practical experience and wisdom, hard-won over a lifetime, make this an invaluable handbook for a new generation of activists committed to a better future.—KATHY GALLOWAY, THE IONA COMMUNITY*

Dyma lyfr sy'n gweld y cysylltiad rhwng pob achos dyngarol - rhwng heddwch a chwarae teg, rhwng cymdeithas wâr ac amgylchfyd iach, rhwng hawl i siarad iaith a hawl i fyw heb ofn trais. Mae Angie Zelter yn myfyrio dros oes o ymgyrchu dros y pethau hyn gan rannu cyngor a phrofiad. Trwy'r cyfan mae'n cynnig gobaith ac ysbrydoliaeth, ac yn ein hannog i wneud beth bynnag sy'n gymwys i ni fel unigolion i wella amgylchiadau'r byd a'i bobl. Y pwythau sy'n rhwymo'r penodau at ei gilydd yw'r tri gair bach, mawr: 'Never give up!

This is a book that will fill you with awe and admiration, suspense and surprise, but above all, it will offer inspiration and hope. From the mundane grind of letter-writing to daring adventures the world over, Angie Zelter reflects on a lifetime of campaigning for a fairer, better society. She shares advice based on real-life experience – what went wrong, what worked – and in the way she recognises that it will take action of every description to bring peace to the planet, she encourages us all to think about how we too can contribute to this goal. The book chimes with phrases that are sometimes practical, sometimes aspirational, always encouraging. The thread that stitches the pages together is three words long: 'Never give up!'—PROFESSOR MERERID HOPWOOD, OUTGOING CHAIR OF CYDEITHAS Y CYMOD (INTERNATIONAL FELLOWSHIP OF RECONCILIATION, WALES) AND VICE PRESIDENT OF THE MOVEMENT FOR THE ABOLITION OF WAR)*

She did not hesitate. She just walked along the Gureombi Rock coast fenced for the Jeju navy base construction. And it was a while later that we discovered Angie with her bright smile inside the fence with the policemen in the background. 10 days later, the Gureombi Rock began to be blasted. The struggle to save the Gureombi Rock coast had reached its peak. Angie stayed with us for a month and was arrested three times for her nonviolent direct actions. When a Korean policeman inquired about her name, she said it is 'World Citizen' and about her nation, she said she came from Gureombi. In her last arrest, she got an exit order. She left us a gift of a flag with an image of the Earth without any artificial nation borders. It is not only me but many people in Gangjeong who have been greatly affected by her legacy. After her visit to Ganjeong, she is one of our greatest inspirations to keep us fighting against this base.—CHOI SUNG-HEE, GANJEONG VILLAGE RESIDENT/PEACE ACTIVIST

Books by the same author:

Snowball: The Story of a Nonviolent Civil Disobedience Campaign in Britain (ed with Oliver Bernard), Arya Bhusan Bhardwaj, 1990
Trident on Trial: The Case for People's Disarmament, Luath Press, 2001
Faslane 365: A Year of Anti-nuclear Blockades, Luath Press, 2008
Trident and International Law: Scotland's Obligations (with Rebecca Johnson), Luath Press, 2011
World in Chains: Nuclear Weapons, Militarisation and Their Impact on Society (ed), Luath Press, 2014

Dedicated to all living beings on planet Earth
at this crucial time of change.

To the humans among us –
let's remember we are global citizens.

We either go forward together to a more equitable,
fair and compassionate global society
or we will destroy ourselves
and our once diverse home.

Let us all join our hearts and minds
and act in the interests of all life forms.

We know the solutions – let's act now.

Contents

Preface

OVER THE YEARS I have often been asked to reflect on various actions or events that I have taken part in. So, when I was invited to Gothenburg in Sweden in 2010, I delivered a talk which encapsulated some lessons for lifelong activism. I later developed these as a slide show for Bradford University in 2015. The 'lessons' proved of great interest to the people who heard them and I was asked to write down more of my experiences.

This book builds on these lessons, and is an attempt to reflect on some of the campaigns and actions I have been involved in. It covers campaigns and movements that include the Greenham Common Women's Peace Camp, the Snowball Civil Disobedience Campaign, SOS Sarawak, the UK Forests Network, the Citizens' Recovery of Indigenous Peoples' Stolen Property Organisation, the Seeds of Hope Ploughshares, Trident Ploughshares, the International Women's Peace Service – Palestine, Faslane 365, Save Jeju Now, Action AWE, the Public Interest Case Against Trident and Extinction Rebellion Peace.

It is 50 years since I left university, started my real education and began thinking about how I could help create a better world. This is the story of my personal journey to make sense of a world that I knew was teetering on the edge of self-destruction. Instead of despairing and becoming a part of the problem, or just putting my head in the sand and ignoring it all, I wanted to find ways to change the age-old patterns of exploitation, power abuse and fear that were fuelling the nuclear arms race, environmental destruction and ecocide on our planet. That meant changing my lifestyle and learning from past nonviolent struggles against oppression.

These recollections focus on my campaigning life and show how an ordinary woman like myself chose to respond to some of the most serious and challenging issues of my era. The Appendices contain documents and reports which provide extra information on nonviolence and solidarity campaigning.

Angie Zelter
February 2021

Foreword by Kate Dewes

Kate Dewes ran the South Island office of the Aotearoa/New Zealand Peace Foundation from 1980 and has co-directed the Disarmament & Security Centre[1] with her husband Robert Green since 1998. She was a member of the Public Advisory Committee on Disarmament and Arms Control for nine years; the New Zealand government's NGO expert on the UN Study on Disarmament and Non-Proliferation Education 2000–02, and a member of the UN Secretary-General's Advisory Board on Disarmament Matters 2008–13.

AS A FELLOW woman peace activist committed to nonviolent direct action, my anti-nuclear campaigning in New Zealand began during the mid-1970s Peace Squadron actions. In small boats we confronted US and UK nuclear-powered and probably nuclear-armed warships visiting our ports. We used these spectacular confrontations, attracting extensive national and international media coverage, to help generate hundreds of grassroots peace groups, which led to our iconic 1987 nuclear-free legislation banning these warship visits.

My first contact with Angie Zelter was during the decade-long World Court Project, pioneered in Christchurch when, as Secretary of the UK Institute for Law and Peace, she distributed information about the international laws of war. She also established the Snowball Enforce the Law Campaign which involved arrests, court cases and imprisonment. This followed her first arrest during the early 1980s women's occupation of the US base for nuclear-armed cruise missiles at Greenham Common. Women returning home to young families and other responsibilities were encouraged to 'think globally, act locally', and 'Carry Greenham Home' to highlight the issues at local military and intelligence-gathering bases. Globally, women's groups protested in solidarity with the Greenham campaigners.

The various campaigns Angie initiated often used creative, courageous, sometimes humorous and colourful actions to uphold international law over national legislation. Media attention raised public awareness about the issues. Her campaigns challenged deeply entrenched UK government practices and reliance on public deference to authority. She even had the principled audacity to write a *DIY Guide to Putting the Government on Trial* in an attempt to get the courts to outlaw British nuclear weapons. Her careful preparation of documents and uniquely inclusive campaigning skills attracted support from sympathetic lawyers, and her actions advanced the many different causes she espoused.

Like Gandhi and other nonviolent peace leaders before her, Angie represented herself in court, enabling her to say things traditional lawyers could not. She demanded that legal proceedings were accessible to ordinary people and were conducted in plain language. While in prison, she agitated successfully for improved hygiene and conditions for women inmates.

This memoir of her life as a dedicated anti-nuclear and environmental campaigner highlights lessons learnt from her extraordinarily diverse experiences. In effect it is a most valuable handbook for all campaigners, especially young people, on how not to waste energy on ineffective protest for its own sake. She learnt that

> effective campaigning needs *sustained* nonviolent direct action combined with education of the public, lobbying, negotiating and... it needs clearly communicated requests or demands that can be implemented by the people or organisations targeted.

Angie's seemingly inexhaustible energy and zeal are balanced by extraordinary humility as she follows the thread of her many courageous actions sustained over half a century. She gently encourages us to 'take each step in good faith and learn and adapt as you go along', 'set a time limit on each action' to prevent burnout, and above all remember: 'it is better to try and fail than not to try' to do what we can to change the world.

Foreword by Alice Slater

Alice Slater serves on the boards of World Beyond War, the Global Network Against Weapons and Nuclear Power in Space. She represents the Nuclear Age Peace Foundation at the United Nations and works with the People's Climate Committee, NYC, working for 100 per cent green energy by 2030.

AT A TIME when our whole world is so painfully experiencing the murderous excesses of patriarchy and untrammelled capitalism, with the very existence of humanity threatened, Zelter's experiences demonstrate how any one of us can make a difference and be effective in ending bad policies and building a better world.

She relates a moment in her life when her eyes were opened to the major crises facing life on Earth, and from then on, it seems like there was just one thing after another in a lifetime of working for a better world. She starts out in Cameroon as a newly-wed, where she observes the dehumanising and oppressive system of British colonialism, returns to the UK where she joins up with the women of Greenham Common to protest nuclear war and the missiles stationed there and continues by engaging in all forms of nonviolent protests, being arrested many times over the years. She writes powerfully about how she challenged the prison system and revealed to the world the terrible conditions that existed in jails, particularly how women were affected. She publicised the folly of the law and the legal system that protected the military installations. She learnt how to organise and broaden community organisations which could engage the media, the press, the legal structures: all to get the word out and move public opinion.

Her activism led her from campaigns within the peace movement to ban the bomb, to working with environmental groups in Malaysia and Canada publicising the truth about forest destruction and the great injustices done to indigenous people who were trying to save their forests from corporate greed and relentless consumerism. She has worked and been arrested providing support and solidarity with Palestinians in the rural communities of Salfit suffering under the harsh illegal Israeli military occupation of the West Bank. She ends with the wonderful new generation of climate activists in the UK's

Extinction Rebellion organising trying to stave off catastrophic climate disaster.

Undaunted, Zelter continues her work for a liveable Earth. She reminds us that any one of us can do it and has written some inspiring rules for engagement. Her passionate and persistent energy devoted to peace and justice is a shining example that we can all be a part of this. If you ever needed a good shot of political will, to encourage you to add your voice and your efforts to the work that lies ahead, read *Activism for Life* and get organised! Zelter's inspiring book reminds me of the famous aphorism from Margaret Mead, which illustrates the principles and encouragement Zelter provides:

> Never doubt that a small group of thoughtful committed individuals can change the world. In fact, it's the only thing that ever has!

The Beginning:
Cameroon, Sustainable Living and Greenham

I WENT TO Reading University to study Philosophy and Psychology. In 1972, my final year, I read the special edition of *The Ecologist* magazine called *A Blueprint for Survival.*[2] It was an eye-opener, as it introduced me to the major problems then facing our world – war, poverty, acid rain, ozone depletion, desertification, species loss, deforestation, greenhouse gases, civil and military nuclear power, pollution, endless economic growth and consumerism. I was astounded that having gone through a university education I had never come across most of these issues before. I realised that I was incredibly ignorant, and had to start taking responsibility for my own education by reading more widely and mixing with a greater variety of people. I had to question the dominant Western culture and open myself up to informal and alternative learning methods. As I read and thought more deeply about the crises facing life on Earth, I knew that I wanted to be a part of finding their solutions. On hearing of any problem I always want to be involved in finding out if there is anything I can do or change that will make the situation better. I cannot just forget it.

After my degree, at the age of 21, I decided to do some voluntary work in Africa with my husband. We spent three years in Cameroon, where I had the first of my two children and learnt lessons that have remained with me to this day. I was shocked to find that colonialism and racism still existed. Yes, I was very naive and ignorant. I still remember my shame and embarrassment when we held our first party one evening a few months after we arrived. The women were at one end of the room, the men at another, the white-skinned people on one side and the black-skinned on the other. The white expatriates (our neighbours) stayed on much later and started expressing their racist views and I could hardly believe what they were saying, nor could I hold back my tears.[3]

Expatriates like us were expected to have servants, which we refused to do, and that decision was criticised by our fellow expatriates. But I wanted to have a more equitable relationship with local Cameroonians and hated the idea of a servant/boss relationship. In any case I have always believed that people who are able to, however busy and important, should keep in touch with reality, do their own dirty work and look after their own daily needs. It is important to be as independent as possible.

It was quite funny to see the reactions when some of our Cameroonian friends came to visit and found my husband on his knees cleaning the floor. It was also very difficult at first to persuade Peter, a local banana plantation worker, who later became our best friend, to call us by our first names rather than Sir and Madam. We let his younger brother live for free in the 'servants' quarters' that were provided with each house in the government residential area where we lived, and we became very close to other members of his extended family.

I soon discovered that local land had been taken over by the UK and French governments and companies for timber, palm oil, rubber, banana, tea and cocoa plantations. I saw poverty in a land of plenty and began to understand the inequities of international trade. I also soon realised that volunteers got a lot more out of their stay than they were able to give to the host communities. The huge disparity between the wages that we expatriates received and those that locals received was shameful. We soon got an insight into the life of local people when we took a walk through the nearby village and got talking to Peter, who worked planting and caring for the bananas at a nearby plantation.

As the months went by we visited him frequently, and his oldest daughter was often sent by her mother to ask for sugar or tea or other foodstuffs that they were too poor to buy. Peter spent time with us at the weekends, taking us to meet his friends in other villages nearby, often to traditional 'elephant dances' where there was a great deal of dancing and singing, drinking of palm wine, and where newly-born infants were blessed by the spirits of elephants. He also took us up Mount Cameroon to explore the cloud forest and black lava fields where we could collect wild honey.

It was here in the forests of Equatorial Africa (from mangrove swamps, to tropical rainforests to cloud forests) that I came to passionately love trees and birds. The diversity was astounding. Once I looked out of the window and saw five different kinds of kingfisher, including the tiny pygmy kingfisher in beautiful blue, red and white. Later, while at the coast far below the town of Buea, where I lived, we saw the black, white and tan giant kingfisher along with sea snakes and an amazing view of the island of Fernando Po on the sea's horizon, which is usually hidden by sea mists but had suddenly emerged to look like a reflection of Mount Cameroon.

During my first year in Buea I was asked by a local man why I had come to Africa and I replied that I had come 'to help'! I was told very clearly that if I really wanted to 'help' Cameroon or any of the poorer countries of the world then I should go back home to the UK as that was where the problems originated. This really got me thinking. I realised it was too easy to think of the 'poor' people in 'third world countries' (as they were then called) and to look no further than the poverty, ignorance and local corruption. There was corruption, of course, as there is everywhere. But it was too easy to look at 'their' problems and issues and ignore the structural and global inequalities and corporate corruption underlying the realities of under-development. There was a need to understand the consequences of resource extraction and destruction of the environment caused by corporations and governments far away. I found that it was true that the majority of the problems faced by ordinary people in West Africa were caused by foreign powers and corporations extracting the oil, minerals, fish, timber and food from the land and seas. The extraction resulted in no gain for local people but in fact impoverished them and their environment, preventing them from developing themselves. My time in Cameroon resulted in my realising that the majority of my life's work would have to be dedicated to trying to stop my own country exploiting the resources of other peoples' lands.

Cameroon is an amazingly diverse place, geologically, culturally and linguistically, with over 250 languages. These languages are quite distinct and seem almost to change from village to village. Most locals that I met could speak up to ten of these different languages as well as Pidgin English. While there, I read widely about African history, the slave trade and often talked to the students at the Pan-African Institute for Development where my husband was teaching. They were mainly middle-level civil servants from anglophone African nations with a great deal to say about development issues.

While in Buea, I used to go to the local market and buy all the books in English in the African Writers Series, devouring the fascinating novels of Chinua Achebe, Camara Laye, Wole Soyinka, Ben Okri and many others. My mother-in-law had been born in Southern Rhodesia and my father-in-law had settled there when he was 21 years old.[4] They were very involved in supporting the Black independence movement. They were visited by many British historians while living in Salisbury and got to know Basil Davidson very well.[5] So of course, I read his books on the history of Zimbabwe. I still have a signed copy from him of his *Black Mother: The Years of the African Slave Trade.*[6]

When UDI (the Universal Declaration of Independence) was declared by the white regime under Ian Smith, people of their persuasion were likely to be rounded up and imprisoned. The family therefore moved to Northern Rhodesia, which was now happily independent and renamed Zambia. Their knowledge of African politics and the iniquities of British colonialism were very informative. When our three-year contract came to an end, I was carrying my second child and we had to decide whether to stay on in Cameroon or go home. We decided that it was time to return to the UK and put into practice our desire to live more sustainably, and try to stop the worst excesses of British companies and corporations that had continued the British contribution to the under-development and exploitation of Africa.

Returning to the UK in 1975, I moved to Norfolk with my two children, husband and parents-in-law. We were an extended family of six people and it was especially good for the children to have different role models. We were determined to live as sustainably as possible, keeping bees and chickens and growing fresh fruit and vegetables organically. I was fascinated to learn about the myriad soil organisms and read *The Living Soil.*[7] I soon got involved and helped start a local Norfolk-based joint Soil Association and HDRA (Henry Doubleday Research Association) group and still buy my organic seeds from Garden Organic which was founded by Lawrence D Hills.[8]

This was a special time for me with the children growing up, spending lots of time with them and growing food in our large garden. I had the extraordinary good fortune to meet and talk to the co-founder and first President of the Soil Association, Lady Eve Balfour, at Haughley, where I spent some time cataloguing her library.[9] At dinners with us volunteers she presided over fascinating talk around the table where everyone listened to each other. It felt so civilised and inclusive, and I was introduced to many of the classic organic books. I was especially impressed with *Farmers of Forty Centuries*, which explained how one could continue to grow food on small plots of land for centuries if you looked after the soil and recycled all waste back into the land.[10]

My concerns about how we produce food sustainably have stayed with me. I learnt to make and sell pottery and cane chairs, and my husband made beautiful hand-made furniture and taught the violin and cello. The children were lucky to have their grandparents living with them, as were we. We had lots of their friends visiting us at the weekends, many of whom were, as you would expect, from southern Africa. But we also had guests from other parts of the world, as my father-in-law was Romanian and my father was Armenian and my side of the family had moved to live in Vienna in Austria.[11] So we had a diverse group of people coming in and out of our home, enriching our lives with their different stories. Some people stayed for weeks and months at a time in our large house set in an acre of land, close to the sea and with our nearest neighbour over half a mile away. The creative and life-affirming practical work within a loving family sustained me over the following years of political activism, helping me avoid major burnout.

One of the books that influenced me and many of my generation was Schumacher's *Small Is Beautiful: A Study of Economics as if People Mattered*.[12] This, along with other books discussing growth economics and capitalism, sparked my interest in economic structures which continues to this day. It seemed that whatever problems I was looking into, the economic structures were holding everything back. Much later on I met Mary Mellor who taught me a great deal about the creation of money and how the banks create it out of thin air from debt (much of it from mortgages) and how it could instead be created on credit by the government and used in the public interest.[13] I now follow the admirable work of Positive Money, a group that educates and advocates for a money system that works for our society as a whole.[14]

We had returned home during the height of the Cold War and nuclear weapons were a major issue. I soon got involved in the peace movement and helped co-ordinate the local Cromer Peace Group, collecting signatures for the first World Disarmament Petition, supporting demonstrations, leafleting and vigils.

My very first arrest was in 1983 at RAF Greenham Common, where nuclear cruise missiles were to be based.[15] These ground-based cruise missiles, deployed all around the country on the backs of lorries, threatening nuclear war, were depicted by the artist Peter Kennard in 'Haywain with Cruise Missiles'. We had no legal briefings or workshops. We just joined hundreds of other women, sitting in front of the gates and blockading, cutting the fences and entering the high-security areas. I used to go for weekends and get in and out of the base as many times as I could.

The court cases were amazing. Women of all ages, classes and beliefs stood up and represented themselves. Polite women explaining why they had broken the law in a very articulate and quiet manner, poetic women reading their verses or singing in court, silent women, angry women, screaming, despairing women, some breaking the rules of the court and refusing to stand for the magistrates' entrance, some defying the court and lecturing the judiciary on the ills of nuclear weapons, some praying and some dancing, all of them being found guilty and many being led away to prison straight away for contempt of court or for refusing to pay fines.

The resistance was wonderful, funny, poignant, empowering and I discovered that there is no 'right' way to protest or resist or defend yourself. Each person must find their own voice: diversity is empowering and a strength in itself. From this time onwards I have almost always represented myself in court and refused to pay fines, and have tried to make sure that the legal system is challenged to be as accessible to everyone as possible.

My brother, at that time, was a policeman in the RAF, and because of the hundreds of women getting into the Greenham airbase he was likely to be deployed there, as the authorities tried to have guards every few yards around the perimeter fence to prevent our incursions. This took hundreds of personnel, so different units were brought in for short rotations, but it was not very effective because we were so many. We managed to get into the base anyway, because as one woman cut the fence in one spot and started to crawl through, lots of the inside guards would crowd around, leaving their posts, so other women could cut the fence and get in at the places they left. The police and guards deployed outside the fences often sat in their cars, so some of us used to talk to them while other women were carefully letting their tyres down, then we would all run off.

There is no 'right' way to protest or resist or defend yourself

Some of it was not so amusing when the authorities deployed the SAS and other troops to try to get rid of us and there were some nasty incidents when red-hot pokers were put through tents and shelters where we were camping, when our fires were put out in the middle of winter with water hoses, when our possessions were stolen and we were abused. But it is amazing what women can do when they work together and support each other, and lots of donations arrived from women who could not come and camp, or who came just for a few hours to keep the camps occupied while others went off cutting fences or doing court support.

My brother came to visit me at home at Valley Farmhouse with some of his RAF friends, and when I asked him what he would do if he saw me inside the high-security areas at Greenham, he said he would shoot me, as those were the orders! We decided that we would make sure we would not be there at the same time.[16]

Around the camp fires at the women's peace camp were truly times of sharing, swapping stories and learning from each other. We discussed the meaning and the importance of nonviolence, of non-hierarchical ways of making decisions and working together, feminism and women's power. We discussed the whole nuclear chain, from mining, production, testing, deployment and use, the impact of all this on people local to the mining and testing sites and especially on indigenous peoples. We thought about weapon systems, the arms trade, geopolitics, racism, poverty and most importantly how to get the UK to stop deploying cruise missiles. We realised that everything is linked. Go into any one issue deep enough and you will find how it connects with another.

We also shared food and songs. So much music and creativity helped us get through the tough times. Many songs were composed and shared around the camp fires. I chose to be at Orange Gate most of the time because of the music.[17] I could only go for a few days at a time as the children were still young but they were being well cared for, and they often came with my husband when he dropped me off at the camp so they could see where I was staying and meet some of my friends.

I thoroughly enjoyed the freedom and creativity of working in a women-only environment for the first time. Many women told us how they were now able to speak freely and really be heard, that in mixed-sex groups their suggestions and comments were often ignored. They might say something that was not acknowledged or discussed, but if a man said the same thing a little later, it was listened to. Many women, myself included, were not as confident speaking up in front of large groups: they preferred face-to-face or small groups where it felt easier to say what they thought. This was why men often dominated in larger groupings or more formal settings. Of course, there were also many women turning up who had been badly abused by men and only felt safe in this women-only environment. There was a great deal of listening and support going on. It was a special time, an experience of a very different culture building up. A song spoke to this – 'Shall There be Womanly Times? Or Shall We Die?'.

I was arrested many times at Greenham, but only one of these resulted in a court case as generally the police and courts could not deal with the hundreds of arrests taking place each month. We mostly just had our details recorded, were escorted out of the base and heard nothing more.

2

Carrying Greenham Home to Norfolk
and the Snowball Campaign

MY SECOND ARREST, the one that resulted in a court case, was in 1984. A group of us from Norfolk chained ourselves to the House of Commons railings with banners against nuclear weapons and refused to leave. We were a small group of around five people, and had decided we would not give our real names when we were arrested unless we were assured we could use international law in our defence. I had been interested in international law ever since hearing about the war laws and it seemed important to be allowed to talk about these in our defence.

We decided on various false names and I chose Winnie Mandela.[18] I did not realise that this 'alias' would continue to haunt me for the rest of my days! So if you choose an alias, make sure you will be happy with it for your lifetime. We had not decided many details before our action, and we were soon carted off to police cells and kept apart so we could not communicate with each other. I explained that my name for the day was Winnie Mandela and that I would not give my real name until the court agreed to an international law defence. The police were not interested at all. They just kept me in the police cells and asked me for my name each day. After the first day, they told me that my colleagues had already given their names and had been released on bail. I did not believe them. After seven days, I realised we had made a big mistake – we had not agreed a finish time! Another lesson learnt and never forgotten: in all your action planning, make as many contingency plans as you can and agree an ending time. However, one only gains experience by making mistakes, by acting and finding out the consequences, and this lesson was very useful.

I decided at last to give my real name and was bailed to appear in court later. I learnt on my release that three of the others had given their real name after only a few hours in the police cells, and that one other person had stayed inside for a couple of days only. I was the only mug to stay inside for a week!

However, I had found out a great deal about how to cope in custody and about the overcrowded police cells. I listened to lots of other prisoners (many of whom were high-class prostitutes) talk about which judges took prostitutes and which took drugs. I saw police officers call some of the women out, who then returned with take-away food after having 'serviced' the men. I received an insight into the hidden world of police custody, a system I knew little about. I also found out how boring it could be, locked up in a small space day after day with little to do. Time spent in police cells is much more difficult than time spent in prison. I never again went into an action without several books to read and a clear agreement of when or under what circumstances we wanted the action to end – not that this would always be in our control.

The '80s were busy years for the anti-nuclear peace movement, but I needed to be with my young children and it was quite a long way to Greenham Common. There was a banner on the fence that said 'Carry Greenham Home' so I decided to do just that, and work nearer at home in north Norfolk.

Thousands of people all over Britain were not only frightened by nuclear weapons but also wanted to do something about it, to take responsibility in some way, and they wanted to do this locally. I was a member of a local peace group and had already organised a few demonstrations in my rural north Norfolk area. It was not very densely populated, was very conservative and full of RAF bases, many of which were actually US bases in all but name. I thought long and hard about what to do, and in 1984 founded and co-ordinated the Snowball Civil Disobedience Campaign to try to persuade the government, by totally nonviolent means, to show that they truly wanted peace by committing to at least one disarmament measure.[19] It was intentionally designed to include men as well as women as I aimed to include the many men wanting to take action, feeling excluded by the Greenham Common Women's Peace Camp but who had not found the energy to start their own campaign or camp around the other numerous nuclear bases.

Britain at that time was characterised as a US aircraft carrier and Liz, a nearby artist friend living in Aylsham, sewed a banner with an outline of the shape of the UK with a huge US flag behind it, several US planes flying over the UK and words saying 'Whose Britain?'[20] I decided that the civil disobedience act should be simply cutting one single strand of wire around the fence of my nearest US military base (USAF Sculthorpe). Cutting a single strand was to limit the amount of damage done and to be perceived as purely symbolic from an individual's point of view, unthreatening in a physical way to the authorities, but serious enough to warrant prosecution under the Criminal Damage Act and for the authorities not to be able to ignore it. We would be able to explain our actions in the courts and bring the issue of nuclear devastation into the limelight.

As a first step I had to find two other people to join me in cutting the fence at Sculthorpe. These two people were hard to find, but eventually I persuaded a friend, Tony, and my mother-in-law Dorothy to join me. And I was given a valuable piece of advice from an older Quaker friend whom I had approached to take part. He said no, such action was not for him as he did not think cutting fences was a good way to change people's attitudes, but that if I still thought the action was worth doing I should do it anyway even if no one else joined in – I should follow my spirit and act in the truth of that spirit. This has been something that has stood me in good stead – to think of the real value of an action rather than how popular it might be.

It was difficult to find colleagues in the peace movement at the time to take part in this first action, as it seemed to be encouraging vandalism. Although what we were doing was open and accountable and very symbolic with the cutting of only one strand of wire in the fence surrounding the us base, nevertheless it would be considered as 'criminal damage' and we were likely to end up with a criminal record.

I had also stipulated that we each write a statement of intent explaining why we were doing it, to clarify for ourselves our motivations and reasons, and be ready to hand the statement into the police and courts. We also had to commit to write to three public figures explaining our actions and to find two more people to join us in a month's time for the next stage of the Snowball, so that it would grow. The campaign was designed to encourage communication and dialogue and was linked with three requests for the government to take achievable steps towards disarmament. We said we would end the campaign if the government took one of these steps, and it did come to an end when the government signed the Intermediate-Range Nuclear Forces (INF) Treaty at the end of 1987.[21]

The Snowball campaign sparked a whole debate that was new to most people at the time, about whether destroying or damaging property was nonviolent or not – with vociferous local public meetings that included local MPs and the press. Our argument was that it depended on the spirit in which the destruction was done and what was being destroyed and why. For instance, destroying a front door to rescue a person inside from a fire would not be considered as wrong because it was to save a life. Similarly, our actions were to save lives.

The Snowball started with three of us, accompanied by the press, openly cutting our strand of wire at USAF Sculthorpe, and was then supposed to triple at each stage a month apart and take off! When the second stage took place with nine of us, the police started taking bets about how long it would take to peter out. A month later we had our 27, but then the next month we could not quite make the 81. So, I learnt something else: don't make things difficult by setting impossible goals, life is not tidy like a game. And, when things don't work out as planned, improvise, admit a mistake, adapt and continue the campaign in another way.

So we spread the idea to other US bases and snowballed horizontally instead of vertically.[22] We made it easy for people to join in by writing a pack and sending it out so people could copy the idea and do it at their own local US base. One of our slogans was 'Don't sit on the fence. Cut it!'. We circulated reusable envelope stickers with this slogan on. We worked hard getting national celebrities and well-known figures to come and cut a strand: *Think of the real value of an action rather than how popular it might be* these included Lord Peter Melchett, Countess Dora Russell, Billy Bragg and Bruce Kent. But of course, there were also lots of local well-known figures who supported us too.

The local courts and papers were full of it all as so many people got involved and had to appear in the local Fakenham Magistrates' Court. The court was reported to be having its longest hearing in its history when 50 of us were tried over a two-week period in February 1986.[23] Usually, the little court only met once a week with local magistrates, and they had had to call in a stipendiary magistrate from London. I remember it was an amazing community effort with the court being full of people wanting to listen. I had quite a few outstanding cases on during the week and I asked on the first day for reassurance that the stipendiary would not hear cases with the same people involved as this would undoubtedly influence him if he had judged the defendant before. He promised that he would not. But on the next day when I appeared again, he started to hear this second case against me. I reminded him of what he had said yesterday and he ignored me and continued as if I had not spoken. So I just walked out of the dock and into a seat in the public gallery, where I took out a newspaper to read. He then continued to address the place where I had been sitting in the dock and made up answers for me! It was most bizarre and really quite funny. I was learning a lot about the idiosyncrasies of judges and lawyers. The judge gave out quite a few prison sentences, from ten days to three weeks, and so lots of us got experiences of being in prison.[24] The local papers had articles about why all these ordinary local folk were going to prison and covered the issues surrounding nuclear weapons.[25] I ended up with ten Snowball cases and served sentences totalling 64 days in total, including six days for 'contempt of court' when I refused to co-operate by sitting at the back of the court. But I also won a case, getting an acquittal at the only Snowball jury trial held in a Crown Court.

The Snowball spread to Scotland and to Wales, and a *World in Action* documentary was made of the campaign and shown on prime-time TV.[26] I still meet people as I move around the UK who say they were involved in the Snowball campaign and who continue to be active. In the three years it operated we were able to add our voices to the growing tumult against illegal and unethical weapons of mass destruction.

I learnt a great deal from this very first campaign I initiated and ran. It is better to try and fail than not to try: when it is hard to start a campaign but it feels right to you, then do it in the right spirit because it is worth doing in itself and do not worry about whether it takes off or not. Take each step in good faith and learn and adapt as you go along.

And more importantly, I had to learn that although I might initiate a campaign, it was not mine, I did not 'own' it personally. I had to avoid the trap of what is called the 'founder's syndrome' – that feeling that I had to be involved in every stage, that I was indispensable. I learnt to reach out and involve others, to ask for help, to make sure that others had the space to initiate, take responsibility and move the campaign on. I learnt to 'let go' of the action and thus enable new 'leaders', or 'facilitators' as we preferred to call them, emerge in other places to co-ordinate the Snowballs in their areas.

Don't make things difficult by setting impossible goals

I collected lots of the statements that we encouraged everyone to write before their actions to clarify their motivations and to be used in court. Oliver, a close friend and fellow Snowballer, helped me edit them, and I included them in an account of our own history and tried to find a publisher in the UK. But the publishing world at that time was awash with books about peace and disarmament. I was lucky however, when I went to India for a peace conference, that I met AB (Arya Bhushan Bhardwaj) and he published the book on the Snowball campaign in 1989 in Delhi.

I have continued with this pattern of trying to make sure that our campaigns are written up and published. I am so grateful that Gavin of Luath Press approached me when I had finished arguing at the High Court in Edinburgh one day and said he would like to publish a book based on the illegality arguments coming out of the Loch Goil acquittal and the Lord Advocate's Reference. He has provided incredible support and encouragement and his publishing house has published all the books I have written or edited ever since.[27] These books have included contributions from the people taking part in the actions. This is important, because we are all inspired by and learn from each other. We are part of a huge movement for social change and have learnt from those that go before, and others learn from us – we are part of an unbroken line, a continuing tide of resistance that emerges throughout time and place wherever injustice and ill-practice emerge. We need to record our part of the ongoing struggle and explain ourselves, so that our experiences can inform those that come after us and our resistance reaches out into the future. It is our struggle and it is good to explain ourselves in our own words rather than leaving it to others, who may misrepresent us.

This also meant writing articles for *Peace News, Disarmament Diplomacy, Red Pepper* and other alternative news outlets as well as for the peace movements in other countries. Taking part in conferences and meetings also took up time but was well worth the effort. Communication in different mediums and forums is essential.

By the beginning of 1990 I had been arrested many times and this had led to around 15 court cases, with quite a few imprisonments for non-payment of fines. I was fortunate and privileged to have had the support of my family, who looked after my daughter and son when I was in prison. Living within an extended family made this possible. I am very aware that not everyone has the support to take their resistance so far, which is why it is important to make sure that there are roles and opportunities for people in different circumstances to join our campaigns and offer their strengths and passions.

I had been able to experiment with how far to 'disobey' the state and the courts and discovered that it could be quite far. The little local Magistrates' Court in Fakenham, Norfolk, dealing with hundreds of Snowball cases, had been overwhelmed and was getting annoyed at the number of unpaid fines. The bailiffs were ordered to take my property. My family was rather concerned, so I organised lots of friends and colleagues (about 40 of them) to come to my home one day and Mike, a local blacksmith, acted as an auctioneer and auctioned off all our family property, including our car for 50 pence, my son's pet snake for 10 pence, the fridge and the washing machine for 20 pence. These were ridiculously cheap prices but we raised a couple of hundred pounds for the Snowball campaign and fun was had by all. Everyone signed a receipt saying they had bought the item, the item had a little numbered sticker put on it, each person signed a receipt which also said they wanted their property to remain at my home until they collected it, and that they would sue anybody who removed this property that was now theirs. It got into the local press and I took all the receipts to the police to make sure the bailiffs were warned that we no longer owned any property. We heard no more about those particular fines.

Different people devised very ingenious ways of paying their fines. For instance, Mike decided to write his cheque on a concrete block that took two people to lift, which he explained in a letter to the court as being a contingency that could survive anything but a direct hit in any nuclear exchange. Steve wrote his on a three-foot-wide cardboard snowball that he had trouble getting into the fines payment department at his court. Another person paid in small coins that they had dunked in a nearby stream which they said was contaminated with radioactive pollution from a nuclear base.

Take each step in good faith and learn and adapt as you go along

Each person must be supported in the decisions that they make, as everyone has different circumstances. Some need to spare their families and partners the trauma of bailiffs and fines collection agencies banging on their doors and entering their houses to take their property so they need to pay their fines promptly, some may need help with funds to pay the fines, others may have no possessions anyway and can therefore be free of that fear. Some people have to get back to their paid work and may pay an on-the-spot fine. Some plead guilty straight away as they cannot bear the anxiety of waiting and dealing with all the administration and court cases. We need everyone and we need to support all the diverse ways our supporters and activists are able to contribute. No one is better or worse, or more important; everyone does whatever they can in whatever way they can. Local musicians, actors, poets and artists often participate in the action itself, but if not, they contribute their skills for fundraising events, and these fundraisers bring us all together for some cultural wonders, and to strengthen our bonds.

It is a shame that these essential people are unsung and unnamed. Those of us who have been privileged enough to be able to resist paying fines and can take time off to spend in police cells, courts and prison, are no better activists than those who cannot even risk arrest but do essential hidden support work. For every activist in court or in prison there are hundreds of others supporting them. We are all part of the same community of resistance. And every obstacle put in our way can usually be overcome by asking our community to help out.

3

Building Networks of Resistance
at Home and Abroad

BY THE EARLY 1990s the worry of a nuclear war had died down. Cruise missiles had been sent back to the US, mainly due to the strength of the anti-nuclear protests. There was some movement towards disarmament negotiations and I felt that I could take some time off from anti-nuclear activism. I therefore concentrated on other issues that were close to my heart: indigenous peoples' land rights, human rights and the destruction of old-growth forests.

I had met a couple of young activists, Jake and Jason, who were just starting the Earth First! movement in the UK. We were locked-on next to each other, occupying a ship carrying essential parts of a new nuclear power station destined for Sizewell in Suffolk.[28] They asked me whether I would be willing to join an international Earth First! SOS Sarawak action in solidarity with the Penan people, who were suffering from loggers cutting down their forest and destroying their hunter-gatherer way of life. I knew about this issue and had been signing petitions and writing letters about it and said, 'Of course.'

In July 1991, I went to Sarawak with Jake, knowing little other than that we were to meet other activists in the Niah Caves area, and would work out what to do when we arrived! It all had to be kept very secret, otherwise we would never have been allowed into the country. We met up with a dozen or so people and found that he was the youngest, at 18, and I was the oldest, at 40 years of age.

This was the first time I had worked with an international team of activists in another country that I was not familiar with, and I had no idea what to expect. I had told my family that I might be away for a week, or maybe several years, but that I instinctively felt that it would just be a few months. None of us had any idea of the law in Malaysia, nor had we met before. We took a week to plan the action once we all met up. And what an amazingly beautiful place to meet. The Niah Caves are massive limestone caves with a long human history going back 40,000 years. They house swiftlets that make edible nests, and also a huge population of bats that fly out each night. There were glowing mushrooms in caves which delved underground for some miles, and the paths through them led out to another far part of the forest on the other side of a mountain. Wonderful views from the caves looked out over sculptural limestone karsts poking through the forests. We met in one of the many cave tunnels overlooking those forests, a reminder of what we wanted to save.

One of the women involved, Anja, who had been working on the issue in Sarawak and Japan for some time, had met with the Penan and local environmental groups and had the local knowledge we needed. Two of the activists were to film the action and get it out of the country, and pass it on to the press people in each of the countries represented by the eight activists (Germany, Sweden, UK, USA, and Australia).

Everyone contributed ideas, and as we got to know each other over a week our plans solidified. I suggested we use false names and hide our passports so that we would not be immediately deported, and could have *Reach out and* a court case which would give us more publicity and allow *involve others* the issue to be aired in Malaysia and the timber-importing countries. We chose names that would give our message – I was 'Chipko Mendes Penan Stop the Logging Save the Rainforest', and others named themselves as 'Clouded Leopard' and 'Stop the Industrial Mega-machine' and other names that gave the public an idea of what we cared about.[29] This time I remembered to suggest a stop time: we decided on two weeks before we would give our real names and tell the authorities where to find our passports. We had hidden these before the action in various places – Anja hid hers under a coconut tree by the sea.[30]

Our action was an occupation of the logging barges loading logs in Miri for export. The logs had been taken from Penan lands without their permission. The use of aliases worked really well this time. We found out later from the lawyers that the authorities just wanted to deport us and get rid of us straight away, but couldn't as they did not know our real names or which countries we came from. The two-week period was just long enough for them to be forced into having to either release us or charge us. Once we gave our real names and nationalities we were able to access our diplomatic consuls and get some messages out. We were held in Miri Prison, the very prison where Penan protesters had been held when they were arrested for setting up logging blockades to stop the loggers getting into their forests, stealing their timber and destroying their environment and homes. The Penan considered the land as their life. Many of these semi-nomadic people, who were used to living freely in the open air, suffered terribly by being locked up in the prisons.[31]

After two weeks in prison we were finally charged. The four of us in the small women's section had already made a nuisance of ourselves by staging a sit-down protest demanding to see our four men and to know whether they were being treated properly. We were told by the guards that this was the first protest the prison had ever experienced, as Malaysians are generally very respectful of those in positions of power. I was put in a cell on my own in the dark at the back of the women's prison section in solitary, as I refused to move when the others did. I was picked up and slung into the cell along with the ants, mosquitoes and other bugs and kept there for a week.

Unbeknownst to us, our presence in the prison had been publicised and we were wonderfully surprised one day when we were taken to a room and found two local lawyers who had come to offer us their help for free. Antalai was an Iban and Raymond a Malaysian of Chinese origin.[32] They were incredibly generous to us all, helping us prepare our cases, representing us, even helping to find funding for bail money and providing Anja and I with a place to stay when we decided to appeal the verdict and sentencing. They also managed to get permission to hand over our mail to us, which was very welcome. It was so good to hear from my husband and children and know they were doing fine.

It is good to explain ourselves in our own words rather than leaving it to others, who may misrepresent us

I was the only one to decide to represent myself, even though I had no idea of the legal system there. Six of our group pleaded guilty and got out of prison very quickly. Only Anja and I pleaded not guilty and had to stay in prison for much longer. I was helped by Antalai and Raymond who told me what the charges were. In court, it was strange having to have a translator and very frustrating to know that not everything was being translated. It gave me a small insight into what it might be like for non-English speakers in the UK having to hear everything through translators.

I learnt once more the power of representing myself, as I was able to get out loads of information about the corruption of the Chief Minister of Sarawak that a lawyer could not risk: he would have lost his licence for doing so. At one stage I was threatened by the court with a piece of old British Colonial emergency legislation and told that if I did not retract my statements about the corrupt practices of the Chief Minister I would be jailed indefinitely. I was advised by the lawyers representing Anja to retract my statements as demanded by the court, as I could be held for years if I didn't, but being rather stubborn I refused and gambled on them not wanting the extra publicity. My hunch paid off and I only got a three-month sentence in the end, the same as Anja.

Our time in prison in Sarawak was most interesting, even though rather uncomfortable. We were not allowed to have mosquito nets and the ants also bit us every night as we slept on thin mats on the concrete floors. But we women were all together (Nirbhao from the USA, Anja from Sweden/Australia, Nitya from Australia and myself from the UK) with the other women prisoners in one room, which was quite sociable. There were about 20 women during our time there. Most were poor prostitutes from Kalimantan who had come up to Sarawak to earn money to help their families.[33] They were cruelly kept in prison until their villages raised the money for their fines and fares back. This left them even more impoverished, so they had to go into prostitution again. The men in the process got off scot-free, of course.

There was one woman in for murder and her story was really sad. She had killed her husband because he had murdered her previous girl babies, and she was scared her newborn daughter would be killed. She had gone quite insane and was kept drugged out of her mind to stop her screaming. There were also two very young teenagers who were in for drugs, which carried a death sentence. Luckily for them, their parents bribed enough officials to get them out. Anja and I heard more of their story after we were released and met them by chance in Miri.

After being found guilty, Anja and I decided to ask for bail while we appealed our verdict and sentencing. With the help of the lawyers, the bail money was raised for us, to be paid back when we returned for the court appearance. During our time on bail we were constantly followed by secret police, but eventually managed to get away from them and go by river taxi up the Baram River to visit some Penan that Anja knew. This was a special and important time for me: hiking in the forest and spending time with the Penan was an amazing experience that I will never forget.

The Penan family we found in the forest knew Anja from her previous trips to Sarawak and they knew we had been in prison, what we had done and why, and so we had an instant bond. The Penan are a quiet, gentle people living in their sulaps, hunting with blowpipes and gathering wild fruits and nuts and other forest goodies. Their forest is their garden and they know it deeply, caring for their special sago and rattan plants. I had never before thought about how these old-growth forests were so intimately cared for by their indigenous peoples, who were an intrinsic part of the forest and shaped it just like other animals living in it. They were skilled at living a full and vibrant life in harmony with their ecosystem and they are, of course, the best caretakers of these important habitats. Unfortunately, their forests are being logged, they are being forced out and the rich biodiversity that they were a living part of is being destroyed by profit-hungry companies.

We spent a couple of nights sleeping on the floor, woven of thin branches, in a sulap built on poles above the forest. These sulaps, built of natural materials, are used for a few weeks or months only, as before the forest is disturbed too much the family moves on and builds another. There is a fire on a verandah, cushioned in clay so the sulap does not burn down, where their staple, sago, is dried and then stored inside large bamboos. I did not mind the leeches that festooned my feet and legs, as they were easily brushed off before I climbed into the sulap, where we were offered a welcome meal. A wild pig had been killed and divided up into equal portions to adhere to the Penan tradition of sharing everything equally. I was told even the little children, if they caught a small insect or snake had to share it equally and could not guzzle it all by themselves. The packages wrapped in leaves would be taken down to share with the other members of the extended family who were unhappily forced to live in longhouses nearby when they wanted to live freely in their forests.[34] We ate communally, using hand-made wooden sticks to eat the gooey sago and unsalted pork. After a day in the forest it was delicious.

Asik took some of the rattan he had harvested and began to make some bracelets, carving designs on them, and with a hot poker made even more beautiful patterns. The Penan wear these on their wrists and legs. He presented me with quite a few that I wore for many years, until they finally broke.

On the way back to Miri, I met Penan in Long Iman who had been forced out of their nomadic lifestyles by the logging companies. I stayed with them a few days. We arrived in time to see a huge python that had just been caught being skinned for supper. I later identified it as a reticulated python, the longest and one of the heaviest snakes in the world. It had lots of small bones and tasted a little like chicken. As I wandered by the riverside that evening, I met an old woman playing her nose flute. She had the traditional long holes in her ears and was festooned with rattan bracelets, and I wish I could have understood her language and heard her stories of her younger years when living her traditional life. The world is losing the skills and knowledge of these wonderful people, who know how to live sustainably and at peace with nature. Another elder took me out among the trees near the village and showed me how to use his blowpipe. He was pointing up into the tall trees to show me things but his eyes were far sharper than mine. The blowpipes are quite light and just a short, sharp puff launches the arrow. I aimed at a mark on a tree and was delighted to find that I hit it. I felt in my element, at peace and so grateful to be with these gentle, welcoming people. We walked together while he searched for traditional medicinal plants, but he said the forests were now so impoverished it was near-impossible to find any in the secondary growth that replaces the ancient primary old-growth forests. They are green deserts. Most outsiders seeing these forests would think they were fine, wondering what all the fuss was about forest loss. Their eyes are not trained, they do not look closely. If they did they would find just a few species, so very different to the hundreds and hundreds of tree species there should be in these tropical rain forests.

I have many fond memories of this time in Sarawak and still follow with great sadness the slow decline of the remaining forests.[35]

Everyone does whatever they can in whatever way they can

I recently met some Canadian friends of Sarawak at an Extinction Rebellion action and we swapped stories of mutual friends. They had just been filming in Sarawak and brought back some sago, which they fed me. They also gifted me a few rattan bracelets to replace the ones that I had been given by Asik. That was special. Sarawak is in my soul. And I had discovered the incredible gifts and benefits of civil resistance in other lands. I learnt the value of international actions and court cases for getting information about an issue out very widely. I realised how good actions can be planned very quickly by sharing resources when working with really committed individuals, and the satisfaction and freedom of being given the space and support to follow my own instincts and take risks.

I bonded with the three other women activists who took part in the action and with whom I shared prison time. I am still in touch with all of them. Nitya came to stay with my family in Norfolk for almost a year and we campaigned together for the forests over several years, Anja visited the UK from Australia and helped out in the anti-nuclear actions I was organising in Scotland and Nirbhao, who lives in New Mexico, USA, has been a constant friend and we have visited each other frequently. Nirbhao and I also travelled together to give solidarity to fellow Polish environmentalists who were protesting to save the Białowieża forest on the Belarus border.[36] I have found that each action and each campaign brings in new colleagues and friends, strengthens our bonds and expands the possibilities for stronger joint actions in the future.

The Sarawak action led, on my return, to my hosting a meeting in my home of those UK-based groups working on the preservation of old-growth forests. The Earth First! SOS Sarawak action had garnered a lot of criticism from some of these groups. During a long weekend we thrashed out differences of style in our campaigning work – some groups in the UK did not approve of direct action, for instance; and the criticism of our action in Sarawak had been because of adverse publicity from mainstream Malaysian press like the *Borneo Post*. It featured headlines screaming 'Environmentalists Declare World War on Malaysia' and accusations that we were 'environmental terrorists' and 'eco-colonialists'! Our allies in Malaysia were not able to publicly applaud our actions, as they would have been closed down, so their support for us had been kept out of the press. This meeting was to clarify some of these issues.

Our groups ranged from the World Wildlife Fund (WWF) to Greenpeace to Friends of the Earth (FOE) and Earth First! plus my own organisation, Reforest the Earth. After clearing the air it was obvious we needed a forum for continuing discussions, as it was the height of the anti-logging movement in the UK. We set up a UK Forests Network, which I helped co-ordinate from 1993 to 1996. We organised contributions to a Forests Memorandum which provided a joint platform for us to coalesce around.[37] It outlined the issues and problems and put together solutions and policies to try to stop the logging of old-growth forests. We organised a lobby of Parliament, and also various joint actions with those groups that felt they could participate in them, but with an understanding by the other groups not to speak out against our nonviolent direct actions.

This experience of co-ordinating the forests forum taught me how useful coalitions and alliances can be, as it extended our contacts and brought in new people with new skills. It also led to me being involved in woodland creation and management in Norfolk and in Wales.[38] I still volunteer in the local woodland management group in Wales, sustainably coppicing woodlands for our firewood needs and planting native trees to improve our environment. In the 1990s I was experimenting with new forms of direct action, and all the additional contacts I now had made it easier to start and maintain campaigns. I was learning that one-off actions, while good in themselves, were not nearly as useful at creating change as sustained protests, and thus the next few years were quite productive.

I had an idea and tried it out with Nitya.[39] The two of us went into a timber yard in Norwich and took out two planks of mahogany. We handed them into the main Norwich police station and reported them as being stolen property, having come from indigenous lands in Brazil. We expected to be interviewed at length about it, but instead we were immediately arrested for shoplifting and taken to the cells and strip-searched. Later, we were released without charge. Luckily, having access to a film crew, we were able to go back to the public desk of the police station and start again – but this time having it filmed! I explained that we had come into the police station some hours earlier to report a crime and had been badly treated: instead of a report of the crime being noted and getting a crime number and reassurance that our allegations would be investigated, we had been arrested, strip-searched and then released. The cameras were whirring and the policeman looked rather uncomfortable. He said he could not understand what had happened; he would look into it, and he took our statement, gave us a crime number and hurried us out as soon as possible. Nothing more was heard from the police so I decided to organise it on a bigger scale.

This was the start of CRISPO (the Citizens' Recovery of Indigenous Peoples' Stolen Property Organisation) which encouraged the 'Ethical Shoplifting' of mahogany out of shops and timber yards and into police stations to highlight the illegal logging which was hastening forest destruction. We concentrated on mahogany, which at the time was mislabelled and had been taken from indigenous reserves in Brazil.

A friend made us badges to wear, based on the Norfolk police badge, which had CRISPO Officer No... and then a specific number for each of us. A list was made of our names and our CRISPO Officer numbers. This list was taken to the police station at the exact time we began what we called our 'ethical shoplifting'; it explained what we were doing and why. It also went out to the local press. This was important, as it made us open and accountable and explained that we were not stealing anything, not really shoplifting, just trying to stop crime. I cannot remember how many of us there were, but probably around 15 or so, and we all got out different pieces of mahogany from Bonds, the biggest department store in Norwich. There was a mahogany clock, a mahogany toilet seat and several other items. It was scary how easy it was to pick up these objects and just walk out with them. We took them straight to the police station and handed them in with our own personal statements. We got lots of publicity but nothing else happened. The goods were returned to the store, and we were not charged because after all we had done nothing wrong. But on the other hand, the shop continued to sell the mahogany.

The idea was developed and I asked a well-known lawyer, Mike, to help us by writing a formal legal letter accusing various timber merchants and shops of dealing in stolen timber. This soon created a huge buzz in the timber industry. We were following and joining in the public debate in the *Timber Trades Journal*. We continued with other ethical shoplifts, including one at Harrods in London at Christmas in 1993, with 60 protesters from Reforest the Earth, Greenpeace and FOE taking part together inside the store, and probably a hundred or so outside the store. A 'Mahogany is Murder' banner was displayed in one of the Christmas window displays. Activists walked out with all kinds of mahogany goods, including several tables. Surprisingly and worryingly easy to do, but great fun too. In fact, several of us had big grins on our faces as we trundled around to hand them into Chelsea police station. We were drawing attention to the illegal and immoral trade in mahogany from the Brazilian rainforest. As the *Guardian* article highlighted, we wanted to show British shoppers that if they bought mahogany they were likely to be participating in the trade of stolen goods and human lives.[40] And we wanted the police to do something about it.

As a follow-up to this action, we organised groups from around the country to join in an ethical shoplift at six different places in the UK, and instead of taking the items to each local police station, we took them to London and dumped them outside the Attorney General's Office. The Attorney General (AG) is the head of the UK Judiciary and appointed by the government. We got Ken Livingstone MP – this was before he became Mayor of London – to meet us there. He went into the office on our behalf to explain what we had done and why, and to ask the AG to investigate our claims of stolen timber, as local police stations were refusing to take it further. Ken asked the AG to prosecute the stores selling this stolen timber, saying he was sure the AG would do something if it were the crown jewels.[41] Unfortunately, big business rather than ordinary citizens asking for justice had more clout, and again nothing more was heard.

Another amusing and press-worthy incident was when we organised a Trade Seminar for timber importers. We arranged for some Nuxalk chiefs from British Columbia to come to the UK to talk about the impact of the timber trade on their forests. While the Nuxalk were in the UK, we ethically shoplifted red cedar that had been imported from British Columbia, took it to a police station in Oxford and then had the Nuxalk chiefs go to the police station where we had handed it in and try to claim it. The police did not know what to do when they came in dressed in their full regalia, accompanied by a *Blue Peter* film crew, to ask for their property back.[42] Faxes were flying between the police and the Canadian Embassy, with the Nuxalk explaining that their lands were not part of Canada as they had never ceded their lands nor lost them in warfare, and with the Canadian Embassy saying all of Canada was Canadian. It was hilarious.

Of course, the issues were not hilarious, and we were fully conscious of the terrible consequences of this illegal trade in timber for the people living in and around the forests that were being hacked out for profit.[43] During the years of this campaign we started actions at major trade importers' offices – James Latham, Meyer International and Timbmet, and at chain stores like Jewson.[44, 45] We organised office occupations and demonstrations, and lobbied far and wide for a lawful, sustainable and ethical trade in timber. All of these actions raised the profile of the issue and got lots of press.[46]

While this was taking place we were also going along to Timber Trade Federation meetings, organising actions outside various embassies, occupying timber yards, blockading dockyards and locking on to ships bringing in 'stolen' timber. I was engaging in regular letter-writing and contributing articles to the *Timber Trade Journal* that helped the debate.[47] I even set up a Women's Negotiating Team to negotiate with the timber industry and persuade them to commit to more ethical and sustainable trading practices, especially in relation to mahogany purchases.[48] The team held some very productive meetings with timber importers and I was invited to give a talk to the timber industry.[49] We also helped persuade Jewson and Meyer International to go to Brazil and see for themselves the damage that logging was doing.[50] On 28 September 1995, we were even part of a 'mahogany round table' meeting between environmentalists, timber traders and IBAMA (the Brazilian Federal Agency for the Environment and Natural Resources). We were able to do so much because there were hundreds of activists, mostly young students, who were keen to get involved, and because several large national organisations like Greenpeace, FOE, the Rainforest Action Network and also young activist networks like Earth First! joined forces. As we were working together in our UK Forests Forum, we were also able to plan a whole series of interlinked actions and no one organisation got overloaded. We had a big impact and policies did change.

When we had started the direct action, which had come some years after major public information campaigns from the big NGOs, none of the timber-importing agents knew exactly where their timber was coming from. They sometimes knew the country of origin but never the actual parcel of land. By the time we ended our campaign, most of them had been persuaded to find out exactly where their timber was coming from and had even seen the management plans. They were employing environmental researchers and many were signing up to the Forest Stewardship Council (FSC) which we had pushed them into supporting, and which at that time we thought would provide a good certification process to ensure legal and sustainable logging.[51]

Unfortunately the FSC has let us down. The standards were not high enough, though certainly better than before, but logging is still proceeding apace and the last old-growth forests are still being cut down. As the CEO of Timbmet said to me during some of our face-to-face meetings, 'Angie, what you are asking for is impossible. It will mean we go out of business!' My response was: 'Yes, your trade would have to be very substantially cut, but this would be better than having no timber to trade at all. Your excessive logging will leave us with no forests and the whole environment that humans rely upon would suffer from the loss of these biodiverse regions of the world.'

Sarawak now has under 11 per cent left of its once-beautiful old-growth forests that have gone mainly to Japan's building industry, and the logging continues. Forests all around the world are still being taken from indigenous people by corporations for palm oil, soya beans, cattle, tea, coffee, bananas and other foods for rich countries, leaving locals bereft of their livelihoods, malnourished and in poor health. Some of these corporations are from the very same countries suffering the devastation, as they *Good actions can be planned very quickly by sharing resources when working with really committed individuals* never act in the interests of the actual people living in their country, they are only interested in profit. The problems with corporations have been clear for a very long time and are a massive threat to the long-term health of all people and our planet. Corporations exist to make money for shareholders; they are not interested in the well-being of people or the environment. This relentless pursuit of economic growth is destroying all life on Earth. It was clear when I started campaigning, and is even clearer now.

A corporation is a legal institution and depends on legal structures that define its mandate as being 'to pursue, relentlessly and without exception, its own self-interest, regardless of the often harmful consequences it might cause to others'.[52] Until we change the law and make corporations culpable for all the damage that they do, things can only get worse. We must also be aware of the power and bullying that go on with threats to take whole countries through the Investment Court System, or Investor-State Dispute Settlement (ISDS). Thus, when a corporation is investing in a country, but the government of that country acts in the public interest and tries to get that corporation out of their country to prevent further environmental destruction, they suddenly find that the ISDS prevents them. It provides legal privileges accessible only to the foreign investor, and whatever the final verdict might be, governments have to cover their own legal fees – which average over £6 million. One example that I found out about from Women in Black in Armenia concerned the Amulsar open-cast gold mine, operated by Lydian, which is backed by UK hedge funds. Amulsar is near a reservoir that feeds into Lake Sevan, which is Armenia's most important source of fresh water. The toxicity of the mine was impacting this water source and poisoning the local environment. Locals held protests which were brutally crushed by the authoritarian regime. When the velvet revolution of 2018 ushered in a more democratic government, the fight was on to remove the toxic mine. This is a fascinating case that involves UK investment.

After the community blockade at Amulsar began, Lydian established two subsidiary companies in the UK and Canada. Both countries hold investment treaties with Armenia that include ISDS provisions. In March 2019, the company 'formally notified' the Armenian government of a dispute it was bringing under both of these investment treaties.[53]

Human rights, land rights and indigenous peoples' rights are all part of our struggle for a more just, equitable, peaceful and truly democratic world. We cannot protect the forests without protecting the peoples who live in and near them. We have to work on many issues at the same time – they are all inextricably linked. The companies and corporations destroying our world are backed up by armies, security firms, investment banks and legal frameworks that put business before people. There is scant regard for ordinary people and their environment. Our privileges and high standards of living, here in Europe, are based on the denial of the basic rights of other peoples. This is closely linked to militarism and thus to peace and disarmament campaigning.

A major lesson I took from the forest protection campaigning was that effective campaigning needs *sustained* nonviolent direct action combined with education of the public, lobbying, negotiating and, most importantly, it needs clearly communicated requests or demands that can be implemented by the people or organisations targeted. Each activist is just one part of a diverse movement for change. In this campaign we were asking the trade to stop dealing in illegal timber, and suggesting that they only trade in certified timber: this did clean up the trade a bit. To do all this work needed the combined forces of several organisations and the mobilisation of hundreds of activists, and took quite some years to achieve.

First Snowball cut at Sculthorpe, Norfolk with three of us, October 1984. (Snowball Campaign)

Second Snowball cut with nine at Sculthorpe, November 1984. (Snowball Campaign)

L: Asik at home in Sarawak, September 1991.
R: Angie, Antalai and Anja in Miri, October 1991.

Solidarity protest at the Malaysian Embassy, London, 1992. (Reforest the Earth)

L: Angie handing in mahogany at Norwich police station to begin CRISPO (the Citizens' Recovery of Indigenous Peoples' Stolen Property Organisation), 1993.
R: Outside the High Court, Liverpool after the acquittal, 30 July 1996.

The yellow tank outside DTI, London, 4 December 1996. (CAAT)

Ellen, Angie and Ulla preparing for the Loch Goil action, June 1999.
(Trident Ploughshares)

Maytime with banners, 8 June 1999. (Trident Ploughshares)

Right Livelihood Award 2001 recipients, Stockholm, Sweden, December 2001. (RLA)

Angie and an Israeli peacenik blocking an armed Israeli settler at Yasouf,
October 2002.

Jayous farmers praying for peace against building of Apartheid Wall on their land, October 2002.

Trident Oratorio, Parliament Hall, Edinburgh, July 2004.

4

Preparing and Following Up Actions

ANOTHER ENVIRONMENTAL, PEACE and human rights issue that affects indigenous peoples, as well as other people, is the UK arms trade. In February 1996, I was involved in the disarmament of a British Aerospace (BAe) Hawk jet which was ready for export to Indonesia. Our group was the Seeds of Hope – East Timor Ploughshares.[54] We were an all-women group of four 'open' disarmers and six 'hidden' supporters. Together the ten of us took a year to plan the action, producing a comprehensive report plus a 20-minute video on the issues and preparing ourselves for possibly ten years in prison. Up to that time there had never been an all-women Ploughshares action, nor a Ploughshares acquittal, nor had any Ploughshares action done much damage.[55] We did an estimated one and a half million pounds worth of damage. The Indonesians later refused to buy the plane when it had been repaired, saying it was jinxed! While we were in prison after the action, an East Timorese freedom fighter imprisoned in Indonesia wrote to us thanking us for downing a plane with no loss of life.

After six months in prison awaiting trial, we were acquitted in July 1996 by the jury, amidst a fanfare of publicity that did a great deal to get the corrupt arms trade into the public eye. The Hawk jets were sold by BAe as 'training' aircraft, but we knew they were to be used to continue the bombing of East Timor where a third of the population had already been killed, including the genocide of whole tribes of unique indigenous peoples.

The threads of previous experiences were joining to strengthen this action. I knew that, although unlikely, there was a chance we could win this case because the sale of such aircraft was obviously immoral and arguably illegal too. If the jury was given the information and we organised ourselves well, we had a chance. The others did not think we could win but I pushed for a serious legal defence and not just a moral defence.

I had been told in a Crown Court case some years before that the symbolic cutting of fences around a military airbase was not an action capable of preventing crime and that therefore I had no legal defence – whereas if I had destroyed an aircraft, then maybe I would have had a defence. Little did that judge realise how he influenced me! I was able to tell the others in our group about this, and we determined to do as much damage as possible to the plane to make it unusable and thus to show that our action was capable of preventing it from being used by the UK government and BAe to commit crimes.

We spent a lot of time making sure that our booklet and video contained a history of events in East Timor and Indonesia, the background to the arms deal and what Hawk jets had done in the past, the international law context and the history of nonviolence and the Ploughshares movement. We included our indictment of the British government and BAe, who we charged with aiding and abetting genocide and murder. The video that was produced for us by film activists was especially powerful: it contained footage from John Pilger's film of the destruction in East Timor and ended with an appeal from a desperate East Timorese woman saying that if we were human we would not allow the export of arms to Indonesia.[56, 57] We included statements from the four 'open disarmers' – the 'hammerers' – about why we were doing the action and made sure that we all had copies of the booklet and the video on us when we were arrested, as well as leaving copies at the scene of the disarmament. We also made sure that we did not talk about our 'crime' but about 'disarmament'. We were preventing crime, not engaging in it!

Throughout that year of planning we all continued to campaign against the export of arms to Indonesia, and tried our best to get the decision to export the Hawk jets stopped. We wrote letters, held vigils, confronted shareholders at BAe's AGM and organised a peace camp outside the BAe airfield at Warton in Lancashire, where the Hawks were being assembled and tested – but all to no avail. We even arranged a meeting in London with Locksley Ryan, a BAe executive, but he told us that the government had granted the licence, so as far as BAe was concerned, the deal was done. He was not interested in the human cost. We were eventually able to use all these efforts to show the judge and jury that we had tried everything we could before we resorted to the disarmament action. This is always important to do as it shows you are being reasonable and not just acting on the spur of the moment without real thought.

I was given contact details for a plane spotter who informed me of the exact number of the plane that was going to be exported to Indonesia. This was essential as we did not want to damage other planes – only those that would be used in East Timor. The plane number was ZH955. We prepared our hammers, which were decorated and carved with messages.[58] Although we were a group of ten, only four of us were in a position to be publicly known after the action as being in the group, because all named people could have been charged with conspiracy to commit criminal damage, and some of the women had jobs, or very young children or an ill parent they had to look after.

The other six women were unsung heroines who were brave enough to be part of our group and trusted us not to give their names away. We were all conscious that although four of us would get the publicity and credit for the action, these six were an essential if unknown part of it. The support work is often the least glamorous and yet the most essential part of an action. Without their work, before, during and after, we would not have got the action, legal defence or court support organised so well. They helped arrange daily marches to the court along the streets of Liverpool, and in front of the court they read out aloud the names of the East Timorese who had been killed. With their banners and presence I am sure they helped influence the local population, who started putting support notices in their shop windows, and of course, the jury probably saw them too as they went into the court.

We (Jo, Andrea, Lotta and myself) called ourselves 'the Hammerers' and at the last minute had to divide even further – three to enter the Warton factory and hangar and do the actual damage to the plane, and one to provide press backup and enter later if the first group did not succeed. We decided that I would be the person who should stay behind and go into hiding until the basic press work was completed.[59]

After several recces to check where the plane was and which hangar it was being kept in, our group was ready. In the early hours of Monday 29 January 1996, Jo, Lotta and Andrea cut through the perimeter fence at Warton, broke into the hangar, found the plane and hammered on its nose-cone and wings, and on the weapons control panel within the cockpit. They hung our banner over the plane and placed our video and report in the cockpit.[60] They placed photos of East Timorese children on the wings and scattered the ashes and seeds from our joint New Year's Eve ceremony.[61] They used the phone in the hangar to inform us and the press that the action had been successful, and were eventually arrested and taken to Lytham St Annes police station. As soon as I got the message I knew I had to leave Valley Farmhouse and get on with the press work.[62] The very next day I managed to find 51 other people in Norwich to join me at Norwich Magistrates' Court to 'lay an information' in an attempt to get a warrant for the arrest of Ian Lang MP, the then Secretary of State for Trade and Industry, for conspiring to aid and abet acts of genocide, and to get an injunction to stop BAe from delivering any Hawks.

On 6 February I met with MPs and campaigning groups at Westminster to inform them of the successful disarmament action, and directly spoke to MPs Tony Benn and Paul Flynn asking for their support and for them to join in the disarmament.[63] Tony Benn was especially enthusiastic and supportive. I took out my hammer and publicly renewed my intention to disarm more Hawk jets and to encourage others to join in. All this helped get us publicity and support. I knew I did not have long before the police found me and arrested me for conspiracy, but was prepared. That afternoon, having taken a train to Preston, I arrived at the town hall to take part in a public meeting, and as I entered the hall I was arrested by two plain-clothes policemen. I handed in my copy of the video and report and soon joined the others at the police station where they were waiting for a second bail hearing. We had a chance for a quick catch-up before being separated.

I was then taken to my own bail hearing, which was held with no members of the public present. I was representing myself. The judge was pretty hostile and said 'Women like you should be locked up for a very long time'. I was shocked and said that I hoped I would have a more impartial judge when I came to the actual trial. He replied that he would be the trial judge. Judge Wickham was known to be harsh and was nicknamed, we later found out, 'Wackham Wickham'. We were rather despondent at the time, but in the event, his outrageously biased comments throughout the trial – like 'if we did not sell these weapons then the French would' – and his attempts to shut us up only served to make the jury more sympathetic.

We all ended up on remand in the high-security wing of HMP Risley. We agreed that we would be better able to influence a jury if we defended ourselves but, to make sure that we also had proper legal advice, we agreed we should have at least one of us on legal aid with a good lawyer. This is a pattern that I recommend – it is not only a safer and more creative way of fighting court cases but also gives activists a chance of finding and working with sympathetic lawyers and allowing for a cross-fertilisation of ideas and tactics.

We were extremely privileged to have an excellent solicitor, Gareth Pierce, who understood our consensus decision-making process and therefore helped us all.[64] She also found us a brilliant barrister. Jo was thus represented by Gareth and by Vera Baird QC. Andrea did a prevention of crime defence, I did an international law defence and Lotta ended with a powerful moral defence.[65] We also used four excellent expert witnesses: John Pilger, the investigative journalist who produced the documentary *Death of a Nation*; Professor Paul

Rogers, an expert on weapons from Bradford Peace Studies Department; Carmel Budiardjo, founder of Tapol, an Indonesian human rights campaign; and José Ramos-Horta, who not long after received (along with Bishop Belo) the Nobel Peace Prize and eventually became the fourth President of East Timor.[66] He was treated abysmally by the judge, who tried to stop him answering my questions about the tribes that had been annihilated by the previous Hawk jets exported to Indonesia, and sharply told him to answer simply yes or no. I could not let this behaviour go unremarked, and thus apologised to him for this treatment in front of the jury. Sometimes it is so good to be representing yourself and able to say things like this that a lawyer would not be able to do. I believe the jury was also ashamed of the way he was curtailed when explaining what had happened to his fellow East Timorese.

Because we had had the forethought to provide the evidence against ourselves in our statements of intent to disarm the plane in the video and booklet, and because we had handed these in on arrest, the prosecution used these as evidence against us, enabling us more easily to get the complete booklet and all of the video evidence in front of the jury. This provided them with the background context of our concerns and the motivation for our actions. When it came time for the jury to make a decision, we were sitting in the dock all holding hands and waiting. What an amazing relief it was when the jury went against the judge's directions and found us not guilty. Coming out of the court and into a crowd of supporters, the first and best hug was from my daughter, who had written long letters to me every week and been in the court to support me throughout the trial.

Our privileges and high standards of living, here in Europe, are based on the denial of the basic rights of other peoples

I have written a little about the prison conditions in Risley in Chapter 10, so will not go into them in detail here. We were often on 24-hour lockdown and not able to talk much together. But one of our conversations was very interesting. We discovered how hard it is for people to keep information secret. In our preparations we knew that such a serious act of 'sabotage', if known about, would have led to the arrest of all of us on conspiracy charges before we could carry out the action. We therefore agreed that only the ten of us in our Ploughshares group could know about the action or the actual date of the action. However, as we needed to inform our nearest and dearest about the possibility of so many years in prison and also to enable us to make practical plans and arrangements about housing, bills, pets, and work, we agreed that the four hammerers could each tell just one other person what they needed to know. When we checked in about this before the action, we each said we had only told one person. While in prison awaiting trial, we decided to find out what had really happened and how many people actually knew about the action before it took place. Guess how many? It was over a hundred people!

An action does not end with an arrest or even at the end of the court case. We did a lot of lobbying and mobilising for the campaign while in prison and some of us then did follow-up for another year after getting released. We were inundated with press interviews and requests to speak. Some found this overwhelming after the six months in prison, with the disorientation and social alienation that this had caused. However, we had some serious evaluations of our action and decided what follow-up was needed and what each of us could take on, dividing up the work according to our energy and personal situations.

Any nonviolent direct action has to be seen within the overall movement for change, which includes the whole gamut of tools for change – research, publications, lobbying, letter-writing, petitions, public meetings, demonstrations, boycotts, nonviolent direct resistance and disruption, legislative changes and their implementation, to mention a few.

I spent the year after getting out of prison working as a volunteer with the Campaign Against the Arms Trade (CAAT) organising demonstrations, including a week of action outside the Department of Trade and Industry (DTI), which facilitated the arms sales.[67] It was especially good to connect up with East Timorese refugees in the UK in the lobbying, protests and direct actions. Some of these refugees welcomed the chance to engage in nonviolent protests aimed at the continuing Indonesian occupation of East Timor and gladly joined in. They enjoyed jumping on the bright yellow tank we hired to drive up to the DTI and point its gun at the front door. They clambered onto the tank and unfurled an East Timorese flag.

I had always wanted to do a series of actions at the DTI as they were responsible for issuing the export licences and took no notice of the human rights abuses caused by their sales. The week was really inspiring and I was glad to be in the group organising it all. Apart from the tank turning up one day, we also had daily vigils and leafleting. One day the entrance was blockaded by a die-in of protesters spattered with blood (red paint). Other protesters climbed up onto the balcony above and showered the bodies below with fake notes marked as 'blood money' and unfurled a large banner that read 'DTI LICENSE TO KILL'. But maybe the most fun action was the Tuesday Blah, Blah Day that I had wanted to do for ages. We found loads of documents that the UK government had produced that claimed to prevent weapons being exported for use in human rights abuses, so we read them out and then hung them on a washing line symbolising 'dirty washing' along with long chants of 'blah, blah, blah'. Another day we had people dressed up as well-known dictators and oppressors coming along to queue outside the DTI to buy arms from the generous British.[68]

An action outside the Indonesian Embassy included one traumatised East Timorese refugee who completely lost it, and started screaming and shouting when confronted by the Indonesian security guards. Luckily, his fellow refugee and friend worked with us to get him to safety out of the action. It was only later that we learnt he had been badly tortured by Kopassus, the Indonesian Special Forces Command, and he was having terrible flashbacks. It is very important when working with refugees to understand what they have suffered, and to make sure they are not put into potential conflict situations where their trauma is reactivated. This is why it is so necessary when preparing actions to know your activists as well as possible and to work in affinity groups where you learn about each other and can provide suitable support.

We did not just act in London. I remember very clearly the action we did at the Glover Webb factory at Hamble, near Southampton, which manufactured armoured vehicles, and the water cannons being supplied to Indonesia.[69] We broke into the factory, after taking a ladder to climb over the security fencing and painted anti-war slogans on all the vehicles we could find before being arrested. These actions continued to put pressure on arms manufacturers, but they are an immensely powerful lobby with high-level connections in the government and our work continues to this day.

I also got involved in helping CAAT with its Judicial Review of the government decision to issue licences for more arms and security equipment to be sent to Indonesia. CAAT continues to do urgent and important work, not only researching the arms trade, but also issuing legal challenges to try to stop illegal arms sales. The most recent are the ongoing UK arms sales to Saudi Arabia, even after a High Court ruling that the arms sales had been illegal. The bombing of Yemen is a catastrophe for the people there and it is shameful that the UK once again is more interested in making money from arms sales than in the lives of people.[70]

Over many years I have continued supporting CAAT by speaking out at shareholder meetings and organising blockades of the arms fairs held at the ExCeL Centre in London.[71, 72] Preparing for the court cases takes more time than preparing the actual blockades, as they require getting all the evidence together and deciding on the legal arguments to use. One of CAAT's expert witnesses, Andrew Feinstein, has now produced a very useful book examining the global arms trade.[73] The issues raised when dealing with these out of control arms manufacturers, like BAe Systems and Lockheed Martin, remind me of the warning that was given in 1961 by the outgoing President, Dwight D Eisenhower, when he described the growing military-industrial complex.[74] He said:

In the councils of government, we must guard against the acquisition of unwarranted influence, whether sought or unsought, by the military-industrial complex. The potential for the disastrous rise of misplaced power exists and will persist... We must never let the weight of this combination endanger our liberties or democratic processes. We should take nothing for granted.

5

Reclaiming International Law
and Making it More Accessible

BY THE SUMMER of 1997, I decided to concentrate on my work for nuclear disarmament once more. The historic judgement of the International Court of Justice on the Advisory Opinion on the Legality of the Threat or Use of Nuclear Weapons in 1996 had brought the international law arguments into focus, and I felt we could use them to better effect in anti-nuclear weapons campaigning.

I had first come across the Geneva Conventions and International Humanitarian Law (IHL) in the early 1980s. It was not very popular in the peace movement as peace protesters were against nuclear weapons on moral grounds, not legal grounds – but I was attracted to it as soon as I heard about it. It seemed to me that the law gained its legitimacy from its grounding in basic morality, that all governments and state leaders used the law and it would be very useful in our struggles for a better world. This has proved to be the case and over the decades the peace movement has come to value and use the law more, thus reclaiming it for themselves.

I had been amongst a group of people led by Keith Mothersson, who co-founded the Institute for Law and Peace (INLAP) in 1989.[75] I became the secretary of this educational charity for its first two years and was engaged in networking and distributing information about the international laws of war, especially as they concerned nuclear weapons. We were involved in the early discussions that led to the World Court Project.[76] In the early 1990s, as part of INLAP and the Snowball Enforce the Law Campaign, I had organised with Robbie Manson a series of 'Information Layings' at magistrates' courts in an attempt to get the courts to outlaw UK nuclear weapons in the light of these international humanitarian laws.[77] I even wrote a *DIY Guide to Putting the Government on Trial*. We organised a lobby of all the High Court judges and arranged public meetings on IHL issues relating to war.

I now felt it was time to integrate these war laws into the very heart of a campaign. The 1996 BAe Hawk action had left me wondering how we could have enabled more follow-up actions to have taken place, and I wanted to experiment with setting up a structure to enable others to take part in Ploughshares actions within a safe, nonviolent and accountable framework, and to base it all upon international law. I decided to write an outline of a Ploughshares campaign based around disarming the Trident system, and sent it out as an open letter in June 1997 to around a hundred people, inviting them to give me feedback on the idea.[78] I asked them to let me know if they would publicly join such a campaign if there were one, ten, or a hundred other activists. From the initial response to my letter I found six or seven people who were willing to act with very few others, and able to take on the risks of possible conspiracy charges – and at that time this felt like a very strong risk. We formed a core group and went on to organise it all.

It took about a year before the public launch of the campaign during which time I wrote the *Tri-Denting It Handbook* with the help of several people including Steve Whiting from Quaker Peace and Service.[79] Zoe Broughton filmed a video to enthuse people to take part and we used it in our mobilising and training of affinity groups. Affinity groups were a tried and tested process for sustaining civil resistance that the peace movement had been employing for many years. It brought between three and 15 activists together to form a hopefully long-term support group for planning and enacting safe nonviolent actions. We found that around ten activists in such a group is ideal as everyone needs to be able to speak, to be heard and able to participate actively. More than 15 usually meant that some people were never fully integrated in the group and their voices and skills were rarely valued

The UK peace movement was very large, with many differing views on how to work towards the long-term goal of ridding the world of nuclear weapons. Faslane was the home base of the Trident nuclear weapon system and our direct nonviolent disarmament actions would mainly be taking place there. The nearby town of Helensburgh already had a thriving CND (Campaign for Nuclear Disarmament) group, so I went to meet them and explain what Trident Ploughshares (TP) wanted to do and to gain their support. It was a productive visit, where I first met Jane Tallents, who said she was very supportive of the project, but that the CND group had enough on their hands and could not get involved. But they would not stand in our way.[80] We also knew we would need a safe place to provide food and shelter for protesters. Although the Faslane Peace Camp had been occupied continuously from June 1982, it was on a small patch of land next to a busy road and had its own work to do. While pondering our options, we were extremely fortunate that Georgina Smith, a woman who had been deeply involved in the Greenham Common protests, was well-known as a feisty protester and for fighting the bylaws there, agreed to let us use her woodland, Peaton Glen Wood, as a campsite.[81]

Peaton Wood is a 14.5-hectare Plantation on Ancient Woodland Site (PAWS) situated in the Rosneath Peninsula in Argyll and Bute in the West of Scotland. It is a wonderful woodland with a burn rushing down the steep hillside, the top of which is only a few metres from the main gate into Coulport, where the nuclear warheads are stored and from which the nuclear convoys are transported to and from AWE Burghfield in Berkshire, England. She had managed to purchase it anonymously, with the help of a lawyer, as the Ministry of Defence would never have allowed an anti-nuclear campaigner to have bought it up! Georgina later offered Peaton Wood to me and I found other women to set up a trust to own it.[82] We are a group of women peace activists keeping the woodland for the peace movement but also as the beautiful ancient woodland site that it is.[83] At the bottom of the wood are a couple of flat fields, covered in bracken but ideal for camping, and Loch Long stretches along a beach just over the road. It was a perfect site and many of us have grown to love and revere the beautiful woodland.[84]

Effective campaigning needs sustained nonviolent direct action combined with education of the public, lobbying, negotiating and, most importantly, it needs clearly-communicated requests or demands

After working flat out for a year we were ready and on 2 May 1998 we organised a simultaneous launch of the campaign in Hiroshima, Ghent Gothenburg, London and Edinburgh. Sixty-two people had signed the Pledge to Prevent Nuclear Crime at this point, and their names were unfurled on a banner in Edinburgh. Right from the start we were determined to be open and accountable to all – in our opinion we were backed up by the law and were acting in the public interest, so we had nothing to hide. We had a huge banner hung under Westminster Bridge and there were police on the bridge and in boats trying to arrest us all. Public meetings and press conferences were held in all five cities – we had begun!

As part of our openness and to encourage the changes we needed the government to make, we sent an Open Letter to the Prime Minister. This began our long series of dialogue and negotiation with government officials.[85] The *Tri-Denting It Handbook* was being widely distributed and after the press got hold of a copy, I received a letter from the Commander of Faslane asking for a copy.[86] I charged him the same £10 that TPers had to pay, thinking that this might make him liable to co-conspiracy charges if the prosecution services ever decided to charge all of us with conspiracy to commit criminal damage purely for owning the handbook! If he ever read the handbook he would have known of our complete adherence to nonviolence. And although we had maps of the naval bases and diagrams of Trident submarines, we had clear warnings of where not to go on the submarines and what not to touch (nuclear propulsion plant space, nuclear-tipped missile tubes, torpedo storage areas) and we stressed the nonviolence and safety ground-rules that all TPers had pledged to keep.

At the first TP disarmament camp of two weeks during August 1998 there were 200 people from 12 different nationalities taking part. Over a hundred of us were arrested (some of us multiple times) doing a variety of actions from cutting fences, painting on the rocks where the nuclear warheads were being stored, swimming to the submarines, entering the base and blockading. I was arrested three times during this first camp and charged with 'malicious mischief' (as 'criminal damage' is known in Scottish legal terms) and contravention of the military bylaws for entering the base after cutting in. TP gained a great deal of experience of likely charges, possible fines, the characteristics of the local magistrates and which local lawyers were friendly and able to handle themselves well with the moral and international legal defences that most wanted to put forward. We encouraged activists to defend themselves and helped advise them on court procedures and possible defences. Many of the TPers spoke so well and passionately in court that they were 'admonished' and left court with no fines to pay at all.[87] Activists, supporters, police, lawyers and judges – all were getting a free education in humanitarian law.

After this TP went from strength to strength: more people joined the core organising group, a newsletter was produced called *Speed the Plough*, donations came in and more affinity groups formed.[88] The court cases were opportunities for people to witness the concern and passion of the defendants and fines were either paid or we went to prison.

Most of the actions were for fairly minor offences, but a few affinity groups planned and carried our more major disarmament actions, and some of their stories are told in their own words in the book *Trident on Trial*.[89]

I made sure that I personally did not do a 'major' Ploughshares action that would result in a jury trial until our campaign was well settled-in and organised. We thus worked to establish regular disarmament camps, trainings, legal and court support networks, and the affinity group structure and members' meetings where decisions were made by consensus. Many of the ideas that I had gleaned over the years from very many different people and organisations came together in the *Tri-Denting It Handbook* that eventually went into three editions, has been used as a model by lots of campaigning groups in different countries and was even translated into Japanese.

None of the ideas were new. We have learnt from what has gone before and have adapted to make it relevant to our times and our issues. The *Handbook* provided background materials, training ideas, briefing sheets, model lobbying letters and petitions and was as open as possible, sharing information, structures and processes, so that each activist had easy access to the latest advice and learning. Eventually all the materials and archives were put up on a website that has been regularly archived by various independent organisations. TP is now in its 22nd year and still engages in regular direct action at the nuclear weapon sites in the UK.

Before moving on, I must tell you about a couple of spontaneous actions. This is because such creativity and enjoyment are essential to enable us to keep motivated year after year and not to give up, even when the changes we want to see are just not happening and we begin to lose heart. It is also important to recognise that a sudden idea for an action can be implemented without months of planning and be just as successful, even if risky.

Just a few months before TP started and as part of a women's camp at Georgina's wood, four of us at the camp-fire one night decided to see how far we could get into the Coulport nuclear base. Sylvia, Jenny, Tracy and I left late that night and walked along the coast in the moonlight over large, jagged rocks, dodging the police boat searchlights that were sporadically piercing the dark coastline.[90] Every time the searchlight came towards us we stood very still and turned our faces away from the light. With our dark clothes this made us virtually invisible. It was very rough going in the dark but we took it slowly until we came to the security fence around Coulport. We cut through it only to find a few more well-lit fences further in. We clustered right under the bright lights and closed-circuit cameras thinking that anyone looking out would be blinded by the lights and maybe not notice us, and the cameras were hopefully not able to see us right at the base of the fence. We managed to get right into the centre of the base, to a jetty where a police boat was tied up. The lights on the jetty were suddenly activated automatically as we walked onto the jetty. We were amazed no one had yet seen us, excited and very keyed up.

We could not resist getting in the boat and were surprised to see the keys were in the engine. I quickly checked in with everyone that we were happy to get the boat started and go on a little exploration of the base by water. Everyone agreed (though there was no time for a proper discussion) and it then took seemingly ages to work out how to get the boat started and for us to untie and take off, slowly making our way out of the base and into the loch. We did not put on the lights on the boat as at that time the police boats were patrolling without lights in order to surprise peace protesters! This meant that no one could clearly see who we were.

We had noticed that as police boats passed in the dark, the police just waved to each other, so that is what we did. It was lucky we were dressed in dark clothes just like the police were. We managed to take the boat right into the explosives-handling jetty, waving to the guards in the watchtower. We had a good look around and then decided to try and go several miles round into the next loch to the Faslane base.

I have always wanted to take off in a police rigid inflatable boat – they are quite powerful and go so fast and are usually employed in chasing us around the loch and keeping locals away from the naval base. One of the women sat in front and called out whenever she saw a rock, which was quite hard in the dark. When we looked at our route the next day we realised we had been very lucky not to put a hole in the boat! Two of us took turns steering, and another was in the back, anxiously clinging on. We got to Faslane and as soon as we entered the busy base, where lights are always blazing out, it was obvious who we were and a police chase began. We went full pelt and managed to land two women on the boom around where the Trident subs are berthed and they leapt into the water and began swimming towards the subs. The police caught up to us and asked, 'Are you filming this?' We just laughed and wished we had been. The police came aboard and sent others off to catch the swimmers.

It was the most fun spontaneous action I have ever been on – it could never have been planned to turn out so well. Keeping going all these years has only been possible because so much of the work is enjoyable as well as serious.

The end of the story was that we were charged with theft, quite a serious charge. However, we argued that we were putting the boat to its proper use, doing a citizens' war crime inspection to see if there were weapons of mass destruction around, that we had driven the boat from one high-security area to another as the police were not doing their duty investigating these massive nuclear crimes. We were certainly not intending to permanently deprive another of their possessions and so we were found not guilty! We were found guilty of the lesser offence of 'clandestinely taking and using the property of another' and got off very lightly with an admonishment. I think the magistrate was secretly amused that a group of four women had managed to embarrass the military and show up how insecure the base was.

However, another spontaneous action did not turn out so well. I was driving a car with Hanna and Katri, two young Finnish women, and Krista, a Dutch woman. They were all part of an international affinity group that I had got to know very well in Belgium when I helped facilitate their two-day TP nonviolence workshop. They were committed activists who had come over for the summer camp and stayed on to help out. We were off to provide court support for one of the many activists appearing at Helensburgh court that day.[91] We had computers in the car, which I had forgotten about, and Hanna and Katri were to be interviewed by a Finnish film crew later that day. I was coming up to the main gate at Faslane and, suddenly seeing the gates open with very lax security, said impetuously, 'Hey, look, shall we go in?' The others thought I was joking and laughingly said yes, so I drove straight in through the gate and only stopped to avoid a security guard who stepped in front of us, blocking the road. The bandit alarm had gone off and the whole base was closed while they dealt with us.[92] It was all rather amusing and we felt quite pleased with ourselves keeping the pressure on the base, reminding them that although the protest camp was over, we were still around and protesting.

We expected to be released fairly soon but found ourselves locked up for three days, with the car, which belonged to someone else, impounded. It was a Friday and we were not put in front of a court until Monday: I was charged with a serious dangerous driving offence and Krista was charged with possession of a dangerous weapon – her peanut-butter knife! I had spent a most miserable weekend alone in my cell blaming myself for letting people down, not having thought of all the consequences and worrying about the serious charge against me. Not all spontaneous actions work out and it taught me to take more responsibility for others and to allow more time for genuine decision-making – I had got the others into a mess without due consultation.

Our court case was held at Dumbarton Sheriff Court, and unsurprisingly the CCTV footage was never produced to prove I had driven safely and had stopped carefully and the guard had been in no danger. The guard in question testified I had almost run him over, which was a complete lie. However, one of the other guards told the truth, and so there was no case to answer: we were all acquitted and the charge of the dangerous peanut-butter knife was also given the disdain it deserved. This was a great relief to us all. It is one thing getting a long record for nonviolent civil resistance but quite another having a record of dangerous driving, or assault.

6

Legal Challenges

TP WAS DEVELOPING well: there were lots of people helping ensure support for all the people getting involved. Several excellent 'maximum' disarmament actions, as we called actions that had the potential for very serious charges and possible long-term prison sentences, had already taken place.[93] We needed to keep the pressure up, and at last I felt the time was right for me to plan my own 'maximum' disarmament action.

Gathering a special affinity group together, we formed an international crime prevention team consisting of myself from England, Ellen from Scotland and Ulla from Denmark.[94] We aimed to disrupt the international crime of threatening the world with mass destruction and decided to take out an essential link in the Trident submarine system and thus effectively prevent crime, even if only for a short while. Having visited several potential sites in Scotland we decided on targeting the floating laboratory complex in Loch Goil which does the research on minimising the radar, acoustic and magnetic noises on Trident nuclear submarines. It was an essential link in the whole system, which was an important legal consideration if we were to have a chance of getting an acquittal.

We were given a boat with an engine by Eric from Helensburgh, prepared our documents, statements and evidence for the jury, and found people prepared to accompany us as supporters to photograph the action and do the press work.

It felt very liberating to leave the administration of TP and support work to others and concentrate on preparing my own action. We practised getting the dinghy in and out of the transporting vehicle, pumped up and motor attached, but every time I tried to start the engine I could never manage to get it going. Eric said not to worry, it would be all right on the day!

On 8 June 1999 we were ready. Our supporters drove us to the loch edge, helped us get the boat ready and our lifejackets on, and after a little struggle the motor did start. We manoeuvred over the loch to the barge *Maytime*, tied up our boat and then we were on the barge. I climbed through a window into the laboratory while Ellen and Ulla hung the banners around the barge. They said: 'BRINGING CRIME INTO THE LIGHT', 'CONSTRUCTIVE DECONSTRUCTION', 'TP OPPOSES RESEARCH FOR GENOCIDE' and with a play on the research acronym, the last one said, 'D.E.R.A. = DEADLY EFFICIENT RESEARCH FOR ANNIHILATION'.

Ulla joined me inside, and we handed out to Ellen loads of computers, printers, computer disks, manuals, papers and telephones, and Ellen gleefully threw them into the loch. In the corner of the lab was a metal cage which housed the mechanism for a model submarine that was used for the tests. I cut into it and then severed electrical wires and smashed circuit boards and control panels. We basically emptied the whole barge. We left it clean and tidy along with our video, the *Tri-Denting It Handbook*, statements and photos of the victims of Hiroshima and Nagasaki.

After doing what we could, we then settled down for a picnic. I had pooh-poohed the idea of preparing food when Ellen had suggested it, thinking we would never have time, as on our two previous reconnoitres there had been a busy police and naval presence. But she was right to prepare refreshments, as we all enjoyed the picnic after our hectic disarmament work.

Newt, another nearby moveable navy barge, was only a few hundred yards away; as the police had not yet turned up, we decided to inspect it. Our dilapidated boat, however, was now hardly afloat so we looked at the life rafts. Haven't you always wanted to have a go? We launched it and it opened spectacularly but upside down, so we turned to release a second one but this one refused to open. So much for saving lives!

By this time three hours had gone by, and as we stood on the deck, finally a police boat arrived. We helped it moor up and explained we were from TP and were totally nonviolent. They had heard of TP and the atmosphere was very friendly. We were all doing our jobs! We got into the police boat for a lovely run down the loch. It had been a really successful action.[95] We spent the next five months in prison in Scotland preparing our legal case, which finally started at the end of September 1999.[96] Ellen and Ulla were represented and I defended myself. With the help of our supporters we got some good expert witnesses into the court, including Professor Francis Boyle, an international lawyer from the USA, and Professor Paul Rogers, who had been one of my teachers at Bradford University in the Peace Studies Department, and another veteran anti-nuclear campaigner, Dr Rebecca Johnson. But the prize witness was Judge Ulf Panzer, whom I had met at a conference of lawyers in Berlin some years previously. He spoke about the Pershing missiles in Germany, and the organisation Judges and Prosecutors for Peace, which had organised a march of 250 judges. He said 'Imagine 250 British judges marching around Faslane!' He described the advert in a newspaper which 550 judges had signed. He then went on explain how he and 20 other judges had blockaded the base at Mutlangen and what the consequences were. It was powerful stuff, and as a fellow judge our woman Sheriff was impressed. At the end of his testimony Ulf said he wanted to congratulate Sheriff Gimblett on the wonderful atmosphere in the court and the fair way that she conducted the proceedings. There was then a spontaneous round of applause from those present, including the jury!

It was an amazing trial and the Sheriff instructed the jury to acquit us, which they did. She said in her summing up to the jury:

> I have to conclude that the three in company with others were justified in thinking that Great Britain in their use of Trident... could be construed as a threat and as such is an infringement of international and customary law. I have heard nothing which would make it seem to me that the accused acted with criminal intent.[97]

It was a strange experience to walk free once again. The newspapers were full of it. There were headlines saying 'Britain's Nuclear Arsenal is Illegal', 'Scotland Outlaws Nuclear Weapons', 'Bombshell Hits Fortress UK', but the one I liked best screamed out: 'How Four Middle-aged Ladies Sank UK Defence'.[98, 99, 100, 101] This was a major breakthrough and we celebrated, but of course, it was a real shock to the government and defence establishments. They could not leave it at this. We had won fair and square but it opened up the possibility that lots more activists would be disarming more naval equipment. Our acquittal could not be overturned, but the legal points could be examined by a higher court, so a year later four legal points were addressed at High Court level at a Lord Advocate's Reference.[102] I was the first non-lawyer ever to argue at this level on my own behalf; that was a campaign in itself involving scores of letters and a stubborn desire to ensure that these legal proceedings would be accessible to ordinary folk and conducted in ordinary language.[103] The legal arguments that I made can be found in *Trident on Trial*. The result was very disappointing, as I had asked for and been assured by the presiding judge, Lord Prosser, that he would look at the exact specifications of the Trident system alongside the international laws. I wonder what kind of pressure these judges were under, because the ruling, when it came out, was quickly shoved on the desk by Prosser who ran into the court without his wig on, dumped it and ran out again. He certainly did not look me in the eye.

The rulings were examined by many international lawyers, who found a lot to criticise in it. Charles Moxley, a distinguished international lawyer, thought the court had 'got it wrong'. After a lengthy analysis of the LAR (Lord Advocate's Reference) he concluded:

> The effects of nuclear weapons are not reasonably subject to dispute and were assumed by the High Court. So too, the nature of the policy of deterrence is beyond reasonable dispute. The only real question is whether it is unlawful to threaten to do that which it is unlawful to do. The ICJ answered in the affirmative. The Scots High Court of Justiciary is in error – and does damage to the rule of law – by its abnegation of this restraint.[104]

The main success gained by our movement to rid the world of nuclear weapons has been the disseminating of the international law arguments to a large number of lawyers and judges as well as to the general public.[105] After the High Court case, several of the prosecution lawyers came up to me to shake my hand and admitted that the case had been fascinating and they had learnt a lot about international law. This was ironic; one of the rulings of the LAR was that we did not need to bring international lawyers in to give evidence, as all lawyers knew enough about international law!

Each activist is just one part of a diverse movement for change

The legal ramifications and challenges continue as TP takes part in ongoing work connected with pressuring the Scottish National Party (SNP) government to take a stronger position by demanding Trident is taken away from Scotland on international law grounds. This would ensure that Scotland is not complicit in preparations for mass murder, which is what basing Trident in Scotland amounts to. In 2009 several of us worked to organise an international conference on *Trident and International Law: Scotland's Obligations*, to which judges and lawyers were invited to hear some of the top international lawyers. The proceedings were written up in a book with the same title as the conference.[106] It was extremely interesting and I was especially glad to spend some time with Christopher Weeramantry, who had been a judge on the International Court of Justice (ICJ) from 1991 to 2000 and Vice-President from 1997 to 2000. I had used much of his work in my legal defences during the original Greenock Trial.

The nuclear weapons possessed by the nine nuclear-armed states have always been illegal and criminal, but because of the denial by the five leading ones – the USA, Russia, China, France and the UK – they and the remaining four, Israel, India, Pakistan and North Korea, get away with it. However, the world community has now challenged that impunity; as I write this, the UN Treaty on the Prohibition of Nuclear Weapons (TPNW) has just been ratified by the 50th nation that was needed to bring it into force.[107, 108] The TPNW prohibits the developing, testing, producing, manufacturing, otherwise acquiring, possessing, stockpiling, transferring, using or threatening to use nuclear weapons, assisting other states with these prohibited activities, stationing, deployment or installation of nuclear weapons belonging to other states on a state party's territory.

As well as prohibitions, the treaty carries positive obligations, which include suppression of violations of the prohibitions on its territory and the requirement to urge non-member states to join. All of the prohibition treaties have an effect on global understanding and interpretations of IHL.[109] They have created stigma and they change the global perception of what is acceptable. To date, none of the nine nuclear-armed states have signed or ratified the TPNW. The use of a nuclear weapon, as an indiscriminate weapon of mass destruction, has always been illegal under the basic principles of IHL and the TPNW, as a specific and targeted legal instrument, has built on that legal basis.

The nuclear powers, especially the USA, had felt so threatened by the imminent coming into force of the TPNW that they wrote to those who had already ratified to try and get them to withdraw.[110] Proof that this treaty was already having a real impact.

Model Trident lock-on, Downing Street, London, 11 October 2004. (Trident Ploughshares)

Angie at Faslane Peace Camp during the Faslane 365 year of blockades. (F365)

F365 academics blockade, 2007. (F365)

Disarm Nukes outside Parliament, London, 2009.

F365 Spanish blockade, 2007.
(F365)

SECURITY FOR WOMEN?
DISARM MASCULINITY DISARM MILITARIES
SPEND £££ ON OUR SERVICES NOT TRIDENT
WOMEN SAY NO TO N.A.T.O.

Women's Gate Big Blockade of Aldermaston, 15 February 2010.

No To NATO demo at St.Martins, London, 20 November 2010.

TP group from UK in Lulea, Sweden, July 2011.

7

International Solidarity

BY THIS TIME I needed to take a break so I switched issues again. I have done this throughout my years of campaigning and have found it to be a way to protect myself from getting jaded or burnt out. Immersing myself in new issues, places, ideas, usually rejuvenates me. Little did I know it would not work this time. I had no idea how much it would affect me.

I was deeply concerned about the problem of peace in Palestine/Israel and wanted to learn more first-hand. My father-in-law, Nathan, was a Jewish Romanian and my daughter was named Zina after Nathan's sister, who had been in Paris training to be a doctor when the Nazis invaded and deported her to a concentration camp. She was never heard of again. I thought keeping the name Zina in the family was a good way to remember her and the personal impact on our family of fascism and authoritarian 'final solutions'.

I had read as much as I could around the issue of totalitarianism, genocides and massacres, and wondered how concentration camps and holocausts could take place in supposedly 'civilised' places. I was in my 20s when the Pol Pot regime organised the Cambodian genocide that killed up to two million people – a quarter of Cambodia's population – and this was also the era of Idi Amin's atrocities in Uganda. I had an Armenian father but he never told me anything much about what it was to be Armenian. Nevertheless, he had taken our family, when I was 18 years old, on a visit to Bursa in Turkey where his family had been weavers.[111, 112] He only found one Armenian left in what had been a large multicultural town with many hundreds of Armenians. I decided to read up about the Armenian genocide that took place between 1914 and 1923 and involved the murder and expulsion of one and a half million Armenians.[113]

But it was the 1963 report by Hannah Arendt, a German Jewish philosopher who escaped to the USA, and wrote about the 'banality of evil' that especially influenced me.[114] Eichmann 'was only obeying orders' and we hear this excuse so often when awful deeds are done. It is a way of pushing the blame onto others

– those giving the orders – and not taking responsibility for our own acts. I was also horrified to learn about Stanley Milgram's famous experiments focusing on the conflict between obedience to authority and personal conscience, just a year after the Eichmann trial. He was a psychologist at Yale University and wanted to know how easily people could be influenced into committing atrocities, like so many ordinary Germans did in WWII.[115] He set up experiments to find out how far people would go in obeying an instruction if it involved harming another person. He found out that ordinary people are likely to follow orders given by an authority figure, even to the extent of killing an innocent human being. He went on to conclude that obedience to authority is ingrained in us all from the way we are brought up and is learnt in the family, school and workplace. This really got me thinking about the dangers of obedience and how important it is to critically evaluate any instructions and orders that we are given.

Although I had Jewish friends and relatives and had visited them in Israel a few times, I had never, to my shame, made the effort to get to know any Palestinians.[116] So, on one of my family visits, while staying with close Israeli friends in Jerusalem, I joined a Women in Black (WiB) conference in Jerusalem in December 1999, and joined in some of their visits to the occupied West Bank.[117, 118] There I not only met Palestinians, but also members of the Israeli peace movement like Jeff of ICAHD who worked with Palestinians to rebuild their houses destroyed by the IDF (Israeli Defence Forces) some of which were then demolished again and again, Uri of Gush Shalom, one of the primary leaders of the Israeli peace movement, and many others.[119, 120, 121] This got me really fired up, as Britain had a huge responsibility for the ongoing political problems in the area after backing the Zionists with the Balfour Declaration of 1917 and because of its actions when administering the territories of Palestine and Transjordan after the League of Nations gave Britain the Mandate for Palestine which came into effect in 1923.[122]

The current situation in Palestine/Israel is yet another example of the long-lasting and terrible impacts of Britain's shameful colonial past that included, lest we forget, the setting up of concentration camps in South Africa during the Second Boer War in 1900–02.The Black Lives Matter movement came strongly into focus in 2020, bringing hope that a more balanced and honest appraisal of our colonial past will be communicated in general and specifically to the children in our schools. A true colonial history may help explain many of the conflicts and problems that still affect the global community. It is time for the UK to confess its many past crimes and to change its foreign policies that are still about narrow and exploitative 'national interests' and to start behaving ethically and compassionately.

Being in touch with the Israeli peace movement, I then joined the International Solidarity Movement (ISM) at its very beginning in August 2001 when it asked for volunteers to go out and help with nonviolent resistance to the Israeli occupation. I had found myself wondering how the vast majority of ordinary Palestinians managed to sustain a nonviolent resistance to such a cruel military occupation when both sides were engaged in bombings and killings during this Second Intifada that had started a year before in September 2000. I joined with four other friends, all of whom were active in Women in Black London, and we formed a little WiB (UK) group to go over for the two weeks of ISM actions in August 2001.[123]

We witnessed the many roadblocks and checkpoints that hindered movement between Palestinian villages and towns, preventing businesses from operating and children and teachers getting to schools, preventing patients getting to hospitals or food getting to markets. We visited refugee camps where those who had been displaced had to live in crowded, difficult conditions.[124]

On 9 August 2001, Orient House in Jerusalem, the diplomatic centre of the Palestinians and a symbol of their statehood, was taken over and occupied by armed Israelis. We met with members of the Husseini family, whose family lived in Orient House, and heard from them that some of the family were being held under house arrest, and many neighbouring Palestinians in the street outside had been expelled from their homes. We decided that we would provide an international presence and witness by holding a quiet demonstration at the roadblocks where the employees of Orient House were demanding to be let into their place of work. Over the next two days, we joined the peaceful protests organised by Palestinians holding signs calling for an end to the occupation of Orient House and an end to all violence and a call for justice for all peoples. As we were standing there the Israeli police and border police used horses to charge at us, started beating people, pointed their rifles at us all, and demanded that everyone go home or be subject to unspeakable things.[125]

Any nonviolent direct action has to be seen within the overall movement for change

This was the first time I experienced the violence and brutality of the Israeli police. I was punched and dragged into a police van and subjected to screaming threats of terrifying violence if I did not sign documents in Hebrew that I did not understand. I refused, of course, but it was very frightening and would have been more so if I had not been standing next to a kind member of the

Israeli peace movement who translated everything for me. I had just witnessed a Palestinian being horrifically beaten up by four or five police. He had been thrown into the back of a van and other policemen rushed into it, pushing out several other international prisoners who had been in the same van. We then all heard lots of screaming as the Palestinian was beaten up. When I later saw him he had blood coming out of his eyes, nose and ears and he was bruised and battered all over. He said he was lucky, as this was minor compared to what Palestinians usually suffered! Fortunately, an Israeli lawyer secured our release, but told us that it was useless to take a case against the police: it was too common and there was no justice within Israeli courts for Palestinians.[126] I could hardly believe this at the time, but over many months I came to know the truth of it. I was especially disturbed by the behaviour of Israeli settlers and soldiers inside Hebron/Al Khalil where Palestinian buildings, factories and clinics had been bombed and turned into rubble, where the rooftops of Palestinian houses were being taken over by Israeli snipers, and where long curfews were in place.[127] As part of the ISM weeks we were based in Bethlehem in the Paradise Hotel, which, because of the violence all around, was empty of tourists and offered to us to use. The road outside was often full of gunfire and we had to keep our heads down when peering out to see if it was safe to leave. We saw an Israeli tank smashing over Palestinian cars and realised we were in a live war zone.

We got to know Ghassan of the Rapprochement Centre, who was dedicated to nonviolence. He told us a great deal about the nonviolent resistance in the First Intifada which took place from 1987 to 1991. He was sad that the resistance was now turning more violent but explained that more Palestinians (though still only a minority) felt that they had a right to self-defence and to use weapons in their fight for independence. My time in Israel/Palestine, a land of dispossession and violent conflict, and yet one where you see the word 'peace' written and spoken about everywhere, tested my own commitment to nonviolence. I began to understand why some Palestinians were taking up arms, when there were daily abuses being carried out by fully-armed Israelis on a largely non-armed civilian population, who every day were losing more and more of their land and water resources to fanatical Israeli settlers. But although shaken, my belief in nonviolence remains steady, as I still believe that violence begets more violence. In these circumstances, international solidarity is even more important. We all need to stand up and resist oppression. We cannot condone by our silence.

Part of our solidarity was becoming 'human shields' for a few families in

Beit Jala. One family showed us the Israeli bullet holes in the bedroom wall where their daughters had been sleeping, and asked us to 'protect' them by staying with them overnight. This also provided an opportunity to get an insight into a peaceful Christian Palestinian home that had been targeted by the IDF. On later trips to Bethlehem I started Arabic lessons with the family's aunt, Samia. My Arabic writing is much neater than my English writing because of her teaching and I love the beauty of Arabic script.

After two weeks with ISM, the four friends that I had come with left to return to the UK, but I stayed on for a further month, visiting other places and listening to people's stories. I was especially privileged to spend ten days in Hebron/Al Khalil with the Christian Peacemaker Team (CPT), shadowing their work and helping out where I could.[128] I learnt about the H2 areas in Hebron where the Israelis had made a closed military zone, and about the constant curfews where people were shot on sight if found outside their homes. These were terrible times and there had been 200 days of total curfew in the previous 11 months of the Intifada, some lasting for many days. People could not get to the hospitals, refuse trucks could not remove rubbish, food ran out, repairs could not be done, people who had died were left in houses as they could not be removed for burial – all of this in a very hot climate. The stench was unbelievable and big black rats and flies were proliferating. The insect bites I received came up in huge welts. As soon as the curfew was lifted, those Palestinians who could leave did so, some getting out of the country altogether. Life was unbearable, which was what was intended by the Israeli State, in order to force as many people as possible to emigrate. But people do not easily give up their homes and the land that their people have lived in for many, many centuries.

I am writing this in Covid times, when British people have now experienced Covid lockdowns. These have involved far, far fewer restrictions than an IDF-imposed curfew done at gunpoint with tanks going round the streets to enforce them. Perhaps more people can now understand at least a little what these curfews meant for Palestinians. The major cause of the problems in Hebron comes from the illegal settlements right in the middle of the city and the way these religious fanatics taunt and harass the Palestinians with the armed backing of the IDF.[129] Locals told us of how soldiers had come in the middle of the night and at gunpoint had raided their cupboards and drawers, stealing their money and jewellery; how they occupied the upper floors and the roofs as snipers. So many heart-rending stories.

My worst experience was on 29 August when we were called to the Avraham

Avino area, where Palestinian shopkeepers were experiencing serious Israeli settler violence. The curfew had just been lifted and so everyone was busy trying to set out their stalls and provide food for the shoppers before the next curfew was called. As I arrived accompanying Dianne, an experienced CPT volunteer from the USA, I saw and was able to take pictures of a group of around 15 teenage Israeli settler girls throwing stones at Palestinians, including an old Palestinian man who was covered in blood and badly hurt, bleeding from the head and neck. I heard one soldier in the area mutter, 'It is a shame to be a Jew.' I think he spoke English so that I would understand him and know that not all the IDF supported the acts of these settlers.[130]

Dianne ran to help the old man and get him to a doctor while I stayed and continued to record what was happening. More teenage settlers came up and started throwing stones at other Palestinians. I saw an armed settler looking on and asked him to stop the kids throwing stones. He started screaming at me – 'Nazi', 'Fascist whore', 'Go home' – literally foaming at the mouth, spitting at me, clenching his gun that was jerking up and down. Meanwhile, more settler kids were arriving and surrounding me shouting 'Nazi, Nazi'. He came closer, saying he would teach me, hitting me over the head, wrestling my camera from around my neck and stamping on it repeatedly. The soldiers all around did nothing: they were there to 'protect' the Israeli settlers not the Palestinians or internationals. The settler kids meanwhile started cheering his action and taunting me. Then one took the film out of the shattered camera, exposing it to the light to get rid of the evidence, and started to attack me. Luckily, Dianne was on her way back with the Israeli police. I was in shock but managed to insist that the police arrest the settler who had attacked me and who had suddenly become very calm and smiling.

We were both taken to the police station and I was treated like a criminal.[131] I managed, however, to get the British Consul on the phone, and between us we managed to get the name of the settler – Karmel Frank, a well-known fanatic – and eventually with the help of an Israeli lawyer we found out that he had been released from the police station with his gun. But we did manage to get him into court months later. By this time, the old Palestinian man had died of his wounds and I was back in the UK. The judge wrote asking for my appearance as a witness in court, to give evidence, which I wanted to do: the settler who attacked me had been urging the girls on and they were all complicit in the killing of the old man. But Israeli justice being what it is, I was denied entry into the country even though I had the court order with me. I was put in the police cells at the airport.[132] I contacted a lawyer who got me into court, where

I was told I was a security risk. The lawyer lodged an appeal for me, which had to be withdrawn due to long delays and threatened huge court costs. I was then deported. During the time I was in the police cells (the courts there can work quickly when they want to!) a small claims court got an apology from the settler and a small compensation payment for the destroyed camera that covered my fare back to the UK. There was nothing else I could do about the original case against Karmel Frank from Kiryat Arba settlement.[133] Nothing was said about the stoning to death of an old man and the destruction of the evidence. Israeli human rights activists told me the settler was a well-known and powerful man in Hebron, and I was lucky to have got his name, and him, into court at all. This kind of impunity from prosecution is common in Israel.

I learnt so much during these six weeks, and wrote a 21,565-word report on the gross human rights abuses I had personally witnessed.[134] When I returned to the UK I distributed it widely around the activist community. This helped to mobilise over 30 UK citizens who came with me over Christmas 2001 for another two weeks of direct action against the Israeli military occupation. It was again organised by ISM.[135]

I found myself unsatisfied, however, with the constant movement from town to village to town, answering calls for help to resist one Israeli aggression after another. Several Palestinian villagers asked us to stay on, explaining that most internationals stayed in the cities but they needed help in their rural areas, where more illegal settlements were being built, taking over Palestinian farmlands. They explained that although they valued the solidarity and support of us internationals as it helped in the short-term, nevertheless, after we disappeared, the IDF and settlers returned and the situation often became even more unbearable than before. I therefore spent several more weeks after the two ISM weeks thinking about all this. Most of the internationals returned to their home countries, but I remained, helping ISM to develop nonviolence training materials. This included introducing role plays so that activists had a chance to think and feel their way into actions before taking part, and would thus be better prepared.

I was introduced to the village of Hares by Neta, an Israeli woman working with ISM (who later married a Palestinian). She told me that ISM had worked in Hares several times before and the village was asking for a sustained presence. She introduced me to Issa, a wonderful man who had been shot in the back by the IDF while trying to get children into the house when the armed soldiers raided the village. He was now paralysed from the waist down and used a wheelchair. His good humour, bravery and commitment to nonviolence were evident and he wanted us in the village.

Hares is near the Green Line – the internationally-agreed border between Israel and the Palestinian West Bank. However, a great deal of Palestinian land had been stolen from the nearby villages to build the large illegal Israeli settlement of Ariel.[136] There were now more Israeli occupiers in the region than the original Palestinians, who were scared of losing even more land and were talking of being ethnically cleansed. The town council of Hares invited us to stay and set up a project, so Neta and I decided to set up the International Women's Peace Service – Palestine (IWPS) and to base it in Hares.[137] I returned to the UK and spent the first seven months of 2002 founding IWPS, fundraising, and recruiting and training the first team of 16 international women.[138]

I returned to spend three months from August to November 2002 in Hares, as part of the first team of four women setting up the IWPS project base in a rented flat in Hares. Our house team met the local townsfolk, including the heads of various clans, the sheikh, teachers and farmers. We also produced a little introduction card in Arabic and English explaining who we were and that we were on call for anyone experiencing any human rights abuses and giving our telephone number for people to contact us.[139] We were soon inundated with calls, especially at night, when the IDF roamed around the village and frightened people by forcing entry into their houses to look for 'suspects', lining up all the family from youngest to old outside in the dark, searching their houses. We were often called to the entrance of the village where the IDF had established a rubble mound to make it impossible for cars and vehicles to enter or leave the village. There was a constant presence of armed Israeli soldiers there, and they often shot into the village.

One particular family who lived right by the entrance were extremely traumatised after witnessing four villagers being shot and killed at different times over the past couple of years. The father used to collect all the bullet casings and could not stop going over all that he had seen in a very agitated manner. The mother was constantly worried about her sons, as after the age of about six or seven years the kids are often rounded up by the IDF.[140] Many of the villagers had experienced spells inside prison on trumped-up charges with no proof, held for months – sometimes years – on 'administrative detention' and then released. When talking to the women in the villages all around Salfit, we heard many stories of their young children who had nightmares, wet the bed and had concentration problems. In the daytime we were sometimes called to witness house demolitions, or called when armed settlers were coming into nearby villages to steal sheep and goats or shoot up the solar water-heaters on the rooftops.

When a new contingent of IDF soldiers arrived at the blocked road entrance into the village, I used to go and introduce myself so that they knew there were international women staying in the village, and why. They would often ask me, 'Why are you staying with terrorists, aren't you afraid?' But I was more afraid of their guns and the human rights abuses that they were engaged in.

We spent time getting to know many of the Israeli and Palestinian human rights groups and NGOs that were also working to monitor and support Palestinians. They were often based in the towns and cities so we had to travel frequently through the roadblocks and undergo IDF questioning. We set up checkpoint watches, wrote human rights reports on the incidents we witnessed and sent them to these human rights organisations and to OCHA.[141]

I will never forget the day I was in the Fatah HQ in Salfit with the head, Nawaf, when Hussein from Yasouf came in to complain of armed settlers from Tapuach, a well-known fanatical settlement, harassing the villagers of Yasouf as they went into their olive fields. They were also stealing the olives from their trees.[142]

I volunteered to go to the village and investigate. As I approached Yasouf I was shown the settlers in the distance – in the Palestinians' olive trees. I was told they had been picking the olives for three days; the Palestinians had rung the Israeli police and District Liaison, but the thefts were continuing. I rang the Israeli police myself and reported what was going on, and then rang the Red Cross, Rabbis for Human Rights and B'Tselem (the Israeli Information Centre for Human Rights in the Occupied Territories). After a short wait, the police said they would meet Hussein and Mohamed at the entrance to the village. In the meantime, I talked to villagers, and asked if they would like me to accompany some of them to go and ask the settlers directly to stop stealing the olives. I suggested that a few very old men and women who could afford to take the risk might be good. I told the police I was going to peacefully ask the settlers to stop their theft. Six old men and one old woman accompanied me through their orchards, past their spring (that the settlers were trying to occupy) and up the hill to the olives.

As we approached the area where the settlers were, I rang the police to tell them we were just about to approach the settlers peacefully. When we were about 500 yards away, we were stopped by a bullet that landed just in front of us, fired by a group of ten settlers. I suggested that the Palestinians all sat down while I continued standing, taking photographs. Soon about 30 more settlers were seen coming from the settlement above; at this point the woman and two of the men with me returned to Yasouf. As the settlers had quite a few guns with them and were getting closer, I rang the policeman again and he asked to speak to the Yasouf men who were still with me. They were told to go back to their village, and so they slowly walked back with their walking sticks. I remained as the settlers started running towards us throwing stones.

Suddenly the settlers were all around me, snatching the camera from me, tearing the backpack off my back and shouting loudly. The Palestinian men were still being chased off by some of the settlers and one of them was injured by a thrown rock. Meanwhile, I sat down when a large dog confronted me and the aggressive settlers pawed through my bag, tearing up papers and taking my passport. They spoke good English; in fact, one was a new immigrant from Britain.[143] They told me that all the land had been promised to them by God and was theirs, none of it belonged to the Palestinians. They told me to leave, but I refused because they still had my passport. After an hour or more, one finally threw my passport back at me. I could not get my bag or camera back and there was no reasoning with the settlers, who just wanted me gone, so I walked back to Yasouf, unmolested but shaken and with much more understanding of the situation. I found that Nawaf was there and had arranged to speak with various authorities.

Eventually, with his help, the police and soldiers took me back up the hill, where I showed them where we had been attacked. I wanted to make an official report and complaint so that the settlers could be held to account. So I was then taken to the police station in Ariel, where I was shown lots of photos of settlers to try and identify the ones who had attacked and taken my camera. I could not recognise any of them. I asked to be taken to the settlement as I was sure I could find the British man with the dog, but this was refused. I was told it would be much better if I had pictures! This was the first time I had met the police at Ariel and I had more dealings with them later. This was the first time I had been to Yasouf. Over the following weeks I met with many of the villagers, and we came up with a plan to pick all the olives safely, as a whole united village, and to have plenty of internationals and journalists around for protection. I really enjoyed the planning and organising of this, making sure that the Palestinians were in control and I was only organising the support. I got supportive internationals and Israelis gathered in the village, and then acted as a go-between, so that the Palestinians would know what we could offer while they were making the overall plan and the final decisions.

The villagers decided to make sure that all children were kept away from the harvesting day so they could be assured of total nonviolence. We would all go out at dawn on 17 October 2001 and we, the supporters, would walk on the outside of the group as protectors. We planned that if any settlers approached and started attacking, the Palestinians would all gather together and sit down, be silent and totally nonviolent. The internationals and Israelis would stand around the group and face outwards to the settlers. We arranged for journalists to be in the surrounding hills taking photos and recording the events. About 250 villagers were involved, and about 30 internationals and Israelis. Not long after we all arrived on the olive terraces, about 13 Tapuach settlers started shooting at us and threatening the Palestinians with knives. We interposed our bodies between the settlers and the villagers, while the villagers left their tarps, sacks and donkeys, slowly gathering and sitting down together in three large groups, remaining calm and disciplined.

We had made sure that the Israeli military and police knew we were going to accompany the Palestinians for their olive harvest, and we had been assured of their protection for the whole of the olive-picking season, but only one military jeep was present at the start. Meanwhile, the settlers were rampaging around, pushing, shoving, throwing rocks, and threatening us with their guns and knives. Some even stole some of the harvesting equipment. Luckily, the injuries suffered were fairly minor, as we were able to have two or three Israeli or international supporters surrounding each settler, calmly telling them to let the Palestinians harvest their olives in peace. It took about 40 minutes of chaos until enough police and soldiers arrived and intervened, disarming some of the settlers and dispersing them.

One military jeep stayed in the area, on the ridge, to keep the settlers at bay and the villagers were able to continue their picking. The day ended with full sacks of olives to take back home, and we were pleased we had all managed to succeed. But it was not the joyous family occasion that olive harvests used to be, with picnics and children scampering around. The very next day there was an Israeli tank at the entrance to Yasouf, stopping all entry into and exit from the village. In the struggle between settlers and villagers, the settlers have the backing of the state of Israel regardless of human and land rights. It is hard not to despair, as a small success is soon cancelled out by the bigger picture.

I managed to collate all the information and pictures and got witness statements too about the assaults and threats that had happened on the day. Various Israeli newspapers covered the events, and I hoped for some justice: I was still naive enough to think that if we had the proof, the authorities would be shamed into doing something. I took the evidence to the Ariel police HQ and spoke to the head of police there, but after congratulating me on the quality of the evidence and jestingly asking me if I would like a job as an investigator, I was told nothing would be done.[144] Apparently, it was not worthwhile prosecuting the settlers as it would only result, at most, in a slapped hand, but they would keep it on file, as every now and then the authorities needed to come down harder on out of control settlers and the information might be useful then. Given that the Palestinian authorities had been told they could collect their olives in peace, this was a rather telling comment: presumably this meant that the settlers were not considered out of control when they were stealing Palestinian olives and attacking the villagers. So much for getting evidence of guns and knives being used against unarmed Palestinians who were just trying to get their olives picked![145]

As many Palestinians had been telling me, there is one law for the Jewish Israeli population and another for Palestinians. The contrast is stark when you think about the terrible treatment that Palestinian children are subjected to – months in administrative detention in Israel prisons – when they sometimes throw stones at armoured vehicles coming into their villages to demolish their houses or to build the Apartheid Wall.[146]While going back and forth to the West Bank, I witnessed many human rights abuses and violent behaviour from armed settlers or the IDF. I was frequently called in to witness yet another ride-by shooting incident when settlers shot up the solar water-heaters on roofs, used tear gas on poultry units so all the animals died, shot into schools where the kids cowered under tables for protection, or when the IDF were arresting children just on suspicion of stone-throwing – with no charges ever brought and no evidence ever presented.[147]

I continued co-ordinating the project, going several more times to Palestine in the next three years before handing the project on to the next batch of volunteers. IWPS-Palestine still exists though many of our records and reports were lost when the Israeli State hacked into our website and put up links to pornographic sites to replace them.[148] Most of our reports were immediately sent out to Israeli-, Palestinian- and UN-based human rights groups, so even though we no longer have records of them all, they were useful at the time.

The extensive network of peace and environmental activists that I was still in contact with received our reports from Palestine and quite a few people made their way over to volunteer with IWPS, CPT, ISM and eventually with EAPPI (the Ecumenical Accompaniment Programme in Palestine and Israel). We all worked together, meeting regularly, sharing information and resources. Each person involved speaks out to their relatives, friends and communities. I believe the constant stream of people from all over the world making the journey to witness the occupation for themselves, to act in solidarity with the Palestinians and then return to speak out, has had a huge impact on public awareness of the issues.

I found the continual exposure to such an aggressive military occupation very traumatic. It was not so much experiencing constant tear gas, rubber bullets and on occasion live fire and bombing raids, or the assaults from Israeli settlers. It was more seeing and hearing directly from ordinary women, men and children their accounts of abuse and terrorism suffered at the hands of the Israelis on a daily basis. It was the witnessing of young Israelis doing their first military service tours, turning from fresh-faced caring boys into hard-faced abusive and racist oppressors; the cruel night raids; constant roadblocks; the destruction of homes, schools, hospitals; the injuries from soldiers firing into unarmed villages; month-long curfews when people could not get out of their homes to buy food or medicines; the continuing loss of lands and water resources; and finally, the building of the Apartheid Wall that was cutting off Palestinian farmers from their olive trees and farmlands, and preventing their free movement to and from other Palestinian towns and villages. The constant ethnic cleansing was happening all around us.

I found that when I gave talks about the situation back in the UK and showed photos, I was unable to stop crying and could hardly speak as the memories came rushing back. I was burnt out. But I could not stop. I had been arrested many times at protests while accompanying Palestinians on their nonviolent marches and demonstrations, so I was getting too well-known by the Israeli police and IDF and thus was finding it more and more difficult to get into Israel/Palestine. I was finally told I was a security threat, was denied entrance, and had to decide what to do.

I changed my name, dyed my hair and got a new passport once I had got back to the UK, and a few months later got back into Palestine. But after being arrested while supporting yet another Palestinian demonstration against land theft, my two names were put together, so the next time I tried to enter Israel I was denied access once more. I was subjected to a long interview with Israeli security and shown a very large dossier of my activities in Israel/Palestine, but when I asked the official to show me one instance of where I had been violent or abusive in any way, or had helped a 'terrorist', he shamefacedly admitted he could not do so. He knew full well that I had only been involved in supporting nonviolent resistance to an illegal and violent Israeli occupation and had been peaceful at all times. He said that he hoped one day I would be allowed back into Israel. I was then put into the Israeli police cells at the airport until I was finally deported, and I have not been able to get back into Israel since.[149] This abrupt and enforced end to my work there has enabled me, however, to recover my balance, and I have continued to work on the issue from the UK.

8

Continuing the Struggles Worldwide

IT WAS TIME to return to anti-nuclear activism back in Scotland. In 2005 I initiated a 'mad plan' to blockade Faslane nuclear base for a whole year and to try and get as many different groups as possible involved. Each would have to commit to bringing a hundred people to blockade for a two-day stretch, overlapping with the next blockading group. Many people said it was much too ambitious and could never succeed. But I somehow knew that people would be attracted to it because of its vision and scope. Three friends I had worked with before in TP agreed to form an initial core group with me.[150] David came up with the name – Faslane 365 – and our group soon expanded.

After raising funds, preparing a briefing pack and mobilising resources, several of us spent around five months going around the country mobilising groups and setting up a blockade rota. It was difficult to fill the rota at first, but to encourage groups to take part I said that we would not go ahead unless we had the first month of the rota filled, so they would know it was worthwhile joining in. This encouraged everyone, and groups slowly came on board, adding to the momentum.

Many different groups were invited to organise the blockades in their own manner, under a non-negotiable nonviolent framework, and to make the links between their issues and nuclear weapons. This enabled people from very different campaigns to unite under the common aim of getting rid of nuclear weapons, but in their individual blockades to highlight their unique messages. For instance, the health professionals emphasised the waste of resources and the health impacts of the whole nuclear chain; environmentalists made the links between military and civil nuclear power and the radioactive pollution of environments all over the world; the Unity group made the links between wars and refugees; religious groups highlighted the moral elements of threatening mass destruction; groups from other countries reminded us all that our nuclear weapons impacted the global community, since radioactivity does not respect borders and if we ever actually used these weapons, the whole world would suffer a nuclear winter. We also tried to encourage a deeper reflection of the ways in which a nuclear warfare mentality affected the real security of life on Earth by distorting the economy and encouraging the global dominance of the military-industrial corporations.

This method strengthened our campaign, as well as those of the groups who took part, proving highly successful in mobilising for the blockades. The myriad links between different issues became much more obvious.

During the year, we covered 131 days with blockades that disrupted the working of the base and put nuclear disarmament at the top of the political agenda, which also helped get the SNP elected with a mandate to get rid of Trident.

It was a great campaign and we were helped and supported by colleagues in the peace movements from many different countries, but especially by volunteers from Finland and Sweden who came over to Scotland for months at a time to help out with website design and training work.

The campaign is written up in *Faslane 365*, which not only gives personal stories but also an insight into how we organised and what the 'behind the scenes' work was like.[151] For instance, there are chapters on training, on police liaison, on legal support and on the impact the blockades had on local people.

I had been supporting anti-nuclear campaigns and actions in other European countries for some decades, taking part in demonstrations and actions and often getting arrested in Germany and Holland where US nuclear weapons were based, France, Belgium in anti-NATO actions and northern Sweden where the military exercises (often involving NATO) were destroying the peace in Sami lands.[152, 153, 154, 155, 156] I found that the contacts and friendships formed in these solidarity actions made it easier to find groups from these countries to come and take part in our actions in Scotland. We had a common agenda. Not only have we gained strength but we have also discovered first-hand that the struggles we face are universal – that many of the corporations that provide us with consumer goods are involved in human rights abuses; that our lives are intricately intertwined in many different ways.

The actions in Sweden had a big impact on me, giving me insight into problems facing the Sami – yet another indigenous group of people suffering from colonisation and militarisation. I had been invited to Sweden for a month of mobilisation with OFOG.[157] The name literally means 'mischief' in Swedish; they are an anti-militaristic network using nonviolent direct action against the arms trade, NATO, military exercises and other forms of militarism in Sweden and abroad. I had worked with many of them over the years, as some were members of TP and had come to Scotland to join our protests.

We were also connected through the European Anti-Militarist Network and thus met together in actions at other European bases. They were generally young people in their 20s, which was quite a contrast to the mostly older people in the UK peace movement. When I had joined the peace movement in the 1970s most of the active members were in their 60s and even older, and this is still true today. But in Sweden they had the opposite imbalance and had few older members. OFOG were gearing up and mobilising for a summer action camp at Luleå which was close to Europe's largest overland military test-range, the North European Aerospace Test-Range (NEAT).

So, in February and March of 2011, I was invited to join an OFOG tour of Sweden to try and get older Swedes involved.[158, 159] It worked and was great fun too. I was able to connect up with many older people, saw a great deal of the beautiful country as we travelled from Gothenburg in the south to Kiruna in the north, and I thoroughly enjoyed meeting some wonderful people. I especially enjoyed my time in Kiruna with the cold snow making strange shapes on the trees, glimpses of reindeer, sparkling crystals shimmering in the frozen air, scooting along on those amazing ski scooters that you can hold onto while standing – and scooting safely across the packed snow to the shops. There were incredible ice sculptures everywhere that you could sometimes climb up and slide down, so playful for all ages. Back in the UK I mobilised a group of about ten to join the summer 'War Starts Here, Let's Stop It Here' action camp.[160]

The long summer days when it never got dark and sunsets seemed to last forever were a brilliant contrast to the long dark days of winter when I was last in Sweden. The camp included a week-long seminar with contributions from around Europe on the problems of militarisation, NATO and how NEAT is used as a training ground for bomb dropping, testing drones and air-to-air missiles. We also met Sami speakers who talked about the impact of all this on their reindeer grazing grounds. We learnt a Sami song and heard more about how Norway, Sweden, Finland and Russia dealt with the Sami; how they had been deprived of their ancestral rights to move their reindeer freely, unhindered by national borders.[161] This is, unfortunately, a global problem for all herding nomadic peoples.

There were several hundreds of people gathered for the anti-militarist camp and we all wore pink clothes for our actions as a colourful non-military gesture. I helped out with nonviolence trainings, press and other essential support work as well as taking part in the actions occupying the military roads into the testing range at Vidsel.

There did not seem to be a single year when direct action was not needed at some European base or another, so I was kept pretty busy. The European Anti-Militarist Network was an excellent way to keep in contact with activists from different countries: we used to meet in a different European country for our conferences most years and end the talking with a nonviolent direct action at a nearby military base. As these meetings and actions were planned by the host groups, we all learnt the different ways we had of organising, of consensus decision-making, of role plays and of course, at the end of the actions, the different judicial systems. For instance, in Belgium, as internationals, although arrested and our details recorded, we were never charged, as they could only prosecute for the most serious offences we were culpable of and not lesser crimes. We surmised they did not want the publicity attendant on higher-profile cases, so we were free to go.

I had been concerned about the spy base at Menwith Hill since getting involved in 2000 with the anti-Star Wars actions planned by the Womenwith Hill Women's Peace Camp.[162, 163] I had followed the excellent work of the Global Network Against Weapons and Nuclear Power in Space and decided to join them and take part in the Jeju International Peace Conference in the Republic of Korea (South Korea).[164, 165] But I planned to stay on after the conference to provide international solidarity and learn as much as I could.

I was therefore based in Gangjeong, on Jeju Island, for a month in 2012. I took part in the conference and learnt about the history and militarisation of Jeju Island, and visited the people who were involved in a really impressive and dedicated nonviolent struggle to stop a US naval base being built there. I was shocked to learn of the massacre on 3 April 1948 by the US military and mainland Korean police, when over a ninth of the population was killed, 84 villages razed to the ground and a scorched-earth policy over the whole island left thousands of internally displaced people.[166] This was finally commemorated by an apology in 2005 by President Roh Mee-hyun, who then designated Jeju an Island of Peace. There was a terrible sense of betrayal when, only two years later, he succumbed to US pressure and agreed to build a naval base on Jeju Island, designed for war not peace.

The issue of a central government and the US determining the fate of Jeju Island is, of course, still at the fore in the ongoing struggle against the naval base.[167] South Korea already had 82 US military bases on its land, creating environmental pollution and taking land away from local people. The naval base at Gangjeong on Jeju Island, if completed, would become a major military base for the ROK-US military alliance, and also for the US-led East Asian military alliance which consists of the US, South Korea, Japan, Australia and India. The Gangjeong base would be available for unlimited use by the US Armed Forces, hosting aircraft carriers, nuclear submarines and AEGIS warships, and was likely to be used in the conflict with China that the US was openly planning and preparing for. But it was being presented as if the current local fishing port could be jointly used by locals and the military once built! In fact it was advertised as the 'Jeju Civilian-Military Complex Beautiful Tourism Port'. Unfortunately, Jeju Island lies in a strategic position where ships on the way to China regularly pass by, so it was a prime target for a US military base.

Putting this into a global context, it was clear even then that the US was in the process of extending its military strategic focus from the Middle East to the Asia-Pacific region, and of transferring up to 60 per cent of its naval forces to the region and securing extra bases and military facilities in the Pacific Ocean area. The US already had almost 1,000 military bases around the world, in over a hundred different countries, with missile defence systems that have proven to be capable anti-satellite weapons.[168] Despite early NATO promises not to move into ex-Warsaw Pact countries that surround Russia, NATO has continued to expand right up to the Russian borders and it was clear that the US was driving a new arms race not only with China but also with Russia.

At the time I was there, the Gangjeong villagers of Jeju Island (many growing high-quality citrus and strawberries) had already been bravely and nonviolently resisting for seven years. They were trying to prevent the construction of the naval base that was destroying 50 hectares of prime agricultural land, as well as the surrounding sea.[169] The South Korean military and central government had claimed that the base construction approval process was approved by a democratic vote. But only 87 people out of 1,800 residents had an opportunity to cast a vote, by applause only. It was later found that some of these villagers had been bribed, and this led to a heart-rending split in the community, which the villagers are still trying to heal.

When the village elected a new Mayor and held their own re-vote, which fairly included the entire community and was done by proper ballot, 94 per cent of all villagers opposed the military base – yet the government and military refused to recognise these results. The democratically elected Mayor of Gangjeong who oversaw the 94 per cent vote was imprisoned for three months for standing up for the rights of his villagers. While I was on Jeju

Island, he was out of jail and working full-time organising the resistance to the naval base.

The village was an amazing example of consistent, sustained resistance, with each family contributing some of the proceeds from sales of their fruit and vegetables to fund the campaign against the base that ran out of the Mayor's office. Each day a van went round the village, calling people out to the blockades, where they gathered in front of the gates to sit for hours to disrupt entry of the vehicles building the naval base. Many of the villagers had faced prison sentences and large fines for their actions, but the campaign was gathering more and more supporters. People from all over Jeju Island, but also from the mainland, were joining the protests; famous people were speaking out and the religious communities (especially the Catholic priests, Buddhists and Quakers) were holding regular services and prayers, and sitting in the blockades. I was grateful for the opportunity to join the protests and help out wherever I could. I was impressed with the dedication of the villagers supporting the campaign.

The role of internationals is, of course, necessarily a minor one but nevertheless important. We provide moral support and help with publicity.[170] We also share ideas and strength. I was made to feel very welcome and was privileged to get involved. I joined in the demonstrations at the civilian port that was being taken over by the military, and locals took me to see their sacred Gureombi Rock which is the only smooth volcanic freshwater rock in Korea. The area is stunningly beautiful with soft corals protected by UNESCO, IUCN-listed dolphins, red-footed crabs and other threatened species that were endangered by the military plans.[171, 172] Locals were meeting almost every day to discuss how to save their environment and were angry that conservation protections were being ignored.

While I was there, the first explosions by the destructive companies Samsung and Daelim took place. The sea was being polluted and there were major fears that the drinking water from the nearby fresh springs was being affected. These springs provided 70 per cent of the drinking water to the southern part of the island. I had been invited to be part of a sea-based group and 14 of us kayaked into the area that was to be blasted the next day in an attempt to stop it. It was a bright moonlit night and it was beautiful to paddle silently along the rocky coast. Three of us were landed near some huge concrete tetrapods where we were to stay hidden until the morning. The others went to different places, to kayak in later. The tide was coming in and we had to keep shifting so as not to get trapped, but eventually as the sun rose, we emerged with flags and tried to get close to the precise blasting area. The place was swarming with riot and coastal police by this time, but eventually all 14 of us were very visibly protesting in front of the blast area. But we could not stop it and it was horrible to watch the exploding rocks. We were so close and yet so far.[173]

One of the most inspiring actions I took part in was with a whole group of Catholic priests who had gathered for a Mass at the port entrance to the naval base. There were about two hundred people standing in ordinary clothes, when suddenly a smaller group of us threaded past the police while they were occupied with the others. We clambered over rocks and razor wire to the wall of a huge concrete pier. One person managed to scale the wall and get a rope down to the rest of us and about 50 of us got up. I was hauled up with the help of four strong men! Suddenly, there we were on the top of the pier inside the base, and 40 of the people around us took off their outer clothing and were transformed into priests in pristine white robes with gold and purple mantles over them. Some of the priests along with some nuns had stayed below where they set up a makeshift altar and PA system. More police surged into the area but allowed the Mass to continue: there was a reluctance to arrest priests when in the middle of their prayers. After the service, many of us on the pier climbed down on to the Gureombi Rock side and I was presented with the pair of bolt-croppers that I had asked for a few days earlier. After being helped by willing priests to get down off the huge tetrapods to the fence at the edge of the waterfront, I started cutting through it. The penalty for damaging the fence would be very high for the locals, and so I had decided to start cutting it.

There is a whole gamut of tools for change – research, publications, lobbying, letter-writing, petitions, public meetings, demonstrations, boycotts, nonviolent direct resistance and disruption, legislative changes and their implementation

I made a hole big enough to get several people through before police came and guarded the hole, preventing others from getting in. So I went on to make other holes, which the police inside scurried over the rocks to defend. Moving slowly along the fence, I continued cutting holes, with the police inside the fence trying to grab the bolt-croppers from me on the outside. I was getting quite tired by this time and asked if anyone else would like a turn. One brave priest volunteered and we took it in turns. We must have cut at least ten holes before it got too dark to continue. Passing the cutters to people to hide for another time, I went back along the fence line and found Father Moon going through a hole, and followed him. I was arrested for destruction of private property and trespass.[174]

I was arrested three times on Jeju Island getting into the base and cutting the fences around it, but no court papers summoned me to trial – the authorities were more interested in making sure that I would leave.[175] After spending some days in the police cells and in the local prison, I was visited by Bishop Peter Kang, who congratulated me on my actions. In the end, I was forced to make an exit from Korea and am unlikely to be able to go back. I keep in touch with the campaign and with various Korean friends, some of whom have visited me here in Wales. The latest sad news I received from Jeju Island was that Dr Song Kang-Ho has been given a two-year prison sentence for his peaceful protests at the base. His last words as he was taken to prison were 'Gureombi will be returned back to us without fail! Don't give up!'[176]

Upon returning home to the UK, I was able to help boost international solidarity by giving talks and encouraging groups to co-ordinate actions outside Korean embassies.[177] This resulted in demonstrations being held in seven countries, and then further demonstrations, including 'Boycott Samsung' events. It was ironic that I had been given a Samsung smartphone before leaving for Korea, only to find, too late, that Samsung was one of the Korean corporations supporting the military with a contract to build the naval base.

Slowly, we are strengthening global anti-militarist campaigns and disrupting the process of the corruption of our politicians, mercilessly lobbied by transnational corporations who are destroying our world in the name of profit. However, the naval base has now been built, the US military are frequently using it, and housing for the military is being built on further land taken from local agricultural production. What a waste! It is hard not to lose hope, but the people of Jeju Island are still resisting and still need our support, so we must persevere. We never know the long-term consequences of our actions, and maybe just witnessing these struggles for a saner, more humane world is a good in itself.

9

It Never Ends

AS A PEACE movement in the UK we have had remarkable success in Scotland. The majority of the Scottish population have rejected nuclear weapons and are angry at having them stored at the Coulport base and deployed from Faslane. These bases are close to Glasgow, the largest city in Scotland. Scottish history and culture, and its legal and education systems are very different from those in England. The story of the Highland Clearances may not be much known in England but is still remembered with some bitterness in Scotland.[178]

When in Scotland I noticed how the 'national' press is English-centred and hardly covers Scottish concerns. When I was young I had picked up the bad habit, as had most of my English contemporaries, of associating English with being British, and England as being synonymous with the UK. Even now there are still some people in England who 'forget' that Scotland, Wales and Northern Ireland are different countries and need to be respected as such. It took my frequent visits to Scotland to get rid of this bad habit. And now, living in Wales, I am trying to learn a little about this country. Learning the language is proving immensely difficult as I have a terrible memory and there are few native Welsh speakers in my border town in the Welsh Marches. However, living beside Offa's Dyke reminds me of borders and their ever-changing character, and how they are so often at the centre of nationalistic battles.[179]

It took some time and much dedication over many years by many people, but there is now a very clear anti-nuclear sentiment matched by corresponding policies in Scotland. However, even since devolution, Westminster still rules supreme in matters of 'defence'.[180] Scottish independence is still a live issue and the disarmament of nuclear weapons is an integral part of the independence campaign. It seemed that most of the work in Scotland had been done, the public was behind us and many politicians were too. It was difficult to see how more nonviolent direct action in Scotland could persuade the UK to demolish its nuclear arsenal. I believed that peace activists now had to concentrate our nonviolent direct action efforts on the English side of the border. This did not mean that actions stopped in Scotland, just that we concentrated more on England, with some actions in Wales as and when it was relevant.

Thus some of us began to transfer our actions to AWE Aldermaston and Burghfield. TP had supported the Aldermaston Women's Peace Camp (AWPC) for many years. Some of us in TP, myself included, considered ourselves part of AWPC and supported the monthly camps when possible, especially those who lived nearby in Oxford or Reading. When their Block the Builders campaign started, we supported it in many ways, joining in their actions as and when we could.[181] We took responsibility for organising some of the blockades, especially those that required larger numbers of women to come along, when we were able to mobilise women from Belgium, Holland, Spain and Germany to join in. There was quite a large overlap between the direct action peace groups, with some of us members of multiple groups including AWPC, Nukewatch, and TP. These groups all continue to be active at Burghfield especially, as this is where the nuclear convoys leave from to deliver their dangerous load of warheads to Coulport.[182]

In 2012 I decided to initiate a campaign called Action AWE. Instead of AWE standing for Atomic Weapons Establishment, we made it into 'Atomic Weapons Eradication'. Once again I managed to find people (mainly TP activists) willing to join a co-ordinating group: a wonderful volunteer, Kate, set up and managed a dedicated website, and we printed an action pack and leaflets and set about mobilising for a sustained civil resistance campaign based on what we had learnt from Faslane 365.

We received a great deal of help from the local Quakers in Reading. We were also helped by Greenpeace, CND and Nukewatch activists in and around Berkshire and Oxfordshire. It was a much less supportive environment than we had in Scotland and harder to get enough people involved long-term. Nevertheless, we did lots of good actions and kept the pressure on both bases, including a very successful two-week disarmament camp on Ministry of Defence (MOD) land very near to the main gate of Burghfield in August 2013. Some of our friends from France, Finland, Belgium and Holland joined us. Our reports and videos were put on the website and we wrote up our actions for *Peace News* and other alternative press outlets. Lots of short films made of our actions at Burghfield remind us of just how much we did, including a month-long presence at the gates of the base, blocking access so that workers had to walk in and convoys could not get in or out.[183]

Some people do not understand the need for this kind of disruptive action, but it serves to keep the pressure on the military and government, and to remind them that there are a substantial number of people who think the activities going on at these bases is unethical, illegal and a terrible waste of resources, and is not being done in our name. In our court cases we raised many issues, including the serious risk of catastrophic accidents, the environmental impact of radioactive emissions, the illegality of threatening mass destruction and how deploying 100-kiloton nuclear weapons with an intent to use them to protect our 'national interests' was in fact a conspiracy to commit a war crime. Our arguments as usual were mostly ignored in our cases before the local magistrates' courts, but we can never know the long-term impact that hearing us might have on police, court officials, lawyers, judges and members of the public.

We decided to be a little more proactive on the legal side and organised an Action AWE 'Reportings of Nuclear Crime' at Reading police station on 8 February 2014.[184] This was followed up by a week of 'reportings' in quite a few other police stations around England and Wales. Hundreds of people went to their nearest police stations and one by one reported the crime and gave whatever evidence they thought appropriate. In Reading, for instance, we had a very long line of people queuing up outside the station waiting to take their turn to report the crime. They would call for the police to arrest government and AWE officials responsible for the warhead production and deployment which facilitated preparations to use nuclear weapons, contrary to IHL. At least 54 witness allegations were submitted to the Thames Valley Police (TVP) that day. Despite the seriousness of our allegations, it took until 1 June 2014 for us to receive a reply from Kevin Brown, Detective Chief Inspector of the Major Crime Unit.[185] He responded saying that the reports had fallen into three broad categories – the manufacture and possession of nuclear weapons; the offences of war crime, genocide, crimes against humanity and a breach of the Nuclear Non-Proliferation Treaty; and the transportation of nuclear weapons. He said he had sought counsel and guidance from TVP's legal services, MOD Police, MOD legal services and the Crown Prosecution Service. This struck us as rather bizarre given that the MOD were the very ones we were making allegations against. He said:

Ostensibly, the issue is whether anything Her Majesty's Government [HMG] does in relation to nuclear weapons is unlawful and therefore capable of amounting to a criminal offence under UK domestic law.

He then went on to say that none of the allegations raised were criminal offences, and therefore there was no duty for TVP to investigate such allegations. In our opinion this was not true: the only thing that differentiates a soldier from a murderer, or protects a soldier from charges of conspiracy to murder abroad, is that a soldier is justified in killing but *if, and only if*, keeping to the international war laws. Planning to cause the death of hundreds of thousands of people by targeting nuclear weapons at cities was a war crime in itself. However, the police response, although very disappointing, was not unexpected. Such a long-held policy of nuclear deterrence is taking a long time to change.

The reportings of crime had been well worth doing as they had raised yet again the issue of national and international law in relation to the UK's nuclear weapons system, and informed and galvanised many people to get involved. Local press coverage had been good and we had an archive of reports, radio interviews and film footage of our attempts to bring the UK government to respect and implement IHL. The UK could never honestly say in the future that they had not been warned they were breaking IHL.

My own attempts to get the international legal implications of threatening mass destruction with nuclear weapons had been going on since the early 1980s and it still continues to this day with the Public Interest Case Against Trident (PICAT) which I started on 1 October 2015.[186] PICAT helped organise around 400 informant prosecutors to lay information at their local magistrates' courts and these coalesced into five PICAT groups, who found that they then had to apply to the AG to get the case against Trident heard in court.[187]

It is so easy for us to be held to account in the courts as defendants when we try to disrupt and stop plans for mass murder, but incredibly difficult to get the government and military officials into court. The powerful have all sorts of ways of stopping the courts from looking impartially at our arguments, the main one being that defence policy and the deployment of Trident are deemed not to be justiciable – so the courts cannot deal with it!

If only they would analyse the evidence, then it would become clear that the UK's nuclear weapons are unlawful. I think it worth publishing once more the words of ICJ Judge Bedjaoui (see Appendix 2A) in which he explains why the UK's nuclear weapons are illegal. The vast majority of international lawyers agree and say it is a 'no-brainer': of course, the nuclear weapons in existence today are unlawful and their deployment with policies to use them in certain circumstances are also criminal, as they could never be used proportionately and in accordance with IHL. However, our struggle to get courts here in the UK to address our evidence has failed so far. We spent several years sending the AG our evidence and asking for permission to proceed with our case. We were given pro bono advice and help and wonderful support from lawyers with great experience including Robbie, Mike, Nick, Kirsty and Megan.[188] You can see all the evidence and the long string of letters that we had to engage in over two years before we finally heard from the Deputy Director of the Public Law and Litigation Team on 10 November 2017, informing us:

> In the Attorney General's view, the material provided by the PICAT Project is insufficient to show that any offence has been committed. Accordingly, the Attorney General has declined to give his consent to the proposed prosecution.[189]

We then took more legal advice and Robbie applied for leave to appeal this decision, but again was turned down in 2018. It is difficult to know what to do next, as the evidence we supplied was certainly enough and we would have needed the court's permission to force the UK government and military to provide more evidence. Probably we just need to keep repeating our requests to police stations and courts until the right moment comes and the door opens and allows us in. We must never give up: change does eventually come, sometimes when you least expect it.

But to get back to our actions at Burghfield and Aldermaston: as part of the Action AWE campaign, I came up with the idea of a seven-mile-long pink peace scarf that could be knitted, joined together and then draped between Aldermaston and Burghfield. I got the idea when a Swedish friend sent me a picture of a tank that had a pink knitted patchwork cover, a peace action which was really effective. Anyway, it was October 2012 and I was sitting next to Jaine, who was knitting socks at the camp-fire during a quiet moment in a long protest against the building of another nuclear power plant at Hinkley Point. I was involved with other groups there in trying to stop new-build nuclear power stations.[190] I asked her if she liked knitting, and what did she think about knitting a long pink peace scarf? She was enthusiastic and so we agreed to meet and talk more about it. I suggested that we ask people to make scarf pieces of such a size that one piece could later be made into a baby's blanket and four pieces sewn together into an adult blanket – so that the knitted pieces would be useful after the rolling out of the seven miles of scarf. Jaine was absolutely amazing. She went all-out for the idea and developed it into the Wool Against Weapons project, advertised it in knitting magazines as well as in the peace magazines, and thousands of people sent her pieces that were joined together into huge rolls. It took over her life for a couple of years. I helped where I could, making sure all my contacts knew about it and were in contact with Jaine.

In my area of Powys, our local Knighton Peace and Justice Group and our local nonviolent direct action affinity group (the Dragonistas) organised knit-ins and made four large rolls of pink scarf that we eventually rolled out down the main street of Knighton from the clock tower to the war memorial on 5 July 2014. We had Derek, our town crier, dressed in his ancient robes, 'calling out' Trident, and over a hundred local people lined the street to unroll the scarf on the road. Roger, a local ex-BBC cameraman, filmed it all for us and we got lots of press coverage.[191] As usual we were supported by peace choirs and musicians. It was a lot of fun.

It was also good preparation for the massive rollout that took place on Nagasaki Day, 9 August 2014, from Aldermaston to Burghfield.[192] We planned this together with CND and the other groups that had come together from all over the UK to take part. Thousands of us crowded onto the seven miles of roads, hanging up the pink scarf. It was quite a logistical nightmare to organise the smooth delivery of the huge rolls of scarf, get the people into position and yet all enjoy ourselves. We had seven places along the route that different groups organised with refreshment and toilet facilities and from which different groups started hanging out their rolls, and we just hoped it all linked up.

It is so necessary when preparing actions to know your activists as well as possible and to work in affinity groups where you learn about each other and can provide suitable support

Our Welsh groups organised one of these places, setting up a tent and getting people there in coaches and cars to deliver the scarf for our section of the seven miles. It did all link up, we even had some parts where the scarf doubled or trebled up along the bushes and tree-lined roads. It was an incredible, innovative action that had Action AWE and CND working together with Wool Against Weapons, and with other peace groups coming from all over the country to take part. It got very little mainstream press coverage but lots in the alternative media and specialist arts and crafts networks. A cyclist went along the whole route with a camera, and this was speeded up into a fast video so we could see what a great job we had done.[193]

It was followed on 24 January 2015 with a Wrap Up Trident action, taking some of the scarf and draping it all around the MOD building in London.[194] Our peace group in Knighton then brought back our rolls and spent several months repurposing the pieces into baby and adult blankets and sending them out to Syrian refugees and also to homeless people in the UK. So many actions took place in these years when the replacement of Trident was being debated and when billions of pounds were being wasted on renewing a criminal and dangerous nuclear weapons system.

Music has always played a large, creative and important part in our actions. In July 2004, a special TP choir of 17 of us performed the *Trident Oratorio* titled *Trident: A British War Crime*.[195] I had commissioned it from my partner Camilla, and it was performed in Parliament Hall, Edinburgh, for the benefit of the Scottish High Court judges, advocates and lawyers. It had been quite a task to get our amateur choir to sing such complicated and unusual harmonies but it was very powerful, emotional and very informative for the listeners. Several lawyers congratulated us on using such an innovative way of getting our views across. Camilla updated the *Oratorio* some years later and we sang it in the Houses of Parliament on 11 March 2015 as a part of Action AWE's month of action.[196] The singers had called their MPs to come and see them in the lobby, and so many of them also heard the *Oratorio*.

A year later a group of us decided we needed to be in the lobby supporting those MPs who would be voting against the replacement and modernisation of the Trident system. Eleven of us entered Westminster on 18 July 2016 just as the debate on the government motion on replacing Trident was getting under way. We removed our outer clothing, revealing messages that read 'No Trident Replacement', 'Scrap Trident' and 'Scotland Says Trident No More', superglued ourselves together and sang anti-nuclear songs for hours. So many MPs, especially from Scotland, came up to thank us for being there and supporting the anti-nuclear MPs that we were left to sing our hearts out, and when the doors opened to the voting chamber we were able to look right down it and sing out loudly. We were certainly heard. The Black Rod himself approached us quite a few times, pleading for us to stop singing. He was getting bored hearing all the anti-Trident messages![197]

Over the decades we have lobbied Parliament numerous times and also done various actions outside. One I particularly remember, as it reminds me of the first time I chained myself to the railings in 1984, was when over 60 of us chained ourselves to the railings of the Houses of Parliament. On 20 June 2018, we stretched from Big Ben to Parliament Square and hung large banners that said 'Denuclearise the World – Sign the Treaty'. We used our mobile phones and called out our MPs, some of whom came out and gave interviews.[198] We were demanding that the UK sign the Ban Treaty.

Angie inside the Gangjeong naval base, 25 February 2012.

Korean Catholic priests holding Mass inside the base, 12 March 2012.

Angie cutting the fence of the naval base, 12 March 2012

Arrival at Hinkley Power Station at the end of Aldermaston to Hinkley Walk for a Nuclear Free Future, 1 September 2012.

Angie in an AWE T-shirt, 2013.

RLA delegation in solidarity with MST at the memorial site of the massacre of Eldorado de Carajás, 1 April 2013.

AWE blockade at Burghfield, August 2013.

Dragonistas AWE Burghfield Trident cake action, 3 October 2013.

Angie and Janet at a Faslane blockade, 13 April 2015.

10

Police, Prisons and Hot Springs

OVER THE DECADES I have, of course, spent quite a bit of time in police stations and prisons in various countries. I once thought of writing a guide to prisons around the world, just for fun, but to lighten the atmosphere I would have added in a guide to hot springs. I just love them, and they were a wonderful element in my campaigning life. I was introduced to a hot spring when visiting Bella Coola in British Columbia on a solidarity visit to the Nuxalk organised by the UK Forests Network. After we had taken part in various actions against the loggers who were destroying the Nuxalk's old-growth forests, the traditional Nuxalk chiefs treated us to a visit to their sacred hot springs.[199]

After a breathtakingly beautiful journey along the coast and up an inlet, we arrived at a rocky place and landed at the edge of a large cave. We swam into it and were told we could talk in this one, but as we went in deeper and entered the last cave we must be quite silent. It was incredibly special. The second cave was quite warm and it was shadowy as the light lessened. Slowly we swam or waded through to the last cave where the hot spring flowed really hot and it was almost completely dark. There was a powerful sacred atmosphere and I was lost in it for a while. The oppressive, depressing feelings that had been building up as we confronted loggers and witnessed the destruction of such a glorious landscape, along with the heart-rending visual memories of the horrifying clear-cuts slowly fell away and I was filled with peace and calm. After some hours, we slowly came out of the hot waters and back out into the daylight where we plunged into the cold seawater, refreshed and invigorated. What an honour to have been given this gift.

I could indulge myself in wonderful memories and talk about the Onsen in Japan, hot pools in Nepal or deserted hot springs on Greek islands – but let me get back to police cells and prisons. What horrid places they are, filled with people who, but for circumstances, might have been living fulfilling lives. Each person had their story to tell, and in the UK especially a vast majority of them came from abusive backgrounds and had had a very limited education, and most were in for petty crimes associated with drug and alcohol abuse. It was an indictment of a society more interested in supporting the 'haves' than the 'have nots'. I believe that no state can claim to be a 'civilised democracy' while it holds a significant proportion of its population in prisons, detention camps, or incarcerated against their will in other places. Rather, such statistics are an indication that deep-rooted social injustices, inequities and conflicts need to be resolved as soon as possible. We should aim for a year-on-year decrease in the prison population and a corresponding increase in social and economic equality.

I found it immensely hard hearing and seeing abuses carried out on prisoners and feeling helpless to stop them. As prisons and police cells are 'closed' environments it is very difficult to get proof of what is happening out into the public domain. I have found in my attempts that it is often my single voice being heard against a whole group of police or prison officers who gang together to stop the truth getting out. But, nevertheless, as fairly well-educated and confident people with support on the outside, we can use these privileges to help ensure that prison conditions are reported and try to get them improved. Prisons are a part of our society, and the conditions in them are indicative of how humane, ethical and just our society is, or is not. I have felt grateful to be able to have an inside view into these institutions that most of us have no idea of. The main thing I learnt is that there is not much difference between those 'inside' and those 'outside' the police stations and prisons, and we can use our time 'inside' creatively and even continue our protests and campaigning while incarcerated. Let me share a few stories with you.

Many of us from around Norfolk involved in the 1980s Snowball campaign experienced rather unsanitary and disgusting conditions in local police stations. Snowballers were a very mixed bunch but included a fair number of teachers, nurses, religious ministers, poets and other middle-class people who had never been arrested before and were shocked by the dirty, squalid, police cells. Carla, who ran a local restaurant, told us about the dirty mattresses on the floor and the lavatory which was 'brown-stained with runnels of dried shit splashed down the outside of the pan'.[200] The floors were dirty, the blankets unwashed. Others had similar experiences: we wrote to the press and local MPs about these conditions and were pleased to find that our outrage had an effect. Almost immediately, conditions improved for everyone and the cells were cleaned up and repainted.

At first, when imprisoned, I just listened and tried to work out what was going on. I did not even understand some of the language used. Sometimes I was quite frightened, like when I was put into a closed cell with a woman out of her mind on drugs, or when confronted with a woman talking about the violence she had inflicted on others. She was up on GBH (grievous bodily harm) charges and it was very disturbing to hear how and why she had used a red-hot iron on someone, and her other angry, disturbed rants. Once, when in the canteen getting food, I witnessed some nasty bullying going on when one prisoner took another's food against her will. I started to confront her and told her to give back the food, but was pulled away by others who said it was too dangerous to confront this particular woman. I had to learn to take note of body language and to recognise whose eyes it was not safe to look into, when I could intervene and when not to, to find other ways around any particular problem that emerged.

I was seeing young women with lots of energy and nowhere to put it, being taken to 'isolation' for doing handstands in the corridors, hearing the constant screaming and banging on the cell doors when my cell was positioned close to the area of the prison where women with mental health issues were being held – women who needed treatment, not imprisonment. I had to cut myself off from some of this when there was little I could do.

Of course, this cutting-off and the physical environment of prisons themselves has deep psychological impacts on all prisoners. We suffered from the lack of visual and sensory stimulation. Just imagine what it is like seeing walls and concrete all the time and hardly ever seeing the sky. Some people living very urban, industrialised lives do sadly have to suffer similar environments, which is why we must insist on more green spaces for everyone to access. I was so fortunate in having friends who sent me beautiful postcards with pictures of the natural world. One friend, Helena, sent me large pictures from a calendar with scenes of forests, mountains and waterfalls. I stuck them on the wall with toothpaste, as other prisoners had taught me to do, and did my exercises to them each day.

But the constant confinement and petty rules, where you have to ask for every little thing (like getting your fingernails cut, or to buy a stamp or get some soap), leads to extreme dependency and institutionalisation – such that women, when finally released after being inside for a long time, often cannot face the outside world and do not want to leave. A gradual dehumanisation takes place for everyone, partly reinforced by being given a prisoner number. Even when leaving the prison you had to remember your prisoner number. I remember the first time refusing to give it and having to wait all day (usually you are released very early in the morning), until they got fed up with me and released me from Holloway prison anyway. Part of my recalcitrance was that I had not been given back all of the possessions that I had entered the prison with. I was meant to sign that I had received them all, and would not do so. I eventually wrote on the form, against their insistence that I did not do this, all the things that had not been returned.

When I was home, I immediately sent a complaint about this to the prison authorities and after an internal investigation I received monetary compensation for the books and badges that had gone missing. Unfortunately, on my return to Holloway I met the same prison officer who had taken these objects and wondered if I would face more trouble. Luckily, I did not. I guess she knew I would not be cowed.

At some point during these short prison sentences I started to learn how to be myself in these situations, to be the kind of person I was outside the prison, not to be too pushed down by the experience, not to get overwhelmingly depressed and to keep a sense of balance. This led to my writing reports and staging protests about prison conditions and about what was going on in the outside world too. Wherever I was, I was still a conscious, caring, political person, and being in prison was not to change that.

In Chapter 3, I gave a brief account of our protest in Miri Jail in Sarawak, but it might be useful to give a few more details here, as I learnt a lot about myself and nonviolent protest when ostensibly powerless. The prison was mainly for men, and the four men in our group were housed in this main section: we had not seen them for almost two weeks. Our small women's section was to one side of the prison with high walls and armed guards in the corner watchtowers who looked down on us. During the hot, humid, tropical daylight hours we were often allowed to roam freely outside in the small compound of grass and trees, where there was a surprisingly pretty flower bed of orchids.

The single-storey building consisted of two rooms, one where we could sit on the floor and eat our meals, another where we slept on thin mats on the concrete floors at night and sometimes sat during the day, and a corridor where we had to sit in a line twice a day to be counted: '*satu, dua, tiga, empat, lima…*'. These numbers – one to five – in Bahasa Malaysia are ingrained in my memory, as we were counted so often. While calling out our numbers, the Malay and Indonesian women prisoners introduced us to the back and neck massages each prisoner did for the woman in front of her. We were often there for up to an hour at a time, so the massages were very comforting. At the end of the corridor were some stand-up toilets and water for washing, and facing them at the very end were a couple of 'punishment cells'.

In some ways being in prison was more humane in Sarawak than in the UK, as we were able to see the sky and be outside so often, but also because Malay people are generally so gentle and accepting. We slept and ate altogether, around 20 women in all, but sometimes as many as 30, so we had plenty of company and a chance to get to know each other, share songs and stories. However, the ants, mosquitoes and humidity were a constant trouble: we were not allowed mosquito nets. More importantly we had no access to the world beyond the prison, even after giving our names and after our passports were recovered. After about 12 days we had still not been charged with any crime or brought before a court and had no access to lawyers or phones, so we decided to nonviolently blockade the only entrance into the small women's section of the prison by sitting together with our backs to the gate. When approached by the prison guards, we handed in a written copy of our verbal demands – that we would not move until allowed access to our embassies, contact with our four male colleagues in order to determine their safety and the use of a phone to contact our families.

The female guards could not persuade us to move and so ten male guards shoved through the gate, followed by the governor, who demanded that we move voluntarily or be disciplined by his men – who by this time were lined up in front of us brandishing their batons and looking very aggressive. We feared a severe beating and so the other three women did move. This was when I discovered how very stubborn I was and not very amenable to threats. Luckily, perhaps because the others had moved voluntarily and because we were internationals, I was merely picked up by the men and slung into the 'punishment cells' for a week with only one blanket and no company.

We heard from the prison guards (some of whom became quite friendly during the weeks we spent there) that our blockade had been the first 'protest' this prison had ever had. It was only a few days later that we were allowed a visit with the four men from our SOS Sarawak action, had visits from our embassies or consulates and were eventually given court dates and charged.

As I said in an article for *Peace News*:

I now consider nonviolent resistance while in prison to be part of our struggle for a better world – a way of confronting and changing the status quo... and that this becomes more relevant as more and more of us end up inside them.[201]

When serving time in UK prisons I found that for my own mental health I needed to talk to other prisoners when I could and find out about their problems, and to write these up into a prison report that I then sent out to prison reform organisations and to the prison ombudsman. I found that these were well-received as they supplemented their official visits and gave an insider prisoner's perspective. I often found that official prison visitors went around with the prison guards or officers, or prison governors, and did not ask to speak privately to the prisoners themselves; some seemed more interested in their status as a prison visitor rather than caring about the prisoners themselves – they did not really want to find out what was happening. This was confirmed much later when a Quaker friend who visited TP activists in Cornton Vale women's prison (near Stirling in Scotland) later became an official prison visitor, and was astounded by the lack of real work and concern that most prison visitors engaged in, and how they were manipulated by the prison system. Whenever I am in prison or police cells and see 'observers' or prison visitors, I go up to them if I can and ask to speak privately with them.

It is one thing getting a long record for nonviolent civil resistance but quite another having a record of dangerous driving, or assault

Speaking to other prisoners and sharing the flowers we were often sent in by well-wishers gave us a chance to share our skills too. I often found myself helping to write letters to solicitors or sharing information, as many of them only had basic reading and writing skills, if that. I was shocked at how many of the lawyers that the women landed up with were jaded and unconcerned, not even getting their facts right because they had not bothered to consult their 'clients' properly or in good time. This contrasted starkly with the solicitors that our activists had, who were so conscientious and supportive.

When out of prison, facilitating mobilising workshops, I used to talk about the risks of nonviolent direct action and preparing for prison. Hoping to get more volunteers to take action, I pondered aloud about how people who meditated or prayed a great deal, or enjoyed isolation, like nuns or monks, or who enjoyed counselling, might be of great service to fellow prisoners and help to improve prison conditions.[202]

My first long (for me!) spell in prison was at the women's prison at HMP Risley, where four of us were held for six months from February to July 1996 on remand for the disarmament of the BAe Hawk jet in the Seeds of Hope Ploughshares action.[203] While there, I put in numerous official complaints to the governor about the appalling quality of the food, lack of exercise and washing facilities, missing mail, dirty clothes, lack of educational facilities and especially about the 24-hour lockups when you only got out of the cells to collect your food and then take it back to eat in your cell. It was quite clear that we were in the midst of a serious breakdown of the women's prison system. I kept a daily record of when and for how long we were allowed to exercise, keeping track of times when we had no access to showers or washing facilities, how long we were locked up each day with no chance to speak to anyone else, when our visitors could not visit and many other things. About a year after my release, quite by chance, I bumped into one of the religious ministers who had visited and taken services in Risley, and she said that our constant official complaints about not getting our statutory allowed one hour's exercise in the fresh air each day and other complaints had borne fruit, and conditions were improving: we had had a great impact.

While in Risley I was determined to do a survey on prison conditions and whenever the lockdowns were eased I asked other prisoners what was happening to them. I wrote a quick report of my findings and sent it out to an MP. I suddenly found myself hauled in front of the governor and told that I could face ten years in prison for breaking the rules! Apparently prisoners are not allowed to do surveys or write reports. I was shocked, as I did not realise basic rights were denied in prison, but I also did not believe a prison had the right to keep me in prison for ten years without at least going to the courts, and I said as much. I heard no more about it but my report never got to the MP either.

There were several suicide attempts while I was there – all of which failed – but a few months after my release, one prisoner did end up killing herself. I kept in touch with some of the inmates after leaving prison and heard that conditions had worsened considerably over the summer. This led me to share my experiences in a report that I distributed as an open letter to the press, the Home Secretary and others on the inhumane conditions I had personally witnessed.[204, 205] I sent it to Sir David Ramsbotham, the Chief Inspector of Prisons, and asked that he include my recommendations in the forthcoming HMP Thematic Review of the Women's Prison System – due in January 1997. A few days later I received a reply from CJ Allen saying that he would make sure that my letter was 'seen by all the inspectors who are taking part in the Chief Inspector's thematic review of women's imprisonment'.[206] He went on to say that many of my comments confirmed their own observations 'but they are all the more valuable as they are "first-hand"'. Perhaps more importantly, he finished by saying:

It is too early to say whether all the recommendations you made will be accepted by the team but I accept entirely your major point that women's prisons are treated as a small adjunct to the male system. I anticipate that the thematic review will concentrate on providing solutions to this very issue and to seek to ensure that women's prisons tackle issues relevant to women.

I believe it was one more of what must have been many reports that helped to get the women's section of that prison closed down. It was in April 1999 that HMP Risley stopped imprisoning women.

Some years later, five of us were on remand for a month in the women's prison at Cornton Vale.[207] This was for our actions at the very first TP nuclear disarmament camp at Coulport. During our time there the fourth Trident submarine, HMS *Vengeance* (what a telling name – 'vengeance', not 'defence'!) was to be launched from Barrow-in-Furness on 19 September 1998. We would have been taking part in the protests there if we were free, but instead we decided to protest where we were. We made some banners from our sheets by tearing out printed words and letters from old newspapers and sticking them on with toothpaste ready to hang out of our windows, and wrote a letter to the governor explaining that our protest was against the government's nuclear weapons policy and against the launching of a vessel of mass murder. We stated that it was not against the prison, would only last one day, was completely nonviolent, consisted of hanging a banner that said 'No escape from nuclear weapons' and we would remain in our cell for one day without speaking or eating. The response was interesting: I would have thought any rational response would have been to ignore the protest as it was so low-key and did not involve other prisoners at all. But authority does not like to be challenged in any way and this was seen as a challenge. In a letter from the Scottish Prison Service, our behaviour was described as 'action which was not only political but likely to lead to the disruption of the prison regime, with implications for other prisoners at Cornton Vale.'[208]

Our plan was discovered the day before, as the prison staff monitored all phone calls and we had notified the press of our intentions. Our shared cells were 'turned over', notes and banners were discovered, and we were removed to single cells in the punishment block, unable to communicate with each other.[209]

The next day, the day of the launch, a prison officer came to my cell and I silently handed in a new note explaining that I was fulfilling my commitment to anti-nuclear protest by refusing to eat, speak or move out of the cell for the day.[210] I was then forcibly removed (having refused to walk) to a disciplinary hearing by having my wrists forced back very painfully by two male officers until I was screaming in agony. I was dragged into a cell and thrown on the ground face-down, set upon by male officers and forcibly strip-searched and left naked for 24 hours. The following day I was allowed clothes and taken back to the original solitary punishment cell. The rest of my remand time was spent in solitary confinement (with no books, radio or TV) with only one hour of solitary exercise each day in a small yard.

Nonviolent protest is seen as quite a threat to prison authorities. I could not just leave it at that and so, on my release (after fortunately being acquitted and out of prison), I took further action. It took three years, with the help of a sympathetic Scottish MP, before I received a half-hearted apology and a small *ex gratia* payment from the Scottish Prison Service for the assault. I learnt to make sure that whenever possible I would write reports of arrests and prison stays and keep copies of letters, and these have proved really useful. For instance, I still have a copy of the letter I sent to the Chief Inspector of Prisons for Scotland, Chief Inspector Clive Fairweather OBE, on 9 October 1998 about my treatment, asking for his advice and enclosing the report I wrote about the assault. The press coverage helped air the issue and some years later my various prison reports on Cornton Vale were used by the media when the number of suicides in the prison was increasing.[211]

This had not been a very good introduction to Cornton Vale. A year later Ellen, Ulla and I took part in the Loch Goil action and I was back on remand, but this time for five months.[212] Much of my time was spent preparing my defence as I was representing myself. Luckily, I had the help of Isabel, a friend who then worked at the British Library, who was able to get me needed references from the Nuremberg Trials. Outside supporters helped by sending in other references and the case law I needed. But a major problem was my terrible handwriting that I often could not read myself! I was used to writing on a word processor and it was difficult to keep writing by hand and crossing out and rewriting. I therefore engaged in a long battle to have access to a laptop and printer, which I eventually managed to get. Defending yourself from inside prison is quite difficult but nevertheless gives you something productive to do that you would have to be doing anyway if you were on bail and living at home. As long as you have good support from friends outside who can send you in papers and look up references for you, it can work well.

The major discomfort and cause of many official complaints, however, was the battle to get access to a toilet. The lack of in-cell toilet facilities was one of the most stressful and unhealthy aspects of our imprisonment. I was reassured that I just had to ring the bell and would be taken to a toilet within 20 minutes at the most, but sometimes had to wait several hours and more than once over 16 hours before a prison officer was free to do this. A cardboard potty might be shoved through a slot in the door and then had to be kept smelling and disturbing other cellmates. There was a high incidence of hepatitis and the constant swilling of urine down the sinks that people were washing in or getting their drinking water from was dangerous for all involved. Access to doctors and dentists were also very difficult for the inmates and although I did not need them, I witnessed one seriously ill woman who was continually denied access to a doctor until she fainted in a corridor. Women experiencing acute dental pain were just given loads of painkillers and were not able to see dentists for many weeks.

The boredom amongst prisoners was acute, as there were never enough education places for everyone wanting to attend them. Remand prisoners were not allowed to use the library, which was very frustrating. I witnessed racial prejudice not only against BAME women but also against Irish prisoners. The lack of airmail letters to buy in the canteen was a major problem for non-nationals, as was the lack of essential prison information in languages other than English. I made numerous official complaints, some of which were dealt with. As an articulate woman with major support in the outside world I was in a good position to be able to demand my rights, or complain, or appeal to people higher up in the prison hierarchy, and was thus able to mitigate some of the problems that I and other prisoners faced. However, as I said in the report I sent out to the prison authorities and politicians:

> The rights I claimed for myself should have been freely available to all prisoners. I was careful to stress to all that I was not claiming them for myself alone. This report is part of the process to try and ensure that all prisoners get better treatment and I write it on behalf of my fellow prisoners.[213]

I was able to compare the changes in prison conditions myself when I returned to Cornton Vale Prison in 2017.[214] I had taken part in the TP disarmament camp, during which we had celebrated at the gates of Faslane on 8 July.[215] The UN had just finished a conference of 130 countries who passed a treaty to ban all nuclear weapons. It was time to celebrate. The TPNW, known popularly as the Ban Treaty, is based on the same international humanitarian laws that our campaign is based on, and showed that, as we had stated so often, the UK's nuclear weapons had always been illegal and were now to be banned.[216] It was to be open for signatures and ratifications on 20 September that year. It would come into force 90 days after 50 countries had not only signed the treaty but also ratified it. As I write this, the 50th ratification has finally happened and I have been out in my street ringing a bell to celebrate with neighbours.[217] As we are in Covid lockdown here in Wales, I was not able to join my friends at any of the nuclear bases, but others did so. It is not often that we can celebrate such good news!

As part of the disarmament camp in 2017, five of us had blockaded the main entrance into Coulport to highlight the continuing illegality of storing nuclear weapons there, and, of course, we were arrested. Brian and I refused to accept the bail conditions not to return to the camp, as we felt this was unreasonable given the situation with the Ban Treaty, and so we were both held on remand. We spent only two weeks inside as the bail conditions were eventually dropped, and at our eventual trial we were merely admonished. But this spell inside gave me a chance to see what, if any, conditions had improved inside the prisons.

There had been a transformation. The general level of cleanliness was so much better than before, and more importantly there were flushing loos in every cell. Prisoners were being encouraged to attend 'breakfast gym' every day by being offered yoghurt, fresh fruit and cereals at the gym, and I noticed more prisoners taking part. I spent part of my time on remand in Edinburgh prison and I also noted they made the 'association' time at the same time as exercise time rather than during visiting, work or education times.[218] This encouraged prisoners (many of whom had been on drugs and were not into exercise or fresh air) to get outside for the hour's exercise where they could smoke freely, talk and occasionally actually walk around the yard. There were enough staff for education classes to take place and access to a library once a week to get books. If society wants to reform prisoners and encourage them into a healthier lifestyle these things are really important. It was much better, and I wrote to the authorities to say so, receiving a 'thank you' letter saying that it made interesting reading.

It stated:

The Scottish Prison Service have made considerable efforts to improve the opportunities for purposeful activity for all prisoners, particularly women.

I had also commented on the difficulty of getting access to computers or word processors, especially for those defending themselves, and there was an agreement that there was a need for greater access in an increasingly electronic world and that my information would be used to 'inform our monitoring and inspecting activities in Cornton Vale and Edinburgh and more widely in Scotland's prisons.'[219] Before I leave off talking about prisons I must emphasise what a difference it makes when you receive postcards and letters, keeping you in touch with the world outside and providing visual stimulation. Not only did I write for the release of political prisoners with Amnesty International after my experiences in prison but also sometimes took on writing regularly to long-term prisoners of conscience.[220]

11

Linking Our Struggles in One World

AS THE YEARS passed I was involved with many others in campaigns that were local, national and international in their scope. Many people were embracing the idea of global citizenship. 'Think Globally, Act Locally' was becoming more than a slogan on coffee mugs and T-shirts. For every issue you can think of, there are global and local ramifications and wherever I could, like many people, I tried to join the dots.

Thus when campaigning for the protection of old-growth forests in Sarawak, Finland, Canada and Brazil, I also tried to make sure I was involved in local tree planting, woodland creation and forest management in the areas I was living in at the time be it Norfolk, Scotland or Wales.[221, 222, 223] I was also part of the environmental group who helped set up the UK standards for the Forest Stewardship Council (FSC).[224] When protesting about the military occupation of the West Bank and East Jerusalem and the continuing siege of Gaza, I linked up with protest groups in the UK and joined in public awareness campaigns including giving talks.[225]

When I moved to Knighton in 2009, my partner and I organised our first demonstration in the town centre after being there for only a few months. This was to mourn the death of the activists on the MV *Mavi Marmara* who were killed in international waters by the Israeli military when taking aid to Palestine as part of the Ships to Gaza project. We later helped fundraise for the Freedom Flotilla, Ships to Gaza project.[226] We are still involved in the Radnor Palestine Links group. I am deeply concerned about the plight of refugees, which I see as a consequence of armed conflicts and environmental destruction caused by military intervention, and out of control corporations exploiting natural resources, all of which the UK has been involved in. Thus, I am a part of our local refugee support group.[227]

Then there is the national and local impact of food and agriculture, which I have been interested in ever since working with the Soil Association. Obviously, apart from growing as much of our own food as possible on an allotment, my partner and I support local organic smallholders. And now there is a local struggle going on to try to get a moratorium on Intensive Poultry Units (IPUs). Powys is the poultry capital of Europe and the cumulative impact on our environment is appalling.[228] Our Sustainable Knighton group has been organising demonstrations in Knighton and in Cardiff, directed at the Welsh government, and is now pursuing a legal challenge (a Judicial Review) to try to reverse the latest planning permission that was given for yet another IPU due to be built on the outskirts of Knighton.There are so many local aspects to national and international issues, and people all around the world are linking these closely together as they start taking climate change seriously.

Greta Thunberg and the School Strikes, David Attenborough speaking out about catastrophic species loss and, of course, Extinction Rebellion have now put climate change on top of the political agenda, where it should have been decades ago.[229, 230, 231] It is becoming clearer to everyone that for life on our planet to survive we must pressure governments, corporations and every institution to change radically from an exploitative, extractivist, growth-at-any-costs society to a sustainable, steady-state economy within an egalitarian and compassionate society. Ever since connecting up with volunteers in Norwich at the Greenhouse in the early 1980s, which was then concentrating on anti-nuclear and climate change campaigning, I was concerned about how difficult it was to engage people in the changes we all have to make to reverse climate chaos.[232]

I remember a cartoon from those days that showed people happily rowing a boat on a river, towards a huge waterfall in the distance that they were obviously unaware of. There were people on the riverbanks desperately waving at them and shouting at them to beware, but they did not hear, they were still larking about and they would soon be at that point when the current would take them over the fall and then, whatever they did, it would be too late. We all felt like those people on the riverbanks. Most people and certainly corporations and governments were ignoring the coming catastrophe.

The Greenhouse put up maps of how much of East Anglia and London would be underwater as temperatures soared and the sea levels rose. This was in the early '80s – almost 40 years ago. As part of Reforest the Earth, Frankie printed hundreds of copies of an excellent pamphlet with 101 ways individuals could lower their carbon footprints: by putting up solar panels, changing lightbulbs, using long-lasting natural fibre bags not plastic bags, recycling and reusing, eating less meat, using public transport and giving up our cars or sharing them, shopping carefully and locally, and consuming less.[233] But, of course, individuals cannot stop and reverse climate change by themselves. Institutions, governments, corporations and smaller businesses have to change too.

Now, 40 years on, it is almost too late. Those in low-lying countries already face unprecedented sea level rises and all over the planet there are extreme floods, droughts, fires, hurricanes and other climatic changes that we foresaw. Too slowly, awareness is growing. I used to have a banner hanging up in the barn at Valley Farmhouse, when I lived in north Norfolk, where so many nonviolence trainings took place. It said: 'WAKE UP THE WORLD IS DYING'. Indeed it is, and it is up to every one of us to demand the changes needed to stop and then reverse climate chaos.

I got involved in Extinction Rebellion (XR) in April 2019 when I went up to London and joined the marvellous, exciting, peaceful occupations in the squares of central London, on Waterloo Bridge and then again in Parliament Square.[234] I was one of many who took it in turns to 'lock-on' to the pink boat in the middle of Oxford Circus. I witnessed the amazing people's assemblies taking place. Ordinary passers-by engaged in deep discussions about climate change and what we could do about it – democracy in process. I was arrested twice and was the first person to face a trial from these April actions, and the judge, although carefully listening to my defence and evidence, did not have the courage to find me not guilty.[235]

A few weeks later I was approached by Gail and asked if I would get peace movements involved in XR.[236] Of course I said yes and invited peace groups to get involved, roped in Jane as a co-facilitator, set up the structure and started getting ready for the next XR event in London in October 2019. I felt very motivated to do this as it was an opportunity to involve more people in making the links between all the different issues I had been involved in for decades. We explained XR Peace as being

> a coalition of peace groups that has come together as an Extinction Rebellion Movement Group to support the overall goals of XR and raise awareness of the role of militarism and war in the climate crisis and to demand that resources that go to the military be used to address the climate emergency.

We also clarified our key messages.[237] Mark volunteered to design our website and keep it updated, and we further explained ourselves as being:

... a movement within Extinction Rebellion that especially highlights the military causes and impacts of climate chaos. We take action for Peace, Disarmament, Human Rights, Real Security and Climate Justice.

Climate Justice and war have the same root causes as structural inequality, racism and violence against women. They are the consequences of military-industrial systems of unsustainable growth, profit, aggression and exploitation.

Armed conflict and weapons contribute to poverty and cause great misery and death. Refugees flee their homes. Climate chaos makes everything worse. When things go wrong, the most vulnerable are at greatest risk. Women and children inevitably pay the highest price.[238]

The build-up to the October 2019 actions was intense and I got very stressed, mainly because of having to fit into the overall planning of XR, with its use of online communication tools, which meant having a mobile phone on all the time. This is not something I usually do, as I prefer to work in silence and not be continually interrupted by messages coming in. But nevertheless, I thoroughly enjoyed working with a mainly young crowd of intelligent, passionate activists. The plans were to take and hold 12 sites in central London, and XR Peace decided to take on organising the site outside the MOD block on the Victoria Embankment. We started the taking of our site earlier than other groups as we were right next to the Metropolitan Police HQ. Over the ten days or so of the actions, over a thousand of us were arrested, 57 from XR Peace.[239]

Creativity and enjoyment are essential to enable us to keep motivated year after year and not to give up, even when the changes we want to see are just not happening and we begin to lose heart

We did actions – mostly blockades and die-ins – outside the MOD buildings, in Trafalgar Square, outside and inside the BAE Systems HQ, and outside the Supreme Court.[240] Some excellent videos were taken of the action and put on the XR Peace website.[241] I was arrested five times, the last time having locked-on to the XR bamboo blockade in the middle of Oxford Circus.[242] But the arrest that I was most distressed about was when the police suddenly swooped on Trafalgar Square on 14 October, after having told protesters the previous week that this was where we should go to 'safely' protest. It is a traditional protest and assembly place. The police suddenly entered the square, demanding that we leave, giving us a mere hour to remove all the gazebos and tents and exhibition materials that were part of our public outreach. Many refused to comply and four of us in the XR Peace gazebos locked-on inside until forcibly cut out of the lock-on tubes and arrested. The police took all the protesters' tents, banners, leaflets, food and other materials and trashed them. There is an ongoing legal challenge to this behaviour, which amounts to theft. There had been a sea change in policing methods and it was becoming increasingly nasty.

Then the Covid-19 virus appeared in our lives. The pandemic is disrupting societies all over the world and affecting protests. Only a few XR Peace activists were able to take part in the last XR Rebellion that took place in September 2020, as we are mostly older and many did not want to risk infecting ourselves or others in crowded cities. Those XR Peace members who lived in or near the cities joined in with their local regional groups. The Covid-19 pandemic has been keeping many people locked down and unable to confront and disrupt the climate destroyers. There has been much debate about whether it is right to engage in activity that is likely to end in arrests and detention, as this will put ourselves and others at risk. We may be socially distanced and masked and taking all precautions, but the police do not always do the same. Thus, the numbers willing and able to take direct nonviolent but truly disruptive action has greatly diminished.

The corporations involved in selling arms, supplying armies and security firms, logging, mining, manufacturing and selling agro-chemicals and pharmaceuticals – in other words the military-industrial mega-machine – are continuing to destroy our planet.[243] The highly-industrialised intensive factory farming of animals is at last getting some publicity, as the general public slowly find out about the drastic increase in animal diseases caused by the unhealthy conditions these animals are raised in, and how these are now impacting on human health – and the link with pandemics.

However, given the increasing urgency of the situation with the two existential threats of climate change and nuclear weapons still with us, we will have to get back to serious, sustained disruptive activity as soon as possible. With our dysfunctional democracies we need to put the pressure on where it will be effective, and this means denting the profits of the corporations who are driving us to extinction.

There are, of course, lots of activities that are taking place online. XR Peace has produced some excellent leaflets for electronic distribution.[244] The one entitled *Climate Chaos and Covid-19 Pandemic: Dangers for our Security When Warnings are Ignored* is especially topical. Ironically, the pandemic has brought people together in ways previously unimaginable. Groups and individuals have shared information, strategised, and found the situation we face is even clearer than before. The pandemic has starkly revealed the inequalities of our world and how the corporations, and the rich people who run them, can make ever-greater profits from any disaster. Witness the squabbles over who will profit from a vaccine, or who gets the contracts for providing the test-and-trace service. Meanwhile people in general are getting poorer, especially those working in the basic services keeping our health services running, ensuring clean water in our taps, cleaning our streets, or educating our children.

Where does this leave us? The major issues of our time are now linked together in the fight for life on Earth. It is important that we still push hard for change and challenge the global system, get out in the streets if we can: yes, socially distanced and wearing masks while the pandemic is still with us. We cannot just let the Earth destroyers continue their destruction. We are the majority and we can stop them. We can find ever more creative ways to stop the destruction and restructure our society into one that we deserve. Utopia, here we come!

12

Lessons Learnt

NEVER GIVE UP.

Take responsibility for your own education by reading more widely and mixing with a greater variety of people. Question everything, including the dominant culture, and open yourself up to informal and alternative learning methods.

Engage in creative and life-affirming practical work within a loving family or friendship circle.

There is no 'right' way to protest or resist or defend yourself – each person must find their own voice. Diversity is empowering and a strength in itself.

In all your action planning, make as many contingency plans as you can and agree an ending time. Practise your action and do some role plays as this helps everyone to be clearer about their role and brings up practicalities that you will need to sort out before the action.

Choose any aliases you use (with the police and other authorities) carefully, as they will be with you all your life on your records.

Follow your spirit. Think of the real value of an action rather than how popular it might be.

Do not make things difficult by setting impossible goals: life is not tidy like a game. Improvise, admit mistakes, adapt and continue the campaign in other ways if the goals have to change.

You are not alone. Reach out to family and friends to get support for yourself to sustain your actions. Involve others, ask for help, make sure that others have the space to initiate, take responsibility and move the campaign on.

Record your own history by writing and publishing books, articles and materials that can explain your actions and campaigns to others. Publish handbooks and action advice for others to learn from.

Wherever possible, form coalitions and alliances in order to extend contacts, bring in new people with extra skills, share resources and engage in interlinked actions. It does not matter if you do not agree on everything. Find something you can agree on and work together, without undermining other approaches and priorities.

Continue your actions: effective campaigning needs *sustained* nonviolent direct action combined with education of the public, lobbying, negotiating, and, most importantly, it needs clearly communicated requests or demands that can be implemented by the people or organisations targeted.

It is always useful if you can prove you have written letters, lobbied, demonstrated and done everything possible before having to resort to direct action to stop dangerous and illegal activities from taking place.

Prepare in advance the materials that might help your defence in court, and that will give the judge and jury the background information they need to understand the moral and legal basis of your action.

If your action needs to be kept a secret (before it happens) to enable it to be effective, do not rely upon encryption or other electronic forms of communication. Face-to-face communication is always best. When you need to phone or email, never put in the date, time, or place.

If possible, defend yourself in court, but if in a group try to have at least one person with a good lawyer to ensure that the legal process is adhered to by the prosecutors, and so that you have a professional to help you through the legal hurdles and prepare for appeals if required.

The legal process can be a nightmare – but never give up. Sometimes you can win surprising cases. Certainly do not plead guilty unless you have serious personal reasons for stopping the process, as quite often the prosecutors lose information or get things in a muddle, and the case is either dropped or you win outright!

Do not forget to share your court and prison experiences to empower others.

Recognise and applaud the importance of all supporters. They are a vital part of all nonviolent direct action, providing essential help in setting up the action, legal and court support, press work, and support to prisoners among the many other tasks that they do.

Be open to supporting and taking part in international actions when they need you.

Encourage openness and accountability in all you do. This increases public awareness and keeps you within a moral framework, as you have to explain yourself to others.

Be nonviolent and aware of safety issues at all times. It is no good saying you are protecting life on the planet while putting life in danger.

Be creative and enjoy yourself. This is essential as it will help keep you motivated year after year. Spontaneity is important and fun to keep the creativity building but you need to think fast to ensure you are behaving responsibly and still allowing enough time for genuine decision-making.

If possible, try to work in an affinity group. These can either be long-term or short-term for a specific action.

When working with refugees, get to know them and understand what they have suffered and make sure they are not put into potential conflict situations where their trauma is reactivated.

Everything is connected, so you can learn about another issue and campaign on that to rejuvenate and re-energise. The linking up of the many problems and issues helps deepen understanding and stops jaded feelings coming to the fore.

Recognise the signs of burnout before you reach the stage where you have ceased to function efficiently and kindly.

From the very beginning keep copies of reports, letters, photographs, press reports and records for later use.

And never, ever give up. Did I say that before?

Answering Questions From a Young Activist

17-year-old Jasmine Maslen from Leicester questions 69-year-old Angie Zelter

JASMINE: What are your thoughts on current nonviolent direct action efforts in Extinction Rebellion? Do you think any recent actions are having their desired effect?

ANGIE: XR is a very timely and necessary mass movement of nonviolent direct action that I wholeheartedly support. There are many creative and effective XR actions taking place, and just by coming out in their hundreds, during these Covid times, the rebels are still having an impact. The general national press coverage is much less than it was in the first year or so, especially compared to coverage in March and October of 2019, but this was to be expected. The main effect will be felt in the conversations and discussions taking place in the families and friendship groups of the rebels as they explain why they are willing to risk arrest and go to court.

There was a very effective action on 21 August 2020 which was really important as it added the impact of ships on the ocean to the climate debate. It was a sea-based action against one of the largest residential ships which is home to around 200 wealthy passengers, and which 'emits ten times more greenhouse gases per person per mile than a jumbo jet.' The projected messages on the hull were eye-catching and the decentralised local action was brilliantly executed.

I also liked the women's action 'Can't Bare the Truth' on 10 September 2020 when women bared their chests and explained the consequences of a hotter world outside Parliament.

JASMINE: In your personal experience as an activist, which nonviolent direct action proved to be most effective to your aims? Why was it so?

ANGIE: The most effective actions that I have taken part in have always been done as part of a sustained and ongoing campaign where my individual action added to others' actions and brought about change. For instance, I was one of thousands of women who took part in the ten-year campaign to rid the UK of nuclear cruise missiles stationed at RAF Greenham Common in the 1980s. The Greenham Women's Peace Camp created a space for a sustained presence all around the base with lots of encampments demonstrating opposition, backed up by many hundreds of actions that involved fence cutting, getting into the high-security areas of the base, into the soldiers' housing complexes, and onto the nuclear bunkers. The resulting court cases, prison sentences, and constant press coverage, plus the fact that so many women from very different backgrounds and of all ages supported the camp and not only took part in the huge demonstrations that surrounded the base but also came back time after time, ensured its success.

The other action that proved very effective to my aim of showing up the illegality of Trident was the TP Loch Goil action. The three of us emptied all the contents of a floating laboratory complex in Loch Goil which does the research on minimising the radar, acoustic and magnetic noises on Trident nuclear submarines. It was an essential link in the whole system. The Sheriff directed the jury to acquit us after having been persuaded that the deployment of Trident nuclear missiles was illegal under IHL. This was a major breakthrough and is part of an ongoing process to get the UK to disarm its illegal weapons of mass destruction. No one action can ever change such a major part of UK foreign and defence ideology, but it was a really important step in the right direction. The reasons it was an effective action was that it was totally nonviolent, well-researched so that we could prove no one would be hurt by the action, was an essential link in the system that we were able to break, and it was well supported by members of a well-known nonviolent disarmament campaign (TP) who organised visits and support for the three of us while we were in prison for five months on remand. The supporters also helped organise our expert witnesses, who included a German judge who explained why he had taken part in a blockade at the Mutlangen base to protest against US nuclear weapons in Germany and why they were illegal.

JASMINE: Have you been met with a violent police response at a nonviolent action? Why do you think this kind of response keeps occurring and what can be done about it?

ANGIE: When various authorities (police, armed forces, security staff) are faced with protest that they feel unable to control easily, or when their orders are to keep the protesters down and out at any cost, then violence is likely to occur.

The recent orders from the Metropolitan Police commissioner Cressida Dick to engage in much tougher policing during the September 2020 Extinction Rebellion protests on climate change resulted in a very changed atmosphere from that of the October 2019 protests.

A change of orders from the top can then empower nasty characters to be let loose. All institutions and organisations have people in them (including the peace and environmental activist communities – we are not immune unfortunately) who have issues that may lead to violent behaviour in certain circumstances. Some people are, in their personal and professional lives, known bullies with violent tendencies and they often choose to be in positions of power in order to be able to express these characteristics. It does not take long for authoritarianism and violence to rear their ugly faces. It is up to all of us to call our institutions and authorities to account and to make sure that these evils do not take over completely. And we can lessen the likelihood of violence by our own actions.

It is important to always be calm and able to think clearly. This is one of the reasons that any nonviolent direct action campaigns I am involved in always stress that there must be no alcohol and drug taking while on actions. I was with a group of peace activists who had entered a military base when police dogs were set on us and the one person who was drunk was badly bitten. We usually trust everyone and had not picked up on this before the action. The rest of us immediately dropped to the ground and sat still with hands and arms close to our bodies, or in my case, in a ball with my head buried in my arms. Police dogs in this country are well-trained and will not usually attack unless told to; they just hold you in position until their handler comes up, so your protection is to stand or sit extremely still, not making eye contact. I have had similar experiences of having guard dogs sent out to find or chase me when entering military bases, and I have never been hurt as I always stop when they are near and get into a submissive position, so the dog knows it is in control and I can wait until the handler comes along and tells me to get up.

Let me give you a few examples of my own experiences of violence. I was inside a us-run military base in Norfolk (RAF Lakenheath) doing a Citizen's War Crimes Inspection inside the high-security area where the us nuclear weapons were based, when a us soldier with a rifle approached me, shouting at me to stop, and prodding the rifle into my chest. He was shaking hard with his hand trembling on the trigger (he was only young) and shouting down his radio that he had given me the three warnings – was he to shoot? He was really scared and nervous. This is the most dangerous time. He was conflicted.

He did not want to shoot, but those were his orders. I immediately sat down and said calmly to him that he was in no danger, I was not going anywhere, he did not have to shoot me. He stepped a bit away, his gun still trained on me, and kept talking on the radio until some UK MOD police came up to arrest me and take over.

You have asked what can be done about this kind of violence – well, one way is not to put yourself into these kinds of dangerous situations. They are not for everyone. Going into high-security areas in military establishments is never going to be completely safe. But sometimes it is only these kinds of civilian nonviolent actions that can help change things. So there is a dilemma. Our frequent incursions into Lakenheath eventually led to all US nuclear weapons being removed from that base, and thus in the UK as a whole, as it was proving too expensive to guard and police them. When going into potentially dangerous situations you therefore have to be really calm and obviously nonviolent and able to assess situations as they arise and try to defuse them.

Another example: I was part of an international solidarity action of about 50 activists trying to enter Gaza from Israel through the Erez Crossing to give support to the besieged Palestinians there. They had been informed and were waiting for us the other side of the border at the end of the long road. We could not see them but knew that once past the border we could go along the road and meet them. Having arrived in a coach and cars at the border, we approached the barrier and just started walking through: some of us, moving quite fast, were ahead of the rest. Suddenly lots of armed border police were running between the two groups shouting at us to stop, and then one mad policeman started shooting live bullets. I ran back and shouted at everyone to sit down and be silent and told the policeman to stop shooting. He looked quite crazy and was still shooting, over our heads but completely out of control, screaming and shouting, and bullets seemed to be flying off at random. I approached another officer and told him to get that guy under control as we were all sitting down now peacefully. He did get him removed and then we were all arrested and taken away. It had been a scary moment, but luckily all the internationals had been sensible and immediately got down onto the ground, and so no one got hurt.

Sometimes, we need to recognise that there is very little we can do to stop violence against us. In Brussels at an anti-NATO demonstration water cannon were used against us and older activists with heart complaints, along with others, were faced by huge pressures of water that scraped us along the roads and injured several people quite badly.

When up a high ladder protesting about old-growth timber imports coming into a port in London, I was grabbed by a security guard who tried to push me off the high ladder on a crane. If a police officer had not come along and removed him and if I had not held on tightly for long enough, I would probably have fallen to my death.

It is important in all these instances, in whichever country you are, to try to pursue official complaints and legal remedies to the violence perpetrated even though these can be very time-consuming and often lead nowhere. A balance needs to be made between trying to get justice and stop the legal impunity, and conserving your energies for the long haul.

In the UK we do not often have to face severe and blatant disregard for human rights and are not faced daily with armed men or women, police and military tanks. But this could change at any time if more of our civil liberties are taken away and more authoritarian and populist governments take over.

There are occasions when violence needs to be stopped in advance. When confronted by civilian police or armed MOD police you can protect yourself by making it very clear that you are nonviolent by your posture and manner, and also by saying 'I am a totally nonviolent protester'. However, it is much better if your group or organisation has had liaison meetings with the police likely to be involved, to explain well in advance of your actions that your organisation is totally nonviolent, and to explain why you are protesting. This does not mean the police are told what you are going to do exactly, or when you might do it, but it makes sure they know and trust your commitment to nonviolence and that you mean them no harm.

TP, Faslane 365 and Action AWE are just three examples of campaigns where we have put police liaison work in the forefront of our preparations. This goes along, of course, with a basic nonviolent and peaceful philosophy of respecting every human whatever their role, job or status. We respect the humanity in each person (however buried it might be!) and only speak out about the behaviours and policies they are engaging in, rather than dismissing them as human beings. However awful their behaviour is, if we cannot recognise that they are human then we risk losing our own humanity. We make sure there is a way out of violent behaviour by meeting them as fellow humans. This can be very controversial as some activists think we are 'collaborating' with the police by doing this. But the police are part of our society: they are someone's sons and daughters, brothers and sisters, mums and dads, and when we can, we need to remind them that they are meant to be policing on our behalf and keeping us all out of danger.

You might be interested in reading some of the letters that have passed between activists and the police. (See Appendix 1d, an example, from the TP Core Group, addressed to Superintendent David Belcher, of the TVP, Newbury, Berks on 9 June 2000).[245] The police liaison work I was involved in with XR in September and October 2019 was good to do, even though it seemed to do little and we did not get very far. The Met are one of the hardest police authorities to deal with. Nevertheless, it was important for the police to have been told that we were nonviolent and why we needed to disrupt the centre of London.[246] Apart from anything else, it helps to be able to say this when defending yourself in court. Resistance and protest are often dangerous, and as Gandhi said, you must be prepared to take the violence that may be meted out to you but not to do violence back. You may want to read the book *Nonviolent Soldier of Islam: Badshah Khan, A Man to Match His Mountains* by Eknath Easwaran. It is about Badshah Khan, who trained thousands of Afghani soldiers to put down their guns and 'fight' nonviolently against the British.

When organising the Faslane 365 year of blockades and discovering that a notorious Yorkshire-based MOD cutting team was being used at Faslane and had used pressure points to get people to release from lock-ons, we talked to the Strathclyde and MOD police and managed to get promises not to use pressure points, and that particular cutting unit was sent back to Yorkshire.[247] This was particularly important as pressure points are dangerous and can result in permanent damage to the activists. The Strathclyde Police were very professional and our liaison meetings worked well in Scotland. When we organised a huge demo at Faslane and the Met sent down their riot team to 'help out', we were told by the Strathies that the Met were kept in the canteen and told not to come out unless asked for. The Strathies knew as well as we did that having riot police out in force made it much more likely that tempers would be inflamed and violence occur. We had our own 'peacekeepers' and knew how to deal with agents provocateurs. But it is very different in other places in the UK. And, of course, the situation might be completely different for those communities that the police have always treated with less respect. For example, if you are a young Black man – or woman – the violence can be horrific and often kept out of sight, and too often has led to death.

The police also often try as hard as possible to stop movements from growing by making it difficult for people to be included. For instance, during the run-up to the October 2019 XR actions in London, the police confiscated ramps, wheelchairs and accessible toilets, and arrested people working to provide this equipment.[248] So what can we do about it?

Firstly, we need to **make sure that the police and authorities know we really are nonviolent.** This can be done by showing them our nonviolent guidelines and explaining that we give nonviolence workshops to our activists.

Secondly, we must **make sure that we have observers taking footage and pictures of our actions,** perhaps have hidden radio mikes and cameras on our bodies that send the data off-site (just like the police on-body cameras that send their data to the cloud). Some observers need to be in plain and obvious sight of the police so they know they are being watched, and some need to be hidden so that they can get the evidence out.

Thirdly, we need to **make sure that everyone is supported.** Given our racist society it is probably a good idea to use various privileges we may have to protect the more vulnerable as well as we can. This may mean partnering up young, male, Black activists with older, white, middle-class women, or having non-disabled activists paired up with disabled people. Of course, some actions cannot divide up people like this as certain groups want to act in their own specific ways, but having support nearby can be a help.

Finally, **remember that support can be found in unexpected places.** Be ready to find and use it. There are always people in any institution who are fair-minded, brave and want a better world, and may be able to provide aid if given a chance. I have found unexpected support from police officers, prison guards, and soldiers. We should never give up hope.

Knitting the pink peace scarf in Knighton, Wales, 2013.

Knighton scarf roll-out on Broad Street, Knighton, Wales, 5 July 2014.

Internationals help to blockade Burghfield, March 2015.

End Coal Now occupation at Merthyr Tydfil, Wales, May 2016.

International Hiroshima Nagasaki Fast in France, 8 August 2016.

Angie being cut out at Coulport, July 2017.

Angie locked-on to the XR pink boat, Oxford Circus. London, 15 April 2019.

Angie arrested at XR in Parliament Square, 17 April 2019.

Angie and Camilla outside the Home Office, 29 July 2019.

Angie and Trish at XR Bamboo lock-on, Oxford Circus, 18 October 2019.

Angie celebrating the 2021 TPNW coming into force.

Timeline

5 June 1951	Angie Zelter born.
1968–72	At Reading University; gained BA in Psychology.
1972–75	Lived and worked in Cameroon.
1973	Tanzania for three months studying Ujamaa villages.
1975–2008	Lived in family home in East Runton, near Cromer in north Norfolk.
1982–88	Co-ordinated the Cromer Peace Group.
1983	First arrest at Greenham Common, Berkshire.
1984	Second arrest at railings of House of Commons, London.
1984–88	Founded and co-ordinated the Snowball Civil Disobedience Campaign.
1989	Took part in local campaign for clean safe seas and against sewage pollution in the North Sea.
1990	Gandhi-in-Action, Delhi, India published *Snowball: The Story of a Nonviolent Civil Disobedience Campaign in Britain.*
1989–91	Helped set up the INLAP as one of the Directors and the Secretary.
	Co-ordinated 'information-layings' in magistrates' courts on the illegality of nuclear weapons as part of the Snowball Enforce the Law Campaign and presented evidence against the UK government to Ramsey Clark (ex-US Attorney General) at the International War Crimes Tribunal held in London on 1 December 1991.
	Actions challenging the USAF Lakenheath Bye Laws with eventual win at the High Court.
August 1991	Founded the North Norfolk Community Woodland Trust.
July–Nov 1991	Took part in the Earth First! SOS Sarawak action in Miri, Sarawak spending three months in prison.
1992	Wrote *Reforest the Earth by Reforesting Britain: A Guide to Creating Your Own Community Woodland.*
June 1992–94	UK co-ordinator for the Rio Mazan Project, a Cloud Forest Conservation project based in Cuenca, Ecuador. Spent April and May 1993 in Cuenca.
1993	Founded and co-ordinated CRISPO. First CRISPO 'ethical shoplifting' action in Norwich, Norfolk.

July 1993	Arrested at the Malaysian High Commission, blockading the entrance Penan style, and acquitted in court.
Sep 1993	Blockaded British Columbia House, London in solidarity with the Friends of Clayquot Sound.
Dec 1993	CRISPO action at Harrods in London.
1993–6	Helped build the UK Forests Network (UKFN) and then co-ordinated it for three years.
	Initiated a Women's Negotiating Team for dialogue with the timber trade.
	Spent six weeks in Para State in the Brazilian Amazon researching the impact of logging and exports to the UK.
	Organised various UK Trade Seminars on the effects of logging on biodiversity in Fennoscandia, Brazil and Canada.
1995–98	Member of the Standards sub-committee of the UK section of the FSC, setting standards for forest certification in the UK.
	Joined campaigners on solidarity visit to Nuxalk territory in BC, Canada, working alongside the Nuxalk and taking part in two blockades of logging activities.
1995	Joined an all-women's group planning the Seeds of Hope action over the year.
Feb 1996	Seeds of Hope – East Timor Ploughshares action at Warton, disarming one BAe Hawk jet ready for export to Indonesia. Spent six months in Risley prison.
30 July 1996	Acquitted at Liverpool Crown Court and released from prison.
Nov 1996	Wrote prison reports about conditions inside Risley.
Aug 1996–May '97	Volunteered with the CAAT and organised a week of action outside the DTI in December 1996.
1997	Awarded the International Peace Bureau Sean MacBride Peace Prize for 1997 with Jo, Andrea and Lotta for the Seeds of Hope Ploughshares action.
Spring 1996	Supported Polish environment movement with actions in Warsaw to protect Białowie a Forest.
May 1997	Working with East Timorese refugees in a Citizens Arms Control Group, painted anti-war slogans on armoured vehicles being exported to Indonesia at the Glover Webb Factory, Hamble, Southampton.
Summer 1997	Founded Trident Ploughshares, writing the Trident Ploughshares Handbook called *Tri-Denting It*.

13/14 Mar 1998	'Borrowed' a police rigid inflatable boat and carried out a citizens' war crime inspection inside Coulport explosives-handling facility and inside Faslane submarine base.
2 May 1998	Official launch of TP in Hiroshima, Ghent, Gothenburg, London and Edinburgh.
August 1998	First TP disarmament camp held at Peaton Wood with over 100 arrested.
19 Sep 1998	Assaulted while protesting in Cornton Vale Prison.
13 Nov 1998	Drove car into Faslane base with three others.
8 June 1999	TP Loch Goil action disarming the DERA floating laboratory complex in Loch Goil. Five months in Cornton Vale Prison.
21 Oct 1999	Acquitted in landmark trial at Greenock by Sheriff Margaret Gimblett.
Nov 1999	Wrote report on prison conditions in Cornton Vale.
Dec 1999	Attended a WiB conference in Jerusalem, Israel/Palestine.
March 2000	A month touring Japan giving public speeches and workshops about nuclear weapons, the law and civil resistance in solidarity with the Japanese peace movement.
19 June 2000	Action at Menwith Hill spy base in Yorkshire.
9–13 Oct 2000	At the High Court in Edinburgh at the LAR in relation to the legal points arising from the Greenock acquittal.
14–17 Nov 2000	At the High Court in Edinburgh at the LAR in relation to the legal points arising from the Greenock acquittal.
2001	*Trident on Trial: The Case for People's Disarmament* published by Luath Press.
Aug 2001	Part of a small WiB (UK) group of four women who joined the start of the ISM in Bethlehem, Palestine.
Aug/Sep 2001	Ten days with the Christian Peacemakers Team in Hebron/Al Khalil, on 29 August 2001 attacked by Israeli settlers.
	Visited Palestinian villages.
	Invited to set up a project (eventually this became IWPS-Palestine) in Hares village to provide international protection against Israeli settlers and army.
Dec 2001	Stockholm, Sweden to accept, with Ulla and Ellen, the Right Livelihood Award on behalf of Trident Ploughshares.
Jan–July 2002	Founded the IWPS – Palestine, raised funds, recruited and trained the first team of volunteers for human rights monitoring and

nonviolent solidarity actions.

Aug–Nov 2002	Part of the first IWPS team in Hares, Palestine.
2002–05	Co-ordinated IWPS. Due to arrests, entry restrictions and deportations was unable to enter Israel/Palestine after 2005.
July 2004	TP choir performed the 'Trident: A British War Crime' Oratorio in Parliament Hall, Edinburgh.
2005	Founded Faslane 365 and helped prepare the Faslane 365 Resource pack.
2006–07	Camped a year at Faslane Peace Camp to support the F365 groups coming up for the blockades.
2008	Wrote part of and edited *Faslane 365: A Year of Anti-nuclear Blockades*.
3 Feb 2009	Co-organised a major international conference on Trident and international law in Edinburgh.
Aug 2009	Moved home to Knighton, Powys, Wales.
2010	Co-founded the Knighton Tree Allotment Trust.
15 Feb 2010	Helped facilitate the TP Big Blockade at Aldermaston.
March 2010	Co-founded the Palestine Links Group in Knighton and helped organise local solidarity actions.
Mid Feb–mid Mar 2011	A month mobilising in Sweden from Gothenburg to Kiruna with OFOG giving workshops on militarism and civil resistance.
2011	Co-edited *Trident and International Law: Scotland's Obligations*.
	Co-founded and became a Trustee of the Peaton Wood Peace Trust.
July 2011	Joined the 'War Starts Here. Let's Stop It Here' protest camp in Luleå, Sweden against the NEAT.
1 Oct 2011	With Trident Ploughshares and as part of the Stop New Nuclear Alliance helped organise their first large blockade of Hinkley Point nuclear power station.
24 Feb–6 Mar 2012	Jeju International Peace Conference on Jeju Island, South Korea, giving a keynote speech.
March 2012	Solidarity month in Gangjeong, Jeju Island supporting the local resistance against the building of a US naval base. After three arrests was forced to exit the country.
1 April 2012	Supported the Belgian *Vredesactie* group and arrested in an anti-NATO action at the NATO HQ – NATO Game Over.
9 May 2012	Demonstration and vigil outside the Korean Embassy in London.

25 July 2012	Founded Action AWE.
16 Oct 2012	Initiated a 'No to Trident in Wales' campaign at the Senedd in Cardiff, delivering a model Trident submarine to the Senedd that was 'eaten' by red dragons.
27 Feb 2013	Action AWE launched in Reading, Berkshire.
March 2013	Joined a Right Livelihood Award delegation to Para, Brazil in solidarity with MST whose leaders, Cicero Guedes and Regina dos Santos Pinho, had recently been murdered.
Aug 2013	Action AWE two-week disarmament camp on MOD land at AWE Burghfield.
2014	Commissioned articles and edited *World in Chains: The Impact of Nuclear Weapons and Militarisation from a UK Perspective.*
	Received the Hrant Dink Award in 2014, Istanbul, Turkey.
8 Feb 2014	The first Action AWE Reportings of Nuclear Crime at Reading Police Station.
April 2014	Gave lectures on UK-based civil resistance in Las Palmas, Gran Canaria, Spain and joined European anti-militarists in a Global Day Against Military Spending action by swimming into the naval base area of the port.
30 June–7 July 2014	Organised a week of Reportings of Nuclear Crime at police stations in other parts of England and Wales.
5 July 2014	Organised the Knighton rollout of the pink peace scarf.
9 Aug 2014	Helped facilitate the national rollout of 7 miles of pink peace scarf between AWE Aldermaston and AWE Burghfield.
2 March 2015	Helped organise the Burghfield Lockdown on 2 March 2015.
11 March 2015	Sang 'Trident: A British War Crime' Oratorio as a flash mob/singing lobby in the House of Commons, London.
1 Oct 2015	Launched the Public Interest Case Against Trident campaign for Trident Ploughshares.
27 Oct–9 Nov 2015	Joined a Trident Ploughshares group supporting the Spanish peace movement in their nonviolent protests against a large NATO exercise in Barbate, Southern Spain.
June 2016	Organised a whole month of nonviolent direct action at AWE Burghfield on behalf of Trident Ploughshares.
8–18 July 2017	TP Coulport disarmament camp just as the draft treaty banning all nuclear weapons was signed by 120 nations.
11 July 2017	Arrested for Breach of the Peace for blocking the MOD road into Coulport, imprisoned in Cornton Vale for 16 days after refusing to

sign special bail conditions.

6 Sep 2017	Helped facilitate and was arrested at DSEI on the No Nuclear Day.
10 Nov 2017	AG informed PICAT he was not giving his consent to the prosecution of government and military leaders for conspiring to commit a war crime.
March 2018	Joined Extinction Rebellion, organising the first meeting of the Marches XR groups – initiated Knighton Town Council to declare a climate emergency.
14 April 2018	London for the XR actions. Arrested twice.
20 June 2018	TP chain-in at Houses of Parliament demanding the UK sign the UN Treaty to Prohibit Nuclear Weapons.
28 June 2019	Trial at Westminster Court for April XR action.
23 July 2019	Asked to head up XR Peace.
7 Oct 2019	XR Peace took part in the two-week October rebellion.
6–9 Aug 2020	Four day Hiroshima to Nagasaki Fast in the centre of Knighton.
22 Jan 2021	Bell ringing celebration of the coming into force of the TPNW.

APPENDIX I: NONVIOLENCE

APPENDIX IA
The Nonviolence Movement

We cannot do anything for peace without ourselves being peace.
Thich Nhat Hanh

A CORE PRINCIPLE of all the actions I have been involved in is nonviolence. From the beginning of my life of protest I learnt from the experiences and lives of many nonviolent activists. The main influences were the lives of Gandhi, Badshah Khan and Martin Luther King, but when I attended the Bradford University Peace Studies department doing the course work for an MA in Peace Studies my horizons were broadened. I was, for instance, introduced to the writings of Gene Sharp and his 198 methods of nonviolent action. My understanding of nonviolence developed over many years and continues to deepen as I take part in civil society movements attempting to transform our societies into more compassionate, loving and inclusive ones. My work developing and facilitating nonviolence workshops to prepare activists to take safe but effective actions has also clarified my understanding of nonviolence.

In the peace movement, nonviolence is spelt as one word with no hyphen. This is to express our belief that it is not a negative but a positive concept, not just against violence but a proactive force for nonviolence, a philosophy in itself. It is active not passive. The aim of nonviolence includes both dialogue and resistance – dialogue with the people perpetrating or leading abuses and resistance to the structures holding up the abusive power to compel change. I have tried to include all of this in the campaigns I have developed and been involved in.

The time I spent at the Women's Peace Camp at Greenham Common was very influential. Lengthy discussions around the camp-fire with women from many different backgrounds and nationalities enabled the sharing of personal stories and we all learnt how women often bear the brunt of violence in their homes and in the wider society. As people who generally have less physical strength than men and who are often caring for the very young and elderly many women had to learn how to confront and challenge abusive behaviour in ways which lessened the chances of those they were caring for getting hurt or getting hurt themselves.

In order to ensure that the campaigns I initiated in the UK were nonviolent, I often insisted that we wrote handbooks and organised workshops on nonviolence. As part of this a set of useful nonviolence guidelines have been used on many occasions. They are quite simple and short:

- Our attitude will be one of sincerity and respect towards the people we encounter
- We will not engage in physical violence or verbal abuse towards any individual
- We will carry no weapons
- We will not bring or use alcohol or drugs other than for medicinal purposes

In the case of blockades or actions that involve the use of blockading equipment we also ensure that there are means to quickly enable emergency access of fire engines and ambulances but not of police vehicles. We also engage in liaison work with the police and emergency services so they know of our guidelines and commitment to nonviolence and why we are engaged in civil resistance. We do not give them details of our actions so that we can remain effective but we do provide room for dialogue and understanding to grow. I find this essential in our attempts to keep nonviolence on all sides.

The nonviolence workshops include lots of activities that ensure people have thought through the consequences of their actions and will not put people, animals or the environment at risk. We try to ensure that the means of our actions are consistent with our aims.

APPENDIX 1B
Gandhi's Seven Sins of Humanity

- Politics without principles
- Wealth without work
- Enjoyment without conscience
- Knowledge without character
- Business without morality
- Science without humanity
- Religion without compassion

Three more have been added since Gandhi's death.

- Rights without responsibility
- Power without accountability
- Development without sustainability

Campaigning Skill Share, May 2010

IF WE ARE campaigning we need to analyse the situation and issues, think clearly about our aims and objectives, know what resources we have or can call on, and have a workable strategy. We must pace ourselves so we do not get burnt out, and integrate our campaigning into our creative and enjoyable way of life.

WHAT IS THE AIM OF OUR MOVEMENT?
Clarify aim – ultimate purpose – in one or two sentences – a peaceful world – utopian/easily understood
Clarify goals
What do you want to happen?
Is it negotiable or not?
What is the least you would settle for?
Strategic goals are achievable and possible – eg change of specific NATO policies?
Tactical goals are limited accomplishments which can be made through a small number of particular actions. They have a short time span, are realistic in terms of resources available within time span, eg a peace camp/blockade
Analysis of the current situation

WHAT IS WORKING FOR AND AGAINST YOUR GOAL?
Do a *force field analysis*
On flipchart headed goal, divide into pluses and minuses and list under each side the forces working for and against the achievement of your goal, including:
individuals
groups and organisations
sectors of general public
ideologies and beliefs
social traditions and assumptions
geographical factors
your own skills and resources
Pick the strongest of the above and think about how you could counter the strong working against you and use the strong working for you.

WHICH HOSTILE GROUPS COULD BLOCK YOUR GOAL AND WHICH FRIENDLY GROUPS COULD BE INVOLVED IN THE CAMPAIGN?

Try a *Social Speedometer* working from very hostile/hostile/unfavourable/neutral/favourable/friendly/very friendly, putting into the relevant spaces the various people and groups that have an interest in the issues. How many on the hostile side have the power to block the achievement of your goal? How can you move people one step nearer the very friendly side – is it enough for hostile people to become neutral?

Strategy
Within the spirit of nonviolence (care and respect for everyone, willingness to accept suffering rather than inflict it, recognition that no one has the whole truth):

Communication: What messages/information do you need to communicate to whom? What are your means of communication?
Persuasion: What would persuade your opponents to make the change you want? Whom do they listen to and take seriously? What methods could you use to communicate to them directly or indirectly?
Coercion: If opponents are unpersuadable, what kind of pressures, non-co-operation or action would make them decide to change? How would you achieve this? Is there a need for direct action?

What are you aiming to do?
        Why?
        How?
        When?

Communication
        Between organisers (who are the organisers?)
        With the public
        With those you want to change
        With press
        Action planning
        Information/briefing pack
        Legal/court support
        Mobilisation
        Training/preparation workshops

Finance
Press
Police liaison

Let me distil some of the patterns which should by now be emerging more clearly and which I think are needed for a successful campaign:

- Knowledge and analysis of a problem facing society – in this case nuclear weapons; an understanding of the issues involved – and then the motivation and passion to create the changes needed.
- An idea for a specific nonviolent campaign with specific achievable aims.
- Producing a summary outline of the issue and campaign, and using this to help reach out to people to find those willing to form a core organising group.
- Working out timelines, resources, and action plans.
- Getting funding to cover basic expenses but relying mainly on volunteers and enthusiasm.
- Producing campaign leaflets/websites, writing articles and talking at meetings to mobilise activists.
- Providing training materials and briefing sheets, and being as open and sharing as possible about information, structure and processes so each activist has easy access to the latest advice and learning.
- Remembering that any direct action campaign is nonetheless working within a movement for social change where all the strands need to be present, and is also relying on the work and information of many others; and therefore valuing the work of other individuals and groups fulfilling those functions, like lobbying, or education, or letter-writing or engaged in dialogue and negotiation work.
- Linking up with other groups and individuals at home and abroad – thinking and being aware globally, even though acting locally.
- Keeping the spirit of a better and fairer world alive, and working in as many creative ways as possible to be an active participant in change at all levels – eg not only making sure that you can represent yourself and that the court language is explained to you, but also remembering that you have rights that can be struggled for in prison as well; you never have to succumb to being a victim, there are often choices and open doors where you do not expect them.

Example of Police Liaison Letter from the Trident Ploughshares Core Group, 2000

Addressed to Superintendent David Belcher, 9/5/2000

Dear Mr Belcher,

Thank you for your letter, faxed to us on 19th April 2000, about the events at Aldermaston from 18th to 25th May.

We are glad of the opportunity to extend our liaison with you. You should however note that Helen Harris and Sarah Lasenby have undertaken to conduct the practical aspects of our liaison and this is the arrangement we would like to continue.

As our website and the *Handbook* (Section 2.5, pages 19 and 20 – also on the website) explain, we are not an organisation in the conventional sense but a campaign made up of autonomous affinity groups and individuals who have pledged to prevent nuclear crime in a peaceful, nonviolent, safe and accountable way. As the AWE at Aldermaston itself demonstrates, a conventional form of organisation can easily become the means whereby individuals can avoid taking responsibility for their actions. The 160 'global citizens' who have taken the Pledge to Prevent Nuclear Crime, individually take responsibility for their action, and for their own and others' safety, and do not hide behind a formal organisational framework or insurance policies. There are no 'organisers' or 'leaders'. Different people take on different responsibilities at different times but the bottom line is always individual responsibility and autonomy along with respect for others. The 160 Pledgers (there may well be more by 18th May as there is another training taking place soon) have taken their pledge after careful consideration and have undergone a two-day training process, which helps them confront and resolve issues of nonviolence and safety.

Anyone who stays with us at any of the Trident Ploughshares Disarmament Camps is asked to attend a half-day nonviolence and safety workshop and sign an undertaking to abide by our nonviolence and safety guidelines. We enclose a copy of this (entitled 'Individual Supporters Nonviolence and Safety Pledge') for your information.

We would also like to raise with you the matter of your response as a law enforcement agency to the existence within your area of responsibility of an industrial complex engaged in preparations for war crimes. We enclose a leaflet (entitled 'Refuse to be a War Criminal') that we hand out to people working in Trident nuclear weapon related sites. It clarifies some of these issues. You will be aware that AWE Aldermaston is where the key components for Trident nuclear warheads are constructed. The UK Trident nuclear weapon system is clearly in breach of those fundamental principles of international humanitarian law which govern the conduct of warfare. The Trident system threatens innocent civilians in their millions and presents a long-term and serious threat to the natural environment. What action is TVP taking on this urgent and desperately serious matter? You will be aware that members of local police forces appearing at the UN Former Yugoslavia War Crimes Tribunal in the Hague are held accountable, not to their own interpretation of local statute, but to international humanitarian law in its full rigour.

We understand that it is difficult for a police force to tackle illegal and criminal acts when done by powerful people, institutions or 'official' bodies and even more difficult to confront its own government. We know that the 'official' mind set is so entrenched that it may be difficult for some people and organisations to recognise the criminality of the Trident system. Although we may have very different perceptions of the role and legality of Aldermaston, we hope that you will support our right to publicly protest at Aldermaston and for Pledgers to engage in their disarmament work. Trident Ploughshares actively engages in open and accountable dialogues and sees its disarmament work as part of the whole democratic process. Nonviolent resistance and protest against criminal and immoral activities by the state and military are an essential part of the democratic process and an essential human right.

Trident Ploughshares was launched over two years ago now and the Prime Minister and other major political leaders as well as members of the military and the AG and Lord Advocate are aware of our aims and objectives and our pledge to engage in active disarmament work. Our aims and methodology are referred to in the *Tri-Denting It Handbook* which is very explicit about the structure of the campaign. We openly send the names of all the Pledgers every three months to the Prime Minister. If you would like a copy of the latest letter to the Prime Minister, which will be sent out in the next few weeks and which will include the updated list of names of all Pledgers then please let us know, although as a visitor to our website you will probably already have found that this list is readily accessible.

These 164 Pledgers have never been charged with conspiracy to do any illegal acts. Three women Pledgers were recently acquitted by Sheriff Gimblett at Greenock Sheriff Court after openly admitting to £80,000 worth of damage to essential components of the Trident system. The grounds of their acquittal were, in the words of the Sheriff:

> the three took the view if Trident is illegal, given the horrendous nature of nuclear weapons, they had the obligation in terms of international law to do whatever little they could to stop the deployment and use of nuclear weapons.

We would like to reassure you that we are respectful, thoughtful people who reluctantly and in sorrow have prepared themselves to safely attempt to disarm Aldermaston because the various official and state bodies who should be doing this work are failing in their public duties. We are assuming that we can work constructively and co-operatively with you.

We have held seven previous large-scale events in Scotland. There have been in excess of 500 arrests. The roads around Faslane and Coulport and the narrow road access to our camps have also provided challenges. However, our police liaisons have worked informally with the Strathclyde Police, and the level of respect on both sides has ensured a high-level of trust, good humour and co-operation. There have never been any violent incidents nor traffic accidents. The Strathclyde Police provide a good model of co-operation both by their skill in minimal intervention and by their publicly stated commitment to ensuring that a citizen's right to demonstrate peacefully must be safeguarded. We were going to suggest that it might be useful for you to contact that force and exchange information and that an appropriate contact might be Superintendent Alan Davis of 'L' Division, based at the Divisional HQ at Stirling Road, Dumbarton. However, we are pleased to learn that you have already become aware of our good relationship with the Strathclyde Police as we understand that you have been in touch and recently made a visit to them in relation to our activities.

We value your comments about road safety around Aldermaston. Apart from each individual taking personal responsibility to ensure safety we would hope that you will work with our police liaisons to ensure the positioning of adequate warning signs for the roads and to work out any other sensible solutions to any problems either side foresees.

We end with a direct appeal to you as an individual. Nuclear weapons for use on Trident submarines are not a political abstraction, but a present and deadly reality. Each one of the Trident submarine's warheads can kill millions of innocent people. The system is actively deployed, seven days a week, 24 hours every day. Every citizen, whether civil or military or a police officer, is responsible. As a law enforcement officer it might be appropriate for you to take advice on how to prevent Aldermaston from continuing to provide essential elements of the criminal Trident system. Even if we agree to differ on this point, we hope that, as in Scotland, we will be able to co-operate and work together on ensuring that our camp at Aldermaston and the march to Aldermaston will be peaceful and safe. Our police liaison people will no doubt be in contact again.

Yours in Love and Peace,

Signed by Angie Zelter on behalf of the TP Core Group: Kathryn Amos, Morag Balfour, Sylvia Boyes, Maggie Charnley, Alison Crane, Marilyn Croser, George Farebrother, Helen Harris, David Mackenzie, Joy Mitchell, Brian Quail, Rev. Norman Shanks, Jane Tallents, Angie Zelter.

APPENDIX 2: NUCLEAR WEAPONS AND INTERNATIONAL HUMANITARIAN LAW

APPENDIX 2A
Judge Bedjaoui Statement of 2009

HE Judge Bedjaoui was the President of the ICJ 1994–97, and wrote the following paragraphs, which were included in the book based on the proceedings of the international conference on Trident and International Law: Scotland's Obligations, *held in Edinburgh on 3 February 2009. The piece was later written up in a book of the same title, edited by Rebecca Johnson and Angie Zelter, published by Luath Press in 2011.*

As a postscript to my Geneva speech above, and for the use of all those in Scotland wishing to ensure full compliance with international humanitarian law, I would like to stress that the International Court of Justice in its Advisory Opinion of July 8, 1996, did not have at its disposal adequate elements of fact to permit concluding with certainty whether a specific nuclear weapon system would be contrary to the principles and rules of the law applicable in armed conflict. The court was asked to rule on a general question of use and threat of use of nuclear weapons. If the court had been asked to rule on the legality of a specific nuclear weapons system or doctrine the conclusion we arrived at might well have been much clearer.

I have been asked to give a personal opinion on the legality of a nuclear weapons system that deploys over 100 nuclear warheads with an approximate yield of 100kt per warhead. Bearing in mind that warheads of this size constitute around eight times the explosive power of the bomb that flattened Hiroshima in 1945 and killed over 100,000 civilians, it follows that the use of even a single such warhead in *any* circumstance, whether a first or second use and whether intended to be targeted against civilian populations or military objectives, would inevitably violate the prohibitions on the infliction of unnecessary suffering and indiscriminate harm as well as the rule of proportionality including with respect to the environment. In my opinion, such a system deployed and ready for action would be unlawful. In accordance with evidence heard by the court, it is clear that an explosion caused by the detonation of just one 100kt warhead would release powerful and prolonged ionising radiation, which could not be contained in space or time, and which would harmfully affect civilians as well as combatants, neutral as well as belligerent states, and future generations as well as people targeted in the present time. In view of these extraordinarily powerful characteristics and effects, any use of such a warhead would contravene international and humanitarian laws and precepts. In other words, even in an extreme circumstance of self-defence, in which the very survival of a State would be at stake, the use of a 100kt nuclear warhead – regardless of whether it was targeted to land accurately on or above a military target – would always fail the tests of controllability, discrimination, civilian immunity, and neutral rights and would thus be unlawful.

In my opinion, any state that aids and abets another country, in the deployment and maintenance of nuclear warheads of 100kt or comparable explosive power would also be acting unlawfully.

The modernisation, updating or renewal of such a nuclear weapon system would also be a material breach of NPT obligations, particularly the unequivocal undertaking by the nuclear weapon states to 'accomplish the total elimination of their nuclear arsenals leading to nuclear disarmament' and the fundamental Article 6 obligation to negotiate in good faith on cessation of the arms race and on nuclear disarmament, with the understanding that these negotiations must be pursued in good faith and brought to conclusion in a timely manner.

The Right Livelihood Awards 2001
Acceptance speech by Angie Zelter, 7 December 2001:
People's Disarmament

OUR PLANET IS dying – both spiritually and physically. Fear, aggression and greed, narrow-minded national interests and immature dominance and control over others is a common theme in most countries. However, there are more and more people who define themselves as global citizens, who know that life is intimately interconnected, and that we can never be fully human while others continue to suffer, and who know that love, justice and nonviolence is the very essence of life. And what gives me hope is the very many different ways in which ordinary people are taking responsibility. They are creating the changes needed to pass beyond war and injustice, control and dominance and towards a free, just, loving, and diverse world.

I would like to share with you just one small part of this web of life and summarise our story of people's disarmament.

I come from a nuclear weapon state, where many of us have decided that, as a first step to ending war and encouraging nonviolent conflict resolution, we need to engage in the nuclear disarmament process ourselves – on a very practical level. We cannot wait for our state to disarm. We therefore started a campaign, called Trident Ploughshares, based upon international law which challenges the legitimacy of the UK nuclear forces.

The UK nuclear weapon system consists of four Trident submarines, each of which has 48 100 kiloton warheads – that is 192 independently targetable nuclear bombs – each eight times more powerful than the Hiroshima bomb. The use of even one of these warheads would be illegal because it is too powerful and indiscriminate to be capable of being used without violating international humanitarian law. When any envisaged use of force is unlawful then any stated readiness to use such force is a prohibited threat. The UK Trident system is deployed under a policy of 'stated readiness to use' – that is what a 'credible minimum deterrence' means.

The seven other nuclear weapon states are also committing crimes against peace which undermine the international legal system. The non-nuclear weapon states seem unable to join together effectively to confront the powerful states and so we are entering a new arms race in space as international law unravels before our eyes.

We have all learnt by now that if we want nuclear disarmament then it is no good waiting for our governments to do it. They have signed many international treaties and agreements promising to disarm their nuclear weapons – the most recent being at the review conference of the Non-Proliferation Treaty last year. But what do these promises mean when at the very same time they are researching the successors to the Trident nuclear weapons system, are backing the USA in its Star Wars and National Missile Defence systems and continuing to say that they rely upon nuclear deterrence?

The government's promises to disarm their nuclear weapons are useless, just as a Trident Ploughshares activist painted on the side of a Trident submarine last April. If we want nuclear disarmament then we, the people, have to take on this responsibility ourselves. This is what People's Disarmament is all about. This is why we started Trident Ploughshares, and this is why we work together with the wider peace movement that has been struggling for over 50 years now to rid the world of these monstrous killing machines.

In 1998, Trident Ploughshares issued a direct challenge to Prime Minister Tony Blair to implement international law by disarming all British nuclear weapons or that the campaign's members would do it. We have organised people to make a personal pledge to disarm the nuclear weapon system themselves and have stated that we will continue with this task until the government takes over the disarmament work and fulfils its promise of complete nuclear disarmament.

Our dedication to peaceful acts of practical disarmament is based on international law and the basic human right to life. People from many different nations come together as 'global citizens' and begin the task of peacefully dismantling the nuclear system. This is not violent, or criminal damage, or vandalism, or a breach of the peace but practical and lawful 'people's disarmament'.

Of course, the UK government and its institutions do not see it this way. Since Trident Ploughshares began in August 1998 – there have been over 1,500 arrests, mainly at the blockades and disarmament camps at Coulport and Faslane. There have been over 220 trials completed and over 1,400 days have been spent in prison, not including the days in police custody. And the vast bulk of the fines so far imposed remain unpaid as a matter of principle, leading to bailiffs confiscating property and to the threat of more prison sentences.

The people, engaged in practical nuclear disarmament, are bringing a breath of fresh air into the antiquated legal systems, bluntly naming nuclear weapons as terroristic murder machines and stating that the law is not worthy of any respect if it refuses to outlaw state-blackmail and mass-destruction. The district court at Helensburgh in Scotland is the scene of an inspiring historical people's confrontation with the evil of a nuclear weapon state. The potential for change in the UK is immense as more and more people discover they are prepared to stand up for their beliefs and say clearly and loudly 'No' to nuclear weapons, 'Yes' to nonviolent conflict resolution.

Trident Ploughshares currently have 158 'global citizens' from 14 different countries who have pledged to prevent nuclear crime and have taken part in a two-day workshop on nonviolence. Having citizens from other countries joining in our disarmament work with us, appearing in the courts and spending time in our prisons, has been much harder for the authorities to deal with. The government and the courts like to pretend that British nuclear weapons are purely a British affair but they find this position untenable when foreigners appear in court to explain why they feel threatened by Britain and why they are joining with many other nationalities as 'global citizens' and why they have pledged to peacefully disarm British Trident. I am talking here of fully pledged members of TP. But of course, we have several thousand active supporters and of these there are quite large groups from Ireland, Belgium and Holland, who come over and join our blockades.

We make sure our plans, motivations and organisational structures are open to the public, the government and military. We have a freely-accessible website which contains all our materials including our *Tri-Denting It Handbook* and our letters to and from the government. We continually ask the UK government a question they have never been able to answer: 'How can a 100 kiloton nuclear warhead ever be used in a way that can distinguish between a military target and innocent civilians?'

We encourage parliamentarians to sign our petition of support, which around 80 have now done. They help get answers to our letters, ask questions for us in their various parliaments and are now beginning to join us in our disarmament actions. At the last mass blockade we organised at Faslane in October, when over a thousand people joined in, there were members of the Scottish, UK and European parliaments arrested for peacefully blockading the base. We have also been joined in past blockades by over 30 Scottish church ministers and a respected senior Scottish criminal lawyer. They sat with us and were arrested for 'breach of the peace'. Tommy Sheridan MSP was recently acquitted on this charge in yet another court victory. The Crown will undoubtedly appeal which may mean another approach to the European Court. But such follow-through is essential in any campaign and gives us more opportunity to challenge the twisted logic of 'nuclear terrorism'.

This kind of support, along with that given by well-known authors, actors, and many hundreds of individuals, shows a wide spectrum of support which prevents the pledgers from being easily marginalised.

We work in this safe, open and accountable manner because we want our methods for opposing Trident to be consistent with our vision of what we would like to see in its place. We see our method as part of a process of good conflict resolution. We do not want to have to do this work but hope to persuade our state to do it for us. Therefore, we keep them fully briefed and keep open to dialogue and negotiation. In the longer term we see our method of disarmament as being an experiment in forming sustainable networks of 'nonviolent resistance to oppression' and hope that these will eventually replace military force all over the globe.

All Trident Ploughshares Pledgers must be in affinity groups and agree to the safety and nonviolence ground-rules but thereafter they work as autonomously as they wish. They have chosen various kinds of disarmament actions which have ranged from blockades, to fence cutting, to swimming onto the submarines and destroying equipment, to dismantling a research lab, disabling military vehicles, to painting war crime warnings on military equipment and handing out leaflets to military base workers urging them to 'Refuse to be a War Criminal'. The majority of these disarmament actions involve people in blockades and fence cutting and have caused minimal damage for maximum court-clogging disruption.

However, there have also been at least nine attempts at substantial disarmament damage in the last 18 months, with three groups managing to complete their actions causing hundreds of thousands of pounds worth of damage and delaying the operation of the Trident related equipment. For instance, Susan and Martin, in November 2000, cut through security fencing at Wittering, broke into a hangar and damaged one of the nuclear convoy vehicles, making it unfit to transport nuclear warheads up to Faslane. We call all of this damage 'disarmament' and 'nuclear crime prevention'.

Our actions are leading to many hundreds of trials. Every trial is important because each one confronts the state and the legal system where they are most vulnerable – on a major law and order issue. This is why our campaign is causing such political and legal ripples. Traditionally the law has been used against the 'people' rather than the 'state' – predominantly against the poor and disadvantaged. Yet now, the people have turned this around and have openly challenged the whole legal basis, and thus legitimacy, of the armed forces – one of the pillars of the state. They are demanding a people-centred law not a state or corporation-centred law.

Our practical people's disarmament campaign has led to some spectacular actions that are challenging the whole legal system. To take just a couple of examples: In February 1999 two women swam into the docks at Barrow, climbed aboard *Vengeance* and dismantled testing equipment on the conning tower. This action delayed, by several months, the departure of *Vengeance* to the USA to collect its missiles. After three retrials over two and a half years, the women eventually had their charges dropped because successive juries could not make up their minds whether their openly acknowledged action was criminal or was in fact justifiable as the women had argued.

Then in June of the same year three of us disarmed a research barge called *Maytime* that maintains the 'invisibility' of Trident under the oceans. We emptied the whole laboratory, by throwing everything into Loch Goil – the computers and monitoring and testing equipment – and then we smashed the control boxes for the model submarines and cut the electricity supplies to various other Trident research equipment. After five months in prison we explained that we were entitled to do this under international law.

Our acquittal at Greenock Sheriff's Court by direction of a brave and humane Sheriff, called Margaret Gimblett, caused a political and legal furore that led to the Lord Advocate asking the High Court to examine some of the international law issues around Trident in an attempt to prevent any other judges from acquitting in the future. The legal debate continues after an appalling opinion by the High Court that incorrectly stated that international law only applies in a time of war and implied that the ongoing bombing of Iraq was not a 'war'.

While lawyers will no doubt continue to argue the rights and wrongs of the Scottish legal system denying the very foundation of the humanitarian law that came out of the war crime tribunals at Nuremberg and Tokyo, we, as ordinary citizens, are not letting the High Court undermine us. We continue to challenge this abuse and distortion of the law, that tries to protect an outdated and corrupt nuclear weapon system. We are attempting to reclaim the law through the common sense and simple morality of ordinary people who have no difficulty in recognising the simple fact that mass murder is a crime. We have filed an appeal at the European Court of Human Rights and continue with our disarmament actions in the faith that all tyrannies fail eventually and that the truth does finally prevail.

Such challenges have, of course, been mounted time and time again over the last 55 years of anti-nuclear campaigning. Nuclear weapons have always been unlawful and the Shimoda case in Tokyo, in the sixties, showed very clearly that the Hiroshima and Nagasaki bombings were war crimes. However, few citizens' campaigns have used the law in such a clear, pointed and consistent manner. Trident Ploughshares has based its whole campaign on international law and has used it to de-legitimise nuclear weapons and legitimise our own actions and we have done it in a highly public and confrontational manner so it cannot be ignored. We have kept the moral arguments to the fore as well, by emphasising the links between morality and law.

The core of our argument is very straightforward. Nuclear weapons are weapons of mass destruction and thus cannot be used with any precision or any pretence at righting any wrong. Their use is basically mass murder on a catastrophic scale with the potential for escalation to the use of thousands of nuclear weapons, which could put an end to all life on Earth. Law is based upon ethical values and is respected in so far, and only in so far, as it conforms to common human morality. Governments, soldiers and armed forces gain their legitimacy and power from the law and thus the law is of immense importance to them. The only thing that distinguishes a soldier from a common murderer is that he has been given legal permission to do certain kinds of killing on behalf of society. This legalised killing is meant to be carefully controlled by laws – the most important of which are international humanitarian laws, which outlaw indiscriminate mass murder. The acquittals at Greenock and the two at Manchester, cleared us of criminal intent and at the same time clearly pointed out the criminal intent of the British nuclear forces.

Trident Ploughshares is based on taking power back and transforming it into processes capable of enhancing fundamental human morality. We are not ashamed but proud that our message can be understood by a five year old.

This is our message – killing is wrong. Mass killing is wrong. Threatening mass destruction is a denial of our own humanity and is suicidal. When something is wrong we have to stop it. Dismantling the machinery of destruction is thus a practical act of love that we can all join in. Please join us – together we are unstoppable.

Witness Statement of Angie Zelter at trial in January 2018 for the DSEI 2017 blockade

I (ANGIE ZELTER) was arrested with Margaret, Douglas who has already pled guilty and is thus not appearing today, Randel, Barbara and Genny. We were all part of the No Nuclear Day, organised by Trident Ploughshares, on 6th September 2017.

I am a founder of Trident Ploughshares. It started almost 20 years ago and is dedicated to the nonviolent and accountable disarmament of the UK's nuclear weapons and it received the Right Livelihood Award (also known as the alternative Nobel Prize) in 2001. TP is founded on international humanitarian law and our belief that the 100 kiloton nuclear weapons on the Trident system are illegal and criminal under international law. In order to show evidence of my nonviolence and accountability I bring to your attention the nonviolent guidelines of Trident Ploughshares that are always part of our actions and were strictly adhered to on the 6th September 2017.

[Hand in Exhibit 1 – TP nonviolence guidelines]

Our guidelines read:

I will not engage in physical violence or verbal abuse toward any individual and will carry no weapons.
I will not bring or use any alcohol or drugs other than for medical purposes.
I will respect all the various agreements concerning the actions.
I will act safely at all times and act responsibly to ensure that no harm comes to any living being including myself.
We will clear blockades to allow emergency vehicles (not police) in or out of a site and resume any blockades afterwards.

I acted reasonably, safely, peacefully and was courteous to everyone I encountered on the day of the action.

I locked on in a tube with Margaret and next to the other four. We were in pairs and covered the whole road just above (ie to the east of) the painted zebra crossing on Seagull Lane just outside the DLR Royal Victoria station. We had plenty of health and safety supporters to ensure that the drivers of vehicles and pedestrians would know where we were and what we were doing and to assure them of our nonviolence. We were intentionally trying to stop any traffic getting into the ExCeL Centre to set up the Defence & Security Equipment International (DSEI) Arms Fair. This is because we believed that some of the arms deals may have been illegal, and furthermore, the indiscriminate sale of arms to *any* buyers, including notorious human rights abusers, has a profoundly damaging impact on the whole world, contributing to poverty, environmental destruction and climate change. I was also there exercising my freedom of expression.

The specific day of our action was the No Nuclear Day so I was particularly concerned about Britain's continuing reliance on illegal weapons of mass destruction which is a serious breach of the Nuclear Non-Proliferation Treaty. I was also deeply concerned about the UK's heavy involvement in out of area NATO military exercises that are hugely provocative and disturbing to global peace and security. NATO is a nuclear alliance and the USA is the 'lead' country in NATO. I have been aware for many years of the 'military-industrial complex' that has led to a massive increase in weaponry.[249] I was also aware that the USA has almost a thousand military bases in over 100 countries and that its 'interventions' and continual military 'exercises' in and around so many conflict areas are a major cause of conflict.[250] My concerns were part of the context in which I took part in the No Nuclear Day.

My own small action on the 6th September 2017 was inevitably short-lived and caused little disruption. But it was part of a whole week of disruption by hundreds of concerned citizens who felt very strongly that it was immoral and illegal to peddle weapons to people and countries involved in live conflicts and human rights abuses.

The Defence & Security Equipment International (DSEI) is one of the world's biggest arms fairs, and the weapons sold here fuel the death, destruction and injustice perpetrated by militaries, police forces, private security companies (such as G4S) and at borders around the world.

The UK government helps to organise these arms fairs, along with private events company Clarion Events. They take place alternate years at the ExCeL Centre here in London. I was aware that DSEI 2017, with full UK government support, was expecting a record number of 1,600 exhibitors from 54 countries to be selling their wares at the four-day fair, many from states currently at war or on the Foreign Office's own list of human rights abusers. The fair was expected to attract 36,000 visitors and 2,500 international delegations. It described itself in its promotional literature as 'the world's leading defence and security exhibition'.

I knew that at former DSEIS, campaigners had exposed the availability of cluster-bombs and torture equipment, banned by treaty. I was also aware that DSEI had been condemned in July by London Mayor Sadiq Khan who said, 'I am opposed to London being used as a market place for the trade of weapons to those countries that contribute to human rights abuses' while admitting that he did not have the powers to stop it from happening.[251]

On our day of action, there was free passage until we blocked the road and then there was a traffic jam. I blocked this traffic deliberately and intentionally as I believe that this kind of nonviolent civil resistance to great wrongdoing can change local, national and, eventually, international policies. I believe our actions can help to end and de-legitimise support for the promotion of weapons and wars and can thus help to prevent major war crimes and protect lives and communities. This was the motivation for my action.

I therefore believed that I was acting in the public interest and had 'lawful authority and excuse' to obstruct the highway.

My actions were not only 'reasonable' in the circumstances but they were also in accordance with my right to exercise my freedom of expression (Article 10) and freedom of assembly (Article 11 of the European Convention on Human Rights).

According to the Global Peace Index the world is becoming a more dangerous place and there are now only ten countries which can be considered at peace and completely free from conflict – in other words, not engaged in any armed conflicts either internally or externally.[252] As a British citizen, in an allegedly functioning democratic nation, I have to admit culpability in this terrible state of affairs because the UK bears a great deal of responsibility for the violence so prevalent in the world today. Not only was the colonial era one of terrible violence and disruption but it also contributes to many current conflicts. And, as the historian Marc Curtis explained:

> Britain's role remains an essentially imperial one: to act as junior partner to US global power; to help organise the global economy to benefit Western corporations; and to maximise Britain's… independent political standing in the world and thus remain a 'great power'.[253]

As a British woman I am and must continue to be concerned that Britain is the sixth largest arms dealer in the world and that Saudi Arabia, where women are still treated as second-class citizens, is the UK's biggest arms customer. According to the Campaign Against the Arms Trade, it is one of

> the world's most authoritarian regimes, its repression at home and aggression abroad is propped up and supported by UK arms sales. Not only does it brutally repress its own population, it has used UK weapons to help crush democracy protests in Bahrain; (and) now UK-made war-planes are playing a central role in Saudi Arabia's attacks in Yemen.[254]

The example of Saudi Arabia is illustrative of many of the problems that concerned me and are a relevant insight into my motivation for lying in the road on September 6th.

Saudi Arabia's war and blockade that started in March 2015 has killed more than 10,000 people more than a third of whom are children and has injured over 40,000. The UN has verified hundreds of attacks on schools, health facilities, markets, roads, bridges and water sources, mostly by air strikes. These violations of international humanitarian and human rights law continue unabated and largely with impunity. Nearly 2.2 million children in Yemen are acutely malnourished and require urgent care and there are 3.1 million internally displaced persons in Yemen as a result of the conflict. Two-thirds of the population require humanitarian assistance to merely survive. The conflict has pushed Yemen into the worst famine the world has experienced for many decades and has caused the worst cholera outbreak on record, with a million malnourished children at risk from cholera. Every ten minutes a child in Yemen dies of preventable causes like malnutrition and diarrhoea. When UNICEF's director was asked how to end Yemen's humanitarian catastrophe, he simply said: 'Stop the war.'[255]

Although in February 2016 the EU Parliament voted for an arms embargo on Saudi Arabia, the UK has consistently refused to suspend arms sales. In the last ten years, the UK government has licensed arms sales to Saudi Arabia totalling over £11bn. Since the bombing began, the UK government has licensed arms sales to Saudi Arabia totalling over £4.6bn which includes aircraft, helicopters, drones, grenades, bombs, and missiles.

As we lay on the ground stopping the traffic going into the ExCeL Centre I could not understand how British politicians could justify UK corporations making money at the expense of so much human misery. We knew that all of these weapons would be on display the next week and that we had to resist this as best we could while remaining nonviolent. We knew that UK-made precision guided missiles and cluster-bombs have been used by the Saudi Air Force and that the UK government has confirmed that it accelerated the delivery of precision guided missiles to meet increased demand. We knew that UK-made Tornado, Hawk and Typhoon jets have been used extensively in Saudi air strikes.

I was also aware that Britain is heavily involved in *many* other current conflicts providing weapons, training and intelligence, for instance, in Iraq, Syria, Afghanistan, Nigeria, Libya, Yemen and Somalia. And even when a conflict has ended, arms, especially small arms, may remain in large numbers, fuelling further conflicts or criminal activity. And of course, I was aware of the desperate circumstances of the millions of war refugees leaving Syria, Afghanistan, Somalia, Sudan and Iraq and latterly (though not yet to Europe in large numbers) from South Sudan, Myanmar and the Central African Republic.

I knew from reading the 'Women and War' report by the International Red Cross that most of the armed conflicts are now, not so often 'cross border' as 'internal' between rival ethnic, religious or political groups, fighting over the control of resources, territories or populations.[256] If there is tension between countries or within a country, arms purchases are likely to increase this tension and make actual conflict more likely. Selling arms to a country already in conflict – whether internal or external – makes the conflict more deadly and last longer.

Today, unfortunately, it is civilians who are all too often directly targeted or caught in the cross-fire. And although men make up the vast majority of those killed, detained or made to disappear during war, women are increasingly targeted as civilians and exposed to sexual violence. They also generally bear all the responsibility for ensuring the day-to-day survival of their families.

The millions of people worldwide brutally uprooted from their homes and livelihoods often find themselves living with inadequate access to food, water, shelter and health care. This impacts all of us over the whole world. As of December 2016, there were 67.75 million displaced people, according to the United Nations High Commissioner for Refugees (UNHCR).[257] Despite this cost in human suffering, the arms trade continues to fuel and prolong war and conflict, and Britain plays a central role in it.

The arms trade is dominated by the five permanent members of the UN Security Council: China, France, Russia, UK and the US, along with Germany and, increasingly, Israel. The permanent members alone account for around three-quarters of exported arms. The leading corporations in the arms industry may have their headquarters in one country but produce weaponry internationally, and include Lockheed Martin (US), BAE Systems (UK), Boeing (US), Raytheon (US), Airbus (Europe) and Finmeccanica (Italy).

Those involved in the trade wield enormous political influence, resulting in a distortion of policy making – not just in the ascendancy of war-making over diplomacy, but also in foreign and economic policy decisions, and in the favour of arms company interests. A crucial dimension of these arrangements is the link between defence companies, arms dealers and political parties, with the trade playing a crucial role in party political funding.

Trident Ploughshares day of action highlighted the involvement of the world's biggest arms manufacturers in production, operation and maintenance of Britain's nuclear weapons, and the disproportionate influence this gives them over government policy, and the ability to lobby the government to promote their military products abroad. BAE Systems, Lockheed Martin, Babcock, Rolls Royce and Thales have, between them, had hundreds of meetings with the UK government, which in turn have promoted their products to some of the world's most oppressive regimes. These corporations were all exhibiting at DSEI 2017.[258] As I said in our press release at the time:

> Our tax payers' money is being used to arm those involved in wars and repression, many of the arms dealers trade in illegal weapons of mass destruction and are implicated in nuclear weapons, and we consider that part of an ongoing conspiracy to commit a war crime.[259]

[Hand in Exhibit 2 – TP press release of 4 September 2017]

There is a revolving door with a steady stream of government ministers and officials moving to companies, where their contacts and influence can then be tapped. A particularly shocking example occurred in 2011 when Sir Sherard Cowper-Coles, former UK Ambassador to Saudi Arabia, moved to BAE Systems. As Ambassador, he had pressured the Serious Fraud Office to drop its investigation into BAE-Saudi arms deals.[260]

[Hand in Exhibit 3 – *Guardian* article of 18 February 2011]

Aside from ensuring unquestioning support for arms exports, this political influence has led to the UK being committed to heavy expenditure on large items of military equipment, including aircraft carriers, fighter aircraft and

Trident. The utility of these in tackling threats to UK security is questioned even by some of those within the military.[261] Some of the largest purchasers of weaponry are in the Middle East and South and East Asia. The sales range from fighter aircraft, helicopters and warships with guided missiles, tanks and armoured vehicles to machine guns and rifles. They also include components and surveillance equipment. As long as the buyers have the money, what they do with the arms is largely irrelevant to the seller. Thus we know that the weapons sold are used to carry out human rights abuses directly, that they increase the military authority of governments and their capacity for abuses and that the sales convey a message of international acceptance and approval.

The UK government's 2017 Human Rights & Democracy Report to Parliament identified 30 countries of concern where they accept that serious human rights abuses and conflicts are taking place.[262] This year, however, that same government approved licences for arms deals to two-thirds of these countries, including Saudi Arabia and Israel. These arms are likely to fuel further conflict and abuses. In my view and that of many others the government is actively arming and supporting many of the most brutal regimes in the world. The government, whatever they say to us, cannot promote human rights and democracy while, at the same time, selling arms to these repressive regimes. It is often difficult to establish where the arms used in conflicts have originated. However, cases of the use of UK arms in conflict zones include the use

by Argentina in the Falklands War
by Libya against rebels
by Israel in attacks on Gaza
by the Indonesian military in East Timor, Aceh and West Papua
by the US in the invasion of Iraq
by Zimbabwe in the Democratic Republic of Congo.

The arms trade is widely acknowledged as the most corrupt of all global trades. One study, conducted by a senior researcher working with Transparency International, calculated that the weapons trade accounts for around 40 per cent of all corruption in world trade.[263] Often it appears to operate with legal impunity; in the name of national security, arms deals and the trade's participants' proximity to political and military establishments, are shrouded in secrecy. *The Shadow World* by Andrew Feinstein reveals the deadly collusion that all too often exists among senior politicians, weapons manufacturers, felonious arms dealers, and the military – a situation that compromises our security and undermines our democracy.[264] The influence of arms companies is felt right at the top of government. Past Prime Ministers Margaret Thatcher, Tony Blair and David Cameron, as well as the present Prime Minister Theresa May, have all led delegations to promote arms sales, including to some of the world's most repressive regimes.

Complementing the high profile visits, the government has had an arms sales agency since 1966, currently the UK Trade & Investment Defence and Security Organisation (UKTIDSO). With around 130 civil servants, it works behind the scenes, arranging contacts and smaller scale visits. They also manage the UK presence at international arms fairs and the official invitations to those in the UK, such as London's DSEI.

This support for military sales is completely disproportionate. While arms account for less than 1.4 per cent of UK exports, the sectors which cover the remaining 98.6 per cent have just 107 dedicated civil servants promoting *their* exports.

Arms fairs play a crucial role in the trade in weapons. They facilitate weapons transactions between companies and governments and/or informal militarised groups around the world. All the world's weapons manufacturers exhibit at these fairs which are attended by government and military representatives, as well as arms dealers, agents and brokers. A significant proportion of the world's weapons transactions are initiated, developed and/or concluded at these fairs.

Historically, it has been shown that companies selling equipment that is illegal (in either the country in which the fair is taking place and/or in terms of international law and treaties and covenants) are admitted to these fairs, as are representatives of governments and groups engaged in conflicts, human rights abuses and/or repression.

The government provides huge state subsidies to the arms industry including R&D funding, diplomatic support (including the occasional deployment of royal family members), absorbing cost when customers of British arms companies fail to pay, and promoting British arms sales – including organising arms fairs. This UK government support is estimated by the Stockholm International Peace Research Institute (SIPRI) to be worth between £104 and £142 million annually.[265]

Since it is government policy to vigorously support arms exports it is hardly surprising that the government's export licensing process does little to impede the trade. It is supposed to take human rights, conflict and other concerns into account, but with, for example, military goods going to Israel while it was bombing Gaza in 2014, it seems little more than a paper exercise. The only meaningful constraint on arms exports is political embarrassment. Which is part of why I am here today and explaining all these facts.

However good the rules are on paper, they are of little value if they are not applied in practice. There are fundamental flaws in the current system: the government's focus is on securing further business not controlling arms sales. And it doesn't use the rules to limit arms sales: instead it uses them to legitimise them while carrying on with business as usual.

The arms trade is a business with a privileged place in the heart of government. In practice, this means arms companies are incredibly adept at taking taxpayers' money and convincing governments that the arms trade should be promoted rather than restrained. However, while the profits gained from the arms trade accrue to international companies, the costs are to the people on the receiving end of the weaponry, the citizens and taxpayers of both buying and selling countries, non-military industry, and national and international security.

I believe that the export controls system is broken. The government continues to insist that the UK has one of the most rigorous arms export control regimes in the world. These rules say that sales should not be allowed when there is a clear risk that the items might be used for internal repression or in the commission of a serious violation of international humanitarian law, or where they would provoke or prolong armed conflicts. Thus, by any common-sense interpretation of the rules, sales to Saudi Arabia and many other countries should never have been allowed.

I am aware and want to bring to your attention the Arms Trade Treaty (ATT).[266]

[Hand in Exhibit 4 – ATT text]

The Arms Trade Treaty is a multilateral treaty which established common standards for the international trade of conventional weapons and seeks to reduce the illicit arms trade. The treaty opened for signature on 3rd June 2013, and entered into force on 23rd December 2014. The UK is a State party, having ratified the ATT on 2nd April 2014. The ATT, came into force on 24th December 2014. The UK was one of the State champions of the ATT, responsible for leading efforts to secure its creation. When I first heard about this some years ago I thought, great, now the UK will stop selling arms to Saudi Arabia or what on earth is the point of this international treaty? Surely the UK will not breach its own treaty?

If you look at Articles 6 and 7 which set out the treaty's core obligations you will see that Article 6, entitled 'Prohibitions', sets out the bases on which the transfer (defined under Article 2(2) as the 'export, import, transit, trans-shipment and brokering') of weapons and related items is prohibited under the ATT. For instance, there is a prohibition under Article 6(3), which provides as follows:

A State Party shall not authorize any transfer of conventional arms... if it has knowledge at the time of authorization that the arms or items would be used in the commission of genocide, crimes against humanity, grave breaches of the Geneva Conventions of 1949, attacks directed against civilian objects or civilians protected as such, or other war crimes as defined by international agreements to which it is a Party.

If, as the government claims, these rules don't prevent arms sales to Saudi Arabia – one of the world's most repressive regimes, using UK-made planes and missiles in bombing that has killed thousands of people, destroyed schools and hospitals, targeted funerals, weddings and food warehouses – then what would they prevent?

The issues I have raised in my testimony and my fears that the government is more concerned about arms manufacturers making money than about preventing war crimes being committed in Yemen with British war-planes has since been corroborated in many ways. To give just one example, an article in the *Guardian* and *The Independent* on 25th October 2017 stated that the Defence Secretary Michael Fallon urged MPs to stop criticising Saudi Arabia in the interests of securing a deal to sell Typhoon fighter jets to the Saudis.[267]

[Hand in Exhibit 5 – *Guardian* article of 25 October 2017]

I will conclude by saying that I have been involved and concerned about the terrible consequences of the arms trade for well over 20 years now. I have written letters, signed petitions, lobbied my MPs, and demonstrated. I have had to live with the shame that I am a citizen of a country that hypocritically talks about being a democracy and respecting the law and yet continues to sell weapons that it knows will be used to commit human rights abuses and war crimes. I hope you can understand the reasons why I felt compelled to peacefully lie in the road to try to prevent this shameful arms fair from being able to proceed as if it was a normal, healthy, lawful business.

History has shown that consistent nonviolent civil resistance against wrong-doing can effect change. We all know about the ending of the slave trade, gaining women's right to vote, Gandhi's Salt March and Martin Luther King and the Black Civil Rights movement. But more recently there was the 1988 Singing Revolution in Estonia, the pulling down of the Berlin Wall in 1989, and the hundreds of thousands who staged peaceful protests and managed to get President Park Geun-hye of South Korea impeached in 2017.[268] I believe that actions like ours can effect change and prevent crime in the long run. I also believe it is my duty as a conscientious global citizen to continue to act nonviolently for a peaceful and just world.

List of Exhibits:

Exhibit 1 – TP nonviolence guidelines
Exhibit 2 – TP press release of 4 September 2017
Exhibit 3 – *Guardian* article of 18 February 2011
Exhibit 4 – ATT text
Exhibit 5 – Guardian article of 25 October 2017

APPENDIX 4A
Eighth Report from Gangjeong, 16 March 2012

While on Jeju Island I wrote eight illustrated reports and sent them to supporters in the UK who had helped fund my visit. This is the last one to give you an idea of the joys and tribulations of solidarity visits like these.

So much to tell you. I started writing this inside the police station and then the Immigration Centre and now am back at Father Moon's home finishing it. It is so good to be back and free again.

Monday 12 March
Up early as usual by 5.30am for the blockade at the main gate. Beautiful clear day with the Halla mountain in the background. Slight scuffles with the crowd not wanting police to take pictures of them, then a Catholic Mass at 10am. I took pics and then quickly went to the community centre to get an internet connection and catch up on emails. Back to the blockade – still going strong – great sushi rolls of rice and veg and drinks handed out to everyone to keep them going, exercises, dances, songs, speeches – the amount of background support work is incredible.

Around 3.00pm I hitched a ride with a friend in the PA van around to the port where the SOS team (the water based group) were attempting to get their kayaks out of the port and into the Gureombi area. I changed vans to the SOS van with the kayaks in it (as I am now a member of this group too) and was treated to a mad, terrifying, accelerated rush around the port roads to find a place to launch the kayaks, the police rushing around after us to try to prevent the launch. Eventually two kayaks were thrown into the water and two activists jumped in after them. I threw them the paddles and they were soon off, to be surrounded by police launches. This kept the attention on them while priests and crowds gathered at the port for their mass.

There must have been about 200 people gathered at the port and suddenly we set off and overwhelming the few dozen police who were still protecting the entrance we threaded our way past them and through some smallish tetra-pods (the location of which is not according to the development plans and are being challenged in the courts). We approached some razor wire, rocks and a huge concrete pier. One of the church ministers managed somehow to scale the wall of the pier and get a rope down and so about 50 of us clambered over the rocks and up the rope. I am terrified of heights but with so much willing help I was soon hauled up by five or six strong men.

Then followed a most extraordinary hour. Around 40 people were suddenly transformed into priests – their pristine white robes with purple and gold mantles worn over their ordinary clothes. Some of the priests stayed below on the rocks with the majority of the congregation and the nuns, where a makeshift altar appeared with a PA system. One of the nuns started a song and prayers and mass followed. By this time a large contingent of police had appeared at the foot of the pier but they let the mass proceed. There is a certain reluctance to arrest priests while actually in the middle of their prayers.

One priest climbed up the lighthouse at the end of the pier and he said his mass from the heights, in full view of the whole port. Meanwhile, some of the early SOS team who had been on the rocks from early morning suddenly entered the site and started to climb up a digger. We saw Seri (a Korean musician) and Benjie (a French activist) climb right on top and stop the work of the crane that was drilling the rock to prepare it for blasting to enable the caissons to be placed. This was a brilliant action that everyone loved and it was effective at stopping the work too. We later learnt that both of them had been assaulted by the Daelim and Samsung workers. Seri had her knee twisted very badly and her neck strained too.

After the mass, we were joined by quite a few of the SOS team who had managed to get to the pier by swimming once their kayaks had been seized. We all decided to climb down from the pier on the Gureumbi rock side and go to the sacred rocks with them. I was suddenly presented with a pair of bolt-croppers (that I had asked for several days previously) and it was clear that I needed to get down too. But I could see no way down the pods that I could manage. I tried to overcome my fear with several people helping me but I just froze up. Finally, the Minister who had spent the night with me and Sung-Hee on the 7th March, when we hid during the dark hours in the smaller tetra-pods, and who knew of my fear, found a couple of people to help me down. I was taken by the arms and lowered onto their shoulders and then they slowly crouched down and I was taken off by another and managed to scramble through a route at the bottom of the pods and onto the rocks. There was a huge cheer and more willing hands helped me for 20 minutes to get onto Gureombi proper. What a relief!

There were now about 30 of us on the rocks before the wire and only me with cutters. The penalty for damaging the fence is very high and although everyone wanted the fence cut no one was really ready to take the risks. So, I started cutting and made a hole big enough to get some people through. This first cut was a surprise to the police and therefore several people managed to enter before the police interposed their bodies to stop more getting through. I went on to make other holes and as I worked police came to guard each hole. I made my way slowly down the fence cutting as much as I could each time. The police tried to snatch the cutters away but the razor wire was an impediment and I stopped before it became too easy for them. A police photographer soon appeared and took plenty of footage. I was told to stop but just stated that the fence was illegal and was stopping the public from their right to pray at their sacred rocks.

By this time I was getting really tired and asked if anyone else would like to help. One brave priest took the cutters and started to help me and we took it in turns. We must have cut at least ten holes when it started getting dark. I passed my cutters to a friend so they could be hidden and used again in the future and made my way back to where Father Moon was lying half in and half out of one of the holes. Father Moon is a very famous priest here since his work with the labour movement during the democracy movement protests under the military dictatorship in the 1980s and currently with his passionate denunciations of the naval base. As night fell, Father Moon was eventually allowed inside the destruction site and I quickly followed and was arrested at 7.00pm for destruction of private property and trespass. I walked over the rocks to the police car as it would have been dangerous for the police to have to carry me on this occasion.

The friendly translator was there again at Seogwipo police station and he laughed appreciatively when I told him that today I was 'Save Gureombi From War Preparations'. Refusing to answer any questions I was quickly on my way to Jeju City police station.

Tuesday 13 March
I spent the next two days getting to know my other three cell mates better. There had been 16 of us eventually arrested with two released immediately as they were under 21. Four of us were women and shared a cell. Apples and strawberries (in season here in Jeju at present), chocolates, a couple of books in English and Korean papers were sent in by supporters and we had visits from lawyers and villagers. We exchanged life stories as Seri spoke good English.

One of the women (about 56 years old) told of her work in the democracy movement in the 1980's and her continuing work against militarisation and for unification.

Wednesday 14 March

By 2.00pm most of those arrested had been released and only two priests were left plus Benjie, Seri and myself. The lawyer told me that by 7.00pm I would either be released or taken to a court for a judge to decide if I would be detained for a further ten days for investigation and then several months until trial. I started preparing my presentation as to why I needed to be released to prepare properly for a trial. At around 6.00pm I was told I was to be released, was given my possessions and taken to the exit door... but was met by a dozen men and women from Immigration with papers who took me to an immigration detention centre. Poor, over-worked Sung-Hee and the valiant Minbyun lawyer witnessed it all and shouted encouragement.

Benjie was also taken but he went straight to a detention centre near Seoul from whence he was deported to Hong Kong but at least he is free now. Seri remained in Jeju City police station but was released around 10.00am on Thursday 15th March. Meanwhile, late on the Wednesday I was able to see the lawyer who explained that I could be kept another 48 hours and then there were various options – I could be deported or sent back to prison to await trial. The detention centre was less comfortable than the police station with a small room where I was isolated and with no access to natural light. My clothes were taken from me and I was dressed in a rather smart blue and black jump suit that would have been great to go jogging in but unfortunately there is no access to any outdoors exercise, so, I did some indoor exercises instead.

Late that night I was allowed to receive a call from the British Vice-Consul (Jamie Bend) who was very pleasant and said he had heard of my arrest from the papers, was I in good health, was my family informed and did I need a lawyer. I thanked him and said everything was in hand, explained the issues and situation and said I would contact him if I needed further assistance. I started my hunger strike at 7.00pm (48 hours after being arrested) and said I would continue until released.

Thursday 15 March

After a rather boring but restful morning I was told I had a visitor. And there was Mi-Kyoung a friend from the village with a book for me to learn Hangul and lots of smiles and hugs. She runs a women's shelter in Seogwipo and is part of the SOS team. She gave me a really amazing gift for my family and said I must visit Jeju for a holiday with her and her husband one day when the struggle is over. I feel quite overwhelmed by the generosity, gratitude and love of so many here for so little on my part compared to their daily struggles. From 3.00 to 6.00pm I was interviewed by the Immigration officers with a Minbyun lawyer present and Regina to help translate.

I admitted to entering the 'destruction' site, cutting the razor wire, taking part in the villagers daily requests to the base to stop blasting Gureombi and to stop building the base. I did not admit to any crimes saying I was upholding international law and trying to prevent preparations for war crimes and crimes against peace, explained about the 1,000 US bases, many of which surround China and Russia, and that the US had openly proclaimed their ambition to be the dominant super-power with control over land, sea, air and space, that the US/Korean agreement enabled the US to use any Korean military base in whatever way they wanted and there was evidence to show that they would bring nuclear weapons to the naval base, that US nuclear weapons were illegal etc etc. I also explained that the razor wire was preventing villagers from their lawful access to a sacred site and that I was supporting them.

They said this was not allowed under a tourist visa. But I argued that a tourist was also a human being and had a right to support Korean friends and accompany them in their daily struggles. I also said that all my actions were lawful and the proper place to have a discussion about the unlawful placing of the fence, the contamination of water sources and the issue of war preparations was in a court of law, that I would like to clear my name of the charges against me and urged them to release me so I could argue these points in a court of law before a judge as neither they nor I were lawyers. I said I would prefer not to be deported but to go home on my scheduled flight and would be prepared not to go to the base again or attempt to get onto the Gureombi rocks. We negotiated the terms of my pledge as I said I still needed to be able to have the right of free speech and to talk to people and the press. We were then told to wait half an hour while they discussed it all.

Suddenly I was called into a meeting with the Chief Immigration Officer, and after a pep talk, signed a pledge and was released at 9.00pm. I think it was the best compromise I could make and was lucky not to be deported straight away, like Benjie, but if I break the agreement I will be forcibly deported immediately. I always try to keep my promises at all times so that my word can be trusted and so will keep away from the destruction site.

I was greeted by supporters, taken to an art gallery where an exhibition of rock rubbings of the Gureombi was being set up, given an amazing Korean meal and then was brought back to Gangjeong. I was taken to the town hall to meet the Mayor who was all smiles and gave me a big hug and asked for a photo. He is on the far left.

Friday 16 March
While spending the morning sorting through my photos and writing out this report I was called out to a meeting in the Peace Centre where the Bishop of Jeju and Priests were holding a mass (yes they do hold masses of masses) with around 60 or so people in attendance (I wish we could get these numbers out to all our events!). I was asked to speak and expressed my admiration for all they were doing, sympathy and solidarity for the Jesuit father, Kim Jeong Wook, still in custody for the actions of the last few days, how we all needed to overcome our fear of the consequences of disobeying the authorities when we were acting to stop militarisation but that I could be deported and suffered little compared to Koreans who would be facing the worst consequences. I also said that the authorities could deal with one or two people cutting the fence but that if many tens of people did it then the prisons would soon be full and the impact would be much greater. There was a great deal of applause at this. I thanked them all for their actions and solidarity and said I was honoured to have been a part of their struggle – it was of global importance – we are all fighting the same battle – to end the culture of war on our fragile planet. The Bishop translated for me. There are more interviews lined up and a full day planned for meetings in Seoul. This may well be my last report from Jeju. I hope it has given you a flavour of the struggles going on here.

Please note that since January 2010 there have been over 400 arrests here and this is likely to increase as the blasts continue to destroy the area. If you plan to come and lend your support to the villagers then do not provide your real name or flight details over the internet as you may have heard of the three US veterans who were denied access three days ago. Meanwhile, there are many ways you can help the campaign.

Please sign the Avaaz petition and send it on to your friends – see www. avaaz.org/en/save_jeju_island/

Nonviolent Resistance to US War Plans in Gangjeong, Jeju Island

Article by Angie Zelter, 6 April 2012

For five years, the Gangjeong villagers on the Island of Jeju, Republic of Korea (ROK/South Korea), have nonviolently and bravely resisted the construction of a naval base on their land. The proposed ROK naval base would cover 50 hectares of prime agricultural land and would be available for unlimited use by the United States (US) Navy and Army and would be used to host aircraft carriers, nuclear submarines and AEGIS warships that are part of the US anti-ballistic missile defence (MD) system. It is also likely that the base would be used in the conflict with China that the US is planning and openly preparing for. The US Space Command have been computer war-gaming a first-strike attack on China (set in the year 2016) and the MD (really missile **offence**) is a key part of US first-strike strategy. MD systems have also proven to be capable anti-satellite weapons and they are driving a new arms race with Russia and China.

The Pentagon is now encircling Russia (which has the world's largest supply of natural gas and significant supplies of oil) and China (a rising economic power) with MD systems. The US knows it cannot compete with China economically but China imports more than 60 per cent of its oil on ships. If the Pentagon can choke off China's ability to transport these vital resources, then it would hold the keys to China's economic engine. The proposed naval base on Jeju Island is just 300 miles from China's coastline and would become a strategic port for AEGIS destroyers and other warships and would also be used by nuclear submarines. The US has over 1,000 military bases around the world, (including 82 in South Korea alone) – China has no significant military bases outside of its borders. Construction of the naval base at Gangjeong only serves to further military tensions and creates an obstacle to world peace in the East Asian region.

The base will create far more problems than it will solve as China is South Korea's number one trading partner. However, the US is trying to change this pattern and has just signed a Free Trade Agreement with South Korea, despite major opposition from South Korean civil society.

The last time a military base was located on Jeju Island, in 1948, more than 30,000 people (a ninth of the population) were killed in a genocide that is known as Sasam. They were killed by the South Korean government under US military rule, 84 villages were razed to the ground and a scorched-earth policy left thousands of refugees. People were not even allowed to openly talk about this trauma until 2006 when the late President Roh Moo-Hyun officially apologised for the massacre and designated Jeju an 'Island of World Peace'. You can imagine how terrible the sense of betrayal was when only two years later he agreed to build a naval base on Jeju.

It is not only those wishing to stop war who are concerned about the building of the naval base but also environmentalists. Jeju Island is a Global Biosphere Reserve and the village of Gangjeong is surrounded by no less than three UNESCO World Natural Heritage sites and nine UNESCO Geo-Parks and was designated one of the 'New Seven Wonders of Nature'. The sea in front of Gangjeong is the cleanest and most beautiful on Jeju and is the only UNESCO-designated soft coral habitat and a site of the Indo pacific bottle nose dolphins (a IUCN-listed endangered species) as well as the red-footed crab (a Korean designated endangered species). The area around Gangjeong was designated an 'Absolute Preservation Zone' to protect it but the military is simply ignoring all these cultural and environmental protections.

The Gureombi Rock, where many of the protests against the naval base take place, is not only environmentally sensitive but also an ancient place of prayer. It is the only smooth volcanic fresh water rock in Korea and the fresh water springs underneath the rock are believed to be the source of the Gangjeong Stream that provides 70 per cent of the drinking water for the southern half of the Island. The first explosions of the rock by the destruction companies, Samsung and Daelim, led to pollution of this water source and there are fears that the drinking water will be badly affected.

The resistance of the villagers and their supporters has been remarkable despite being repeatedly subject to arrest, imprisonment and heavy fines. The South Korean military claim that the base construction approval process was approved by a democratic vote was exposed as a lie. Only 87 people, some of whom were bribed (out of 1,800 residents) had an opportunity to cast a vote, by applause only. When the village elected a new Mayor and held their own re-vote, that fairly included the entire community and was done by proper ballot, 94 per cent of all villagers opposed the military base – yet the government and military refused to recognise these results. The democratically elected Mayor of Gangjeong who oversaw the 94 per cent vote was recently released from three months in prison for standing up for the rights of his villagers.

The village have organised press conferences, lobbied the Island Council in Jeju City and the central government in Seoul, organised peaceful demonstrations and vigils and in return have been subjected to police harassment, assaults, corrupt bribery which has divided their community, and illegal measures that have taken away their ancient rights to pray at their sacred rocks and to use the local public port.

As the destruction work progressed the nonviolent resistance developed into daily blockades with around one or two hundred people regularly taking part. Their protests are peaceful and nonviolent but the force exerted against them is increasingly violent, especially with the general election approaching on 11th April. The Lee Myung-Bak government is enforcing destruction as fast as possible so that the situation becomes irreversible. Over 400 people have been arrested since January 2010 and that number is now rising rapidly since the blasting of Gureombi Rock began on 7th March. Ominously over one and a half thousand riot police have been deployed from the mainland – something that has not been experienced on the island since the days of the 1948 massacre. The protesters are now peacefully entering the site to try and disrupt the destruction, they are breaking down the fences and cutting through the razor wire, taking boats and kayaks over the sea to gain access to the sacred rock – and each action is being met by more and more violence. The courage of these protesters is remarkable as they face harassment and violence perpetrated by police and by the Daelim and Samsung security guards. People have been beaten, had their teeth knocked out and suffered concussion and broken bones.

None of the cases filed against these assaults have been allowed into the courts. Nor have the road closures, the public port closures, the maritime police stealing of public kayaks and the illegal erasure of the environmental protections been subject to judicial inquiry.

The resistance continues however. For instance on 3rd April five pastors broke through the fence in the early morning and were arrested after entering the military construction site to try to stop the blasting.

This brave resistance needs the support of peace loving people all around the world. There will be a demonstration outside the Korean Embassies in London and Paris on 9th May. If you can organise similarly in your own country then let me know.

Appendix 4B References and Further Reading

www.youtube.com/watch?feature=player_embedded&v=G-d6lpbFhoA

www.tridentploughshares.org/article1679

Matthew Hoey's article on the Save Jeju website at www.savejejuisland.org

Bruce Gagnon's articles on www.space4peace.org

www.facebook.com/groups/nonavalbase/10150836007689815/

APPENDIX 5A

'Spring in the Countryside'
First of the IWPS – Palestine Occasional Reports
from Angie Zelter in the West Bank, 22 March 2004

TALL GRACEFUL ASPHODELS, bright red anemones, blue lupins, pale orchids, orange tulips and a myriad of white, yellow, pink and blue ground level flowers adorn the mountainsides here in this rocky, hilly country and the birds are nesting. The olives seem at rest while the almonds are blooming.

My Israeli friends invited me to Galilee and we shopped in malls for food choosing from long shelves of immense variety, drove to Tiberius to eat by the lakeside, drove to various places to hike from and enjoyed ourselves in this lovely countryside. Cows were wandering in the fields and wheat and barley was long, lush and green. People were walking and driving to and fro and the atmosphere was light. Life was proceeding, with problems no doubt, but of a kind that one could devise a solution to. The threat of suicide bombs though in the background never really intruded on our daily lives here in Israel, except for the constant security checks whenever one entered a public space and my friends told me of their plans for the future and of their recent six month travels in the Far East – they said they seemed to meet Israeli's travelling everywhere they went.[269, 270]

The Jewish Festival of Purim was being celebrated and we could hear and see youngsters dressing up and music blaring out of cars passing by. We discussed whether to drive down to the Negev for an outdoor festival and life seemed to be full of choice and hope and normal conversations. My friends are long-standing friends whom I have known for over 20 years, good people who care about others. They hate the occupation, think the settlers should be removed, think the wall an abomination but when asked what they are doing about it all reply saying it is all too political for them – their hearts are touched by the humanitarian catastrophe that is the lot of the Palestinians but all they can offer to do is to help buy up a few plastic jerry cans of olive oil from the village that I live in.[271]

Ruth had helped the previous year with olive picking in the villages in the Salfit area where I worked, she had brought some of her friends and family, this was something they could do, come and pick olives and try by their presence to lessen some of the settler violence that was preventing the Palestinian farmers from getting onto their land.[272, 273] However, they were scared to become more involved, it might change their lives too much, and the simple human connection in the olive fields might degenerate into awful discussions of the rights and wrongs of past history with their two different narratives and all the recriminations and dreadful animosities of their existential fears would surface and in any case what was the use of demonstrating, they hated the very thought of politics and said they were only interested in doing something if it is purely humanitarian. They offered to drive me into the West Bank right up to the village where I live. Just as well as all Palestinian transport had been cancelled and most of the Palestinian villages and towns were sealed off for Purim – supposedly to still the fears of surprise terrorist attacks – in fact, of course, fears are not so easily disposed of. Yacob had not been into the West Bank since the start of this Second Intifada and was feeling fearful as Israeli cars have been stoned and shot at on the settler roads.[274]

The village, where I live and work, is right next to one of the major settler roads connecting Tel Aviv to Ariel, the biggest settlement in the West Bank and although they could not drive me into the village due to the large stone and rubble roadblock preventing access they could see the house where I lived from the settler road.[275] My Palestinian friends had delivered the oil and we loaded it into their car and I waved them off on their way to Jerusalem. Ruth to give a seminar for an anthroposophical audience and Yacob to give cranial sacral treatment to those needing it (including some who are settlers in Hebron). Village life in the West Bank, however, was dominated by the effects of the occupation – life did not even have a semblance of normality.[276]

On the mundane level, our washing machine had ceased to function due to the constant electricity cuts and no one in the village was really capable of repairing it nor did they have the right parts due to travel restrictions and there was just not time to organise a long and risky roundabout journey over the hills, into a nearby town where maybe someone might have managed to find spare parts. Like most other people in the village I would have to hand-wash my clothes. There was no post either and I had forgotten to post some letters home to my family in the UK.[277]

However, there were more important worries. As usual we were receiving a stream of calls from various villages calling for an international presence in the hope that it might lessen the violence they were experiencing. Soldiers had entered Marda and gassed the children on their way to school and were there in the village with their guns threatening anyone who came out of their houses, would we come? We did and we saw the soldiers still in the village and heard them shooting. The villagers told us that the soldiers had been entering regularly, and that the evening before they had desecrated the Mosque by entering it with their shoes on and calling the curfew from the Mosque loudspeakers, and they were painting marks on various buildings marking them for demolition.[278]

We were shown maps by the villagers that showed that the village would be split in half by the building of the Separation Wall. Then someone from Qarawat Bani Zeid called to say that soldiers had entered the village there yet again and threatened to shoot more people. We were really worried at this as six people have been shot dead in this village in the last ten months.[279] The village were asking for a permanent international presence. We helped arrange for some volunteers to go and stay. But there are just not enough of us. Various grass roots international peace teams are co-operating in providing volunteers for such villages but there are too many villages needing protection and too few volunteers or perhaps to look at it another way there are too many armed soldiers and settlers in the occupied West Bank.[280]

So, a few days later there was a gap in the rota and the soldiers entered again and this time they took the opportunity to shoot and injure two schoolboys on their way to school.[281] The volunteers, who had left to go and support the nonviolent resistance to the wall in Biddu where four villagers had recently been shot, felt terrible. Nothing had happened while they had been in the village and they had felt it was probably safe to go to another village.[282]

Soldiers seem to be increasingly active in our area – perhaps because the Wall is approaching fast. A friend of ours who lives right by the roadblock in Hares called us one night because they had heard and seen soldiers creeping through the olive trees and then throwing tear gas outside their house. Talking to others in the village they told us that soldiers had been creeping around several nights that week and they made sure they stayed inside and pulled their curtains closed – they did not want trouble. March 9th we heard that soldiers had been creeping around in Kufr Dik too had then opened fire, damaging several houses and then shooting at a passing car, had shot and wounded a local teacher.[283]

The roadblocks and checkpoints have brought most ordinary life to a stop. Many students cannot get to their schools and universities and village life has turned in upon itself. Cultural and social life has been stunted. Women who used to go out in the hills to gather herbs and to picnic have not felt safe enough to do so for over three years now. People attempt to travel mainly for work, school, and medical services – the risks are too great for pleasure alone, even weddings can become a nightmare.[284] I was told of a recent wedding in a village almost entirely enclosed by the Wall where family members in a village next door, only a few minutes away in normal times, took over 6 hours to get to the wedding that had to be delayed because the wall gate had been closed by the Israeli soldiers. The lack of freedom to move around impacts on everything – one cannot get to the public libraries in the cities for instance. Kindly people in other lands try to help as best they can and we recently received some books kindly donated by a school in the UK (mainly encyclopaedias, reference books and some novels) and while discussing where best to locate the books so that villagers would have easy access to them a series of phone calls started to come in to tell of soldiers in Salfit (the regional capital) who had entered the town to arrest some people and shot and wounded several people in the process.[285] A local grocer was shot in the stomach and died a few hours later, the arrested men were released several days later with no charges.[286]

As I was writing this I received a phone call with the distressing news of a woman on her way to see her doctor – she had presented her ID at Huwara checkpoint and the soldiers had suddenly marched off with her. No one knew what had happened. Six hours later and we still have not managed to track her down. The human rights organisation that helps track the whereabouts of those detained by the Israeli authorities says it may take two or three days to find out where she is. She has four children between the ages of two and eight.[287]

But let me not wear you out with all these incidents – they go on and on – this is a land where there is little rule of law – soldiers and settlers are rarely put before the courts to explain their actions and thus more and more abuses are occurring – after a while all of us become used to them. What a terrible thing to admit – that one takes as 'normal' these kinds of incidents. Let me get back to the rural agricultural scene that I started with. This is the end of the rains, the time of green so different from the yellows and thorny browns of the summer. The white and pink cyclamen grow in clusters in and around the scattered rocks. The peas and beans are in white scented flower under the olive trees. Farmers need access to their lands at this time and Palestinians want the same as the Israeli farmers or indeed as any farmers anywhere want – to go about their ploughing and planting and weeding, to harvest without fear or hindrance. And to the rural Palestinian communities cut off from any other way of earning their livelihood they depend more than most on access to their land. Hence the terrible anguish of the farmers in this region as the Wall encloses them in their villages and shuts them away from their land.

The Israeli government had stated that the walls would have wall gates which would be open and that farmers would be able to gain access to their land. However, we talked to farmers at Mas'ha who showed us their permits and explained that even with them they were still being denied entry and exit through the gates and into their fields and groves. We also met with the three Mayors of Sanniriya, Azun Atma and Beit Amin, neighbouring villages that share land and whose inhabitants are closely related to each other – they consider themselves as one big family – and now the wall was not only cutting them off from each other but also from their land.

They explained a little bit about the problems they faced getting the permits to go through the gates to get to their land. Firstly, each farmer has to go to the local Palestinian municipality to get his registration papers, and then go to the Palestinian Court in Qalqiliya to get a registration from the court and then finally to Kedumin, the Israeli settlement where the land documents are held. Apart from the delays, difficulties and costs involved, once at Kedumin they encounter many problems – firstly they may not be dealt with for hours or even days, due to queues and delays, then when they get to see an official they may discover that the land in question is wanted for Israeli purposes (military needs or for settlement expansion or some other reason) or they may be on a list as a security problem, then again the named landowner may have died and the paper at Kedumin may still be in his name so no one else can claim ownership of this land, or sometimes they are not given any reason whatsoever as to why they cannot get a permit.

The person they see at Kedumin just seems to make his own mind up there and then. Only a small proportion of them have managed to get a permit. Also, only one person in a family may manage to get a permit and that is useless as the land needs many of the family members to work it. And there are many businesses outside the village who buy and sell the produce produced by the farms and who cannot now go and collect the produce from the fields as they cannot get permits. So the farmers are reduced to hauling out their produce on donkeys or on their backs. In some places soldiers have been demanding that donkeys and animals are issued with permits too.

One can see the utter frustration and hopelessness in everyone's eyes. Many of the people we meet have resigned themselves to the slow, steady erosion of their basic human rights and to their land, feeling that there is nothing they can do. They keep their heads down and hope against hope that something will save them, that somehow, sometime they will get their land back. Some of these gentle country folk are following the slide towards violence that you find in some of the big cities and then again some have decided to resist nonviolently.

Over the last few weeks we have supported several villages which are fighting the wall and the occupation nonviolently and having some success too – the stories from Budrus, Mas'ha, Deir Balut, Biddu are inspiring examples.[288] Communities not yet affected by the wall are beginning to meet with those villages already affected by the wall and more demonstrations are being planned. Women are meeting in many different places and discussing what they can do as women to resist the occupation. One thing they are sure about is the need to include all women of whatever political faction and to work as women against the wall rather than for narrow political aims. One local women's anti-wall group (which IWPS is regularly supporting) has just held a successful demonstration on the 20th March. By successful I mean that no one was shot at and the soldiers that prevented the women coming close to the wall at least did not throw tear gas or fire at anyone. Unlike so many of the anti-wall protests occurring up and down the West Bank.

Life goes on, we continue to witness and support the resistance to the occupation, and against the wall, to try to build the bridges towards a just and lasting peace. To try to keep hope alive.

Lessons Learnt
by the International Women's Peace Service – Palestine

Talk by Angie Zelter, 8 August 2008, London

The International Women's Peace Service – Palestine (IWPS) was founded in 2002, and began by establishing a presence in a rural village in the Salfit Governate within Occupied Palestinian Territory. I initiated IWPS, but because I am no longer allowed to enter Palestine, I have ceased to be closely involved with it. Up to date information is on our website (www.iwps.info). IWPS was set up in order to:

- support nonviolent civil resistance by Palestinians and Israelis, and to create space for people to become more involved in resistance
- monitor human rights abuses, provide accompaniment and intervene to nonviolently prevent human rights abuses
- alert the world community to human rights abuses in the Salfit Governorate and to effect change in world opinion about the occupation, and also to
- provide an experiential model that can be used to create international women's peace teams in other areas.

The lessons we have learnt are:

Relatively few Palestinians have so far been able and willing to organise nonviolent resistance. A few resort to violent resistance feeling they have to fight, and the vast majority survive by keeping their heads down. Mohamed, a friend of mine in a Salfit village, explained why his village would not support a neighbouring village in nonviolent protest to protect their best land from the Wall Israel was building to divide Palestinians from Jewish settlers on the West Bank: 'We are a small village of only a few thousand people, we cannot afford to have anyone else killed'. But where Palestianians are taking nonviolent action, then internationals can and do support. This is our space, that can expand or contract depending on the quantity and quality of nonviolent resistance and on local factors.

The violence and control by the Israeli military makes it difficult to organise and sustain nonviolent civil resistance. The IDF is expert at using tear gas, sound bombs, rubber bullets and live ammunition to break up demonstrations (they have even resorted to spraying sewage on villagers to stop them demonstrating against the Wall); they raid villages and towns and arrest anyone known to be organising the demonstrations; create closed military zones; use administrative detentions to keep those arrested behind bars for years without charge or trial and at risk of torture. Internationals are merely deported – it is the Palestinians who bear the consequences of any form of resistance.

The deportations, and refusing entry of many thousands of international volunteers into Israel/Palestine, is a deliberate policy by the Israeli authorities, who understand how important international support is for Palestinians. This policy interrupts continuity, making it harder to build and sustain relationships, and to gain a deep understanding and knowledge of local circumstances. When the frequent infrastructural damage to buildings, computers, libraries, resources generally are factored in then it is clear how difficult any kind of organised resistance is.

Poverty strangles process. The Israeli stranglehold on the Palestinian economy has turned a relatively self-sufficient community into a malnourished, dependent on food-aid and desperately poor community. People's energies are sapped by the struggle to survive and feed their families. 'Internationals' are inundated with requests for money and resources for development, and the need for money skews and sours their relationships, and encourages in-fighting, corruption and fraud, as well as reducing the energy for nonviolent resistance.

There is no fair legal system. The Palestinians mostly do not even bother to try to get justice. Those 'internationals' who try to get the Israeli legal system to deal with crimes face intimidation, high legal costs and obstacles to getting to the court. For example, with the help of the British Consulate, I managed to bring to court a well-known violent settler from Hebron for assaulting me and destroying my camera, that held film of his teenage followers attacking an old Palestinian man who later died of his wounds. But first I was denied entry into Israel for the court case where I was appearing as a witness. Then I was imprisoned and deported from the

Occupied Territory after the settler pleaded guilty to the trivial crime of destroying my camera. He was never questioned about why he had destroyed the evidence of a murder.

IWPS has tried in several cases to take evidence and institute legal proceedings against violent incidents they have witnessed themselves. They have taken their evidence to the Israeli police, of shootings and woundings of Palestinian villagers by violent Israeli settlers, in the form of photos and signed witness statements. But none of these cases have been prosecuted through the courts, even when Israeli human rights groups have helped.

Factionalisation undermines the possibility of a national nonviolent movement. Imprisonment of the Palestinian population by the use of frequent curfews, road blocks, imprisonment and now the Wall has led to huge tensions within the villages and towns. There is much internal fighting, and often violent confrontations between different clans and different political factions. Some villages have a history of killing suspected collaborators. Although there is a great experience and wealth of examples of nonviolent resistance by Palestinians, there have been no effective calls for a national nonviolent struggle and little national leadership. In some extraordinary cases, good local leadership has emerged – for example Abu Ahmad of Budrus, a village in the Ramallah District, managed to unite families and different factions in the Budrus Popular Committee against the Apartheid Wall and to stop work on the Wall several times (see chapter by Veronique Dedouet). The strong nonviolent resistance at Bi'ilin is another excellent example of sustained nonviolent resistance which has resulted in the killings by Israeli Forces of several Palestinian children.

But the Wall, though delayed, has been built.

Cultural insensitivities, lack of Arabic speakers, and tendency to interfere in local politics by 'internationals' are all problems that have emerged and have added to tensions. A well-known Palestinian Christian who leads a Palestinian nonviolent resistance movement says he values the work and solidarity presence of internationals but wishes they would only come for a few months at a time. 'Those who stay longer begin to think they understand everything, and start to interfere in local politics making things much worse.' Groups like ISM may like to think that they are Palestinian led, but they do often tend to initiate nonviolence campaigns and they have their own agendas.

* * *

For nonviolence to work I believe that there needs to be:

A clear exposure of the crimes being committed by Israel. The reality of the occupation is continually distorted by government officials (especially in the USA and UK) and by Western media. The added complications of European guilt over the holocaust, and the Israeli use of the anti-Semitism label, makes people scared to raise their voices over Israeli crimes. The 'organised' harassment of anyone who criticises Israel as being anti-Semitic is very hard to deal with.

I wrote an article for a local magazine in Aylsham, a small town in East Anglia, England, explaining in graphic terms what it would look like if all the things I had seen in Palestine were taking place locally in Aylsham. As a result this small magazine was inundated with hundreds of letters from angry Jewish people who accused me and the magazine of anti-Semitism and created such a furore that the editor decided he would never again print anything 'political'.

A powerful outside international moral authority that can be a source of appeal. This could then put pressure on Israel to stop their war crimes and human rights abuses, their blatant ethnic cleansing and their theft and colonisation of Palestinian land and water resources. However, the major funder/backer of Israel is the USA and they have a strong geopolitical reason for backing Israel. Unfortunately **all** the major states that could have some influence over Israel, are committing their own war crimes in their various areas of strategic interest.

International support for the nonviolence movement inside Palestine. This is happening. When IWPS started work, we were the only international solidarity and nonviolence NGO based in a rural Palestinian village (most internationals were based in towns and only visited the villages briefly). We now have a series of village profiles and a record of the kinds of human rights abuses visited upon the people. Our presence was important in helping provide sustained support and space for nonviolence, in encouraging women's involvement in the nonviolent resistance, and in helping to set up some of the anti-Wall protest camps that also brought Israeli and Palestinian movements together.

Encouragement of the internal divisions in Israel. There is a growing Israeli peace movement, including the Refuseniks to military service, Gush Shalom (Peace Bloc), the Israeli Committee Against House Demolitions and the Anarchists. Nevertheless too few Israelis actually know, understand or care about the reality of life in the Occupied Territories, and they are often too scared to even try to find out. A good example of Israeli nonviolence that is having an impact is Machsom Watch – an Israeli based organisation that organises, monitors and intervenes at some of the major checkpoints. IWPS used to do quite a bit of checkpoint monitoring, but can now leave this work to the Israeli group. The monitoring provides a good learning experience for Israelis who can then use this understanding back inside Israel to break down the ignorance and encourage empathy.

* * *

So what is the role of the international peace and nonviolence movement in relation to Palestine and Israel?

a) Education and political lobbying at home

Maybe our most important role is witnessing, then writing and distributing reports, articles and presentations to counteract the US/UK media distortion. To help more 'internationals' to experience and see for themselves what is going on and then, on getting home, to speak out about it, so that the mainstream view of the Israelis as being the victims of terrorism is countered by accurate reports of the state terrorism of the occupation. Direct experience helps in confronting lies and distortions. A group of returned IWPS volunteers are now engaged in regular lobbying of the UK Foreign Office and in letter-writing to the press and their MPs, as well as actions at the Israeli Embassy. The level of knowledge in the UK, Europe and in the USA is much higher than even a few years ago, and to some extent this is because of the quantity of volunteers who have gone over to Palestine and on their return have spoken at small local meetings.

b) Support for Palestinians and Israeli activists (other than monitoring and protective accompaniment)

An underestimated role for international volunteers is to empathise and listen – just being there and witnessing and hearing makes Palestinians feel less cut-off from the outside world and brings hope. Similarly, interaction with Israeli activists also lessens their sense of isolation and supports them in their vital work.

Then there is a role in supporting nonviolent resistance: being a calm and steady presence, helping out with international media contacts, and discussing ideas and strategies, bringing a wealth of experience of struggles from all over the world. The women that IWPS brought over to Palestine were from

South Africa, the Philippines, Colombia and India. They provided some useful insights for the women in Salfit.

c) Creating a safe space for Israeli/Palestinian dialogue

Certainly, when we first arrived in Salfit there were few Israelis who felt able to go into the villages alone. We helped provide safe spaces where the two sides could meet more easily, and now we are often, happily, redundant.

Response to 15 August 1991 *Borneo Post* article
'Environmentalists Declare World War on Malaysia'

written by Ms Angela C Zelter on 20 August 1991 in Miri Jail, Sarawak

OVER THE PAST two months the local newspapers have been full of tirades against foreign 'environmentalists'. The 15/9/91 article in the *Borneo Post*, excerpted from the 'Executive Intelligence Review', is the latest expression of the fear and paranoia being exposed.

Let us firstly examine the language used in the article. It speaks of declarations of 'world war', of 'assaults', 'carried out with great precision', of people being 'flown in from a base of operations', of 'targets' and 'logistics'. All these words have been carefully chosen in order to influence the reader's mind and build up a picture of a well organised army unit whose main purpose is to destabilise Malaysia. Taken with the other press articles, one can see the relentless preparations being made to try and show how the security of Malaysia is being threatened.

We are told that the purpose of this 'world war' is apparently to 'attack and topple the sovereign governments of third world nations, using the excuse of saving the environment'. And, apparently, 'Malaysia was chosen as the first target as it is small and isolated' and 'vulnerable' whereas the 'ultimate targets' of Brazil and India are 'yet too powerful to challenge'.

This is a strange distorted and twisted picture that has been built up. If any war is going on then it is the relentless and unthinking spread of uncontrolled industrialisation within an inequitable global economy which is killing and polluting our life support system and which is threatening the very life of the whole planet – third world and industrialised nations alike.

I am one of the so-called 'Sarawak 8' – at present, serving an 87-day sentence at the jail in Miri. I would like to set the record straight and tell my story as clearly as possible. I find it disturbing and frightening that people should publish such dangerous propaganda rather than sincerely and objectively analysing the issues and problems raised by this action of ours.

Let me first explain that rather than being the crack unit of some warring environmental army that wants to take over all third world countries, we are a mixed bunch of rather idealistic environmentalists, with a sound knowledge on many of the issues, who deeply care about all forms of life on this fragile planet of ours. We are all nonviolent and don't believe in force. However, we do believe in standing up and saying our truth clearly so it can be heard and we do believe in peaceful resistance against policies and actions that hurt and damage people or the environment.

We came from five different industrialised nations from a variety of different backgrounds in order to protest about the logging in Sarawak. We had never met before and were unsure what we would do. We raised our own money for the airfares with the help of our friends, relatives, different environmental groups and arrived from our different countries at the end of June. We had made contact with each other because we all felt concerned that Sarawak was suffering the fastest rate of logging in the whole world.

We knew that if a viable rainforest ecosystem was to survive and if the few remaining hundreds of Penan were to be enabled to save their knowledge, distinctive culture and way of life, then there were only a few years left to do it in (I would now say there are only a few months left!). We knew that these people were asking for international help.

We knew that the problem of the destruction of fragile ecosystems was one caused by both third world nations and industrialised nations. There has to be a buyer and a seller. We wanted to tackle both ends of the problem – to try and persuade the Sarawak government that the logging of primary rainforest was not in their long-term economic, cultural or ethical interests and to persuade our governments not to continue exploiting the natural resources of the third world. Our countries have got rich on the resources of the third world – as one area is devastated so our multi-national companies move into the next area – they don't care what happens to people, animals, plants, land, water or air as long as the profits keep rolling in.

Of course, the multi-national companies/corporations also work hand in hand with the small rich elites in each country and these elites often include politicians as well (which is even more dangerous for the real interest of these nations). These elites often control the press and mass-media and therefore, the quality of the public debate on these issues.

In Sarawak, the problem is compounded because the issue of logging is so central to the whole political set up. It is public knowledge that over half of the land given out as timber concessions have gone to the relatives and friends of the Chief Minister (Datuk Pattingi Abdul Taib Mahmud) and the previous Chief Minister (Tun Abdul Rahman Yaakob) who became very rich in the process.

It is also a well-known fact that logging (or the forestry industry) contributes around 50 per cent of the total state's revenues. So there are huge vested interests at stake. But, it must be remembered that these vested interests are not the same as the long-term interests or security of the vast majority of the people of Sarawak.

Looked at objectively, the economy of Sarawak could be very healthy if equitably distributed amongst the relatively small population. The revenues from the oil industry, for instance, could be directed to help Sarawak. At present, 95 per cent of the oil revenues from Sarawak go to the Federal government and only 5 per cent are returned for Sarawak's use.

The overall environmental problem of logging is more complicated than just creating a biosphere for the plants, animals and Penan. The article mentions the proposed Baram District biosphere as if this will solve the problems. It must be clearly pointed out at this stage that the truth is that most of the so-called biosphere has already been logged, the so-called biosphere has not even been demarcated yet, the genetic pool has already been irreparably damaged and the Penan have not even been consulted and probably don't want to be rounded up and confined to a very small area.

Logging has disrupted the lives of tens of thousands upon thousands of other Dayak peoples and their blockades and protests have been a constant thorn in the side of those that gain from logging. The traditional, self-sufficient lifestyles of Kayan, Kenyah, Iban, Kelabit, Bidayuh, etc has been impoverished and destroyed and their right to their own customary land has been stolen from them.

When we talk to these people, we hear how there used to be plenty of fish in the rivers, plenty of fruit trees, plenty of sago and rice to eat, and materials to build houses and boats. Now, they are impoverished and suffering from illnesses due to malnutrition and a damaged and polluted environment.

I find it predictable but nonetheless disappointing that the now outdated prejudices about slash and burn agriculture are still being propagated. There is now plenty of scientific evidence to prove that this system of agriculture is ideally adapted to the tropical rainforest when the whole of the customary land is used according to traditional culture. Instead, modern intensive agriculture presents more problems than it solves, relying as it does on polluting and dangerous chemicals and fertilisers leading to more third world dependence on the industrialised nations agribusinesses.

The newspaper article asks us 'what alternatives do the environmentalists have to feed the people?' – not realising, or perhaps trying to hide the truth, that it is the very logging and plantations that bring hunger. These people were always able to feed themselves. They were independent and shared the wealth of their land, forest and rivers between themselves. It was the colonialists and now the loggers and plantation owners and politicians who have created their poverty and their hunger and also now must accept the responsibility of their dependence. What kind of development is it, when the rich elites get richer and once independent, strong and healthy people are driven to work in near slave conditions in the plantations, or to squat in miserable conditions on the edges of towns, and who lose their culture, or opt for prostitution, rather than grinding poverty?

But, as we have been asked, I will reply. The alternatives we suggest are:

To sincerely recognise Native Customary Land Rights, have the lands properly surveyed and protected in order to allow the Dayaks to become self-sufficient once more. They have the answers to their own problems and don't need anyone to tell them, they just need to be heard, respected and left in peace to work through their own problems. They say their land is their life – why not give them their land and life back and allow them to get on with their own development?

Logging should be limited to certain secondary growth areas away from the remaining primary forest areas (which will give these primary areas the chance to gradually enrich the surrounding area) and where there are no outstanding land claims. Sustainable forestry should be set up in the already logged areas to see if it really is possible in the tropics.

The bulk of the oil revenues should be used in Sarawak and invested in village and town level bio-gas and solar energy production infrastructure and to help diversify the economy.

Malaysia as a whole should press for compensation for the theft of genetic material and for the genetic property rights of the plant material that has been taken by transnational horticultural/agricultural industries.

But, what has all that got to do with us, you might be asking, surely we have pressing environmental problems of our own at home, and certainly it is the industrial countries that have created the environmental problems of our era. This is true, and the readers must realise that we are all very active in our own countries trying to get our own people and governments to change their lifestyles so they use less cars and reduce the greenhouse gas production, so they consume less, and so they stop their factories and industries polluting the world environment. The majority of our time is spent in our own countries working for better policies and practices. Many of us have been imprisoned in our own countries for standing up against pollution, environmental damage, nuclear weapons and nuclear energy production etc. But, we have learnt in our many years of work in our home countries that multinational companies move around the globe – that as we impose greater pollution controls in our own countries, then the companies move to third world countries, where the people and governments are less vigilant or poorer, with less power to resist and therefore where these companies can continue to pollute and make their profits. The knowledge we have gained of birth defects, respiratory diseases, long-term poisoning and damage to the land and water, are hidden from our brothers and sisters in other parts of the world. It is this that motivates us to come and make direct links with people in those other affected countries. We all live on one planet and we need to share our knowledge and expertise and help and aid each other, otherwise the profiteering multi-national corporations of the world will destroy much of the diverse life and culture on our fragile planet.

There is no understanding of these problems of industrialisation in the newspaper article I am responding to. Instead, the article says we should 'support a crash programme to industrialise the third world and bring modern energy technologies such as nuclear and hydroelectric power'. But, the article doesn't tell the readers that nuclear energy is a curse, bringing cancer and genetic abnormalities in its wake and creating a still unsolved dangerous waste problem. Communities all over the industrialised world are rising up in protest at this expensive and dangerous technology. As for hydroelectric power, although useful on a small scale, the big dams have been catastrophic all over the world. The evidence of the destruction of wilderness areas and indigenous lands, the terrible human costs involved in resettling people in much worse conditions than they originally enjoyed, and the problems of watershed destruction, silting up, have offset any good gained from the energy produced. If Malaysia is really interested in cheap, safe and environmentally sound energy production for people, then she should concentrate on biomass generation and solar power.

And yes, we environmentalists do support, with cash and educational programmes, the development of these alternatives in our own countries and in third world countries.

As for reforestation, I come from Britain and shamefully admit that only 9 percent of our land is covered by trees. But, Britain has been without trees for many centuries. We are one of the most densely populated countries in the world (taking the number of people per square mile) and our trees were cut down for agriculture and towns hundreds of years ago. However, we are busy trying to preserve our remaining forests and to increase our tree cover to at least 20 per cent in the next decade. Coming from such a country – one where most of our indigenous animals and plants are now extinct, I value even more your land of rainforests and feel so sad when I see these rich, abundant forests being replaced by the green deserts called plantations. Plantations on a small scale are fine but on a large-scale face the same environmental problems as our temperate mono-cultural agriculture – pest and soil fertility problems. It seems ironic that just as the industrialised world is turning a new page to more viable, organic and diverse agriculture, the third world is strangling its own multi-cropping expertise. The economic value of gentle, sustainable multi-cropping from re-grown secondary forest managed by viable, independent and strong indigenous communities would far outweigh the vagaries of a few vulnerable cash crops sold on a world market dominated by industrialised countries who control the marketing and prices.

Finally, I would like to address the paranoia and fear shown in this article. Colonised countries who have suffered the terrible racism and the ensuing degradation of their own cultures and confidence are necessarily still recovering. They have had enough of foreigners coming to their land and telling them what to think and do. They rightly reject the arrogance and implied superiority of economic and cultural imperialism. And they are right to beware. The industrialised countries and their multi-national companies will not easily give up the exploitative world economic system they have set up. They want to continue to take the natural resources from the third world, use their cheap labour, dump their dangerous goods or waste on their lands, and keep the lead in what they see as a 'dog eat dog' world. Third world countries should be vigilant.

But, a more sophisticated attitude is now needed. There are friends in the west as well. People who really care about other people and who want to live in a co-operative world where everyone gains by sharing their knowledge, skills and resources. They cannot enjoy their lifestyles and luxury knowing that it is bought with the tears and blood of the poor in their own countries and of others in the third world. Why don't you accept our hands of friendship and engage in a fruitful exchange of ideas and love?

Angie was charged with committing criminal trespass by unlawfully remaining at the barge Tae Harbour Works with the intention of annoying Simin Bin

Awang Kassim from 7.15am–2.30pm on 5 July 1991. She spent a total of three months in Miri Prison. She returned to the UK to continue campaigning against the logging of old-growth forests around the world.

Witness Box Statement at Extinction Rebellion Trial

Angie Zelter, Hendon Magistrates' Court, 25 June 2019

Personal background

I am now 68 years of age but when I was 21, in my final year at university, I read the January edition of *The Ecologist* magazine, called 'A Blueprint for Survival'. This had an enormous impact on me as it introduced the major problems then facing the world – war, poverty, acid rain, ozone depletion, desertification, deforestation, species loss, civil and military uses and abuses of nuclear power, pollution, population growth, consumerism and climate change.

I had been through a university education and been unaware of these major problems. I determined to educate myself and devote my life to helping solve these problems. After spending three years in Cameroon, learning about the long-lasting impact of British colonialism and racism, the deforestation for timber, oil palm production and other cash crops, and the exploitation of the rich resources of Africa to the detriment of locals and enrichment of corporations and Western societies, I returned home to the nuclear weapons Cold War crisis.

I joined the Greenham Common protests, founded the Snowball Civil Disobedience Campaign and then later Trident Ploughshares which won the Right Livelihood Award in 2001. Alongside the nuclear crisis that still haunts us today, I became involved in work on climate change. Lecturers in Climate Science at the University of East Anglia provided expert witness statements for me when defending my nonviolent direct actions against nuclear weapons. And this is how I was first acquainted with the nuclear winter that would result if only a very few nuclear warheads were used. I learnt that everything is connected and that it all has an impact on the climate, on biodiversity and on the sustainability of life on Earth. I discovered more details about how our reliance on fossil fuels was causing the greenhouse effect and soon joined with climate scientists and local environmentalists, to start a group in Norwich that tried to educate the public about greenhouse gases and climate change.

We had maps up of how much of East Anglia and London would be under water as temperatures soared and the sea levels rose. This was in the early '80's – almost 40 years ago. We concentrated on what individuals could do to lower their carbon footprints, by putting up solar panels, changing our light bulbs, recycling and re-use, eating less meat, using public transport and giving up our cars, shopping carefully and locally, and consuming less.

After discovering the impact that UK timber imports was having on the loss of old-growth forests and their biodiversity I even got involved in carbon sinks and sustainable forest management. I was part of the UK Forest Network and worked with major UK timber importers to persuade them to stop importing old-growth timber stolen from indigenous reserves in South America and Asia and was part of the process that set the UK standards for the Forest Stewardship Council.

But of course, this was never going to be enough. Governments had to get involved and make systemic changes. Individuals changing their personal lifestyles was not enough. However, very few people and governments listened to us. We were considered Cassandras, doom mongers, nihilists, mad. But if governments had acted then we would not be at crisis point now.

I will not go into more details about my personal activities over the last 40 years, but I hope it shows that my actions during the week of 15 to 20 April this year were not taken spontaneously or lightly but came out of lifetime concerns and that I have tried everything I could think of to create the changes necessary to combat climate change and prevent catastrophic collapse.

The basis for my belief that there is a climate emergency
I will now quickly present some evidence of the materials that have had most impact and influence upon me and the basic information that was in my possession and which I was aware of before my action. These will show why I believe that without urgent and systemic changes in our society it is likely that civilisation will collapse along with global ecosystems. They will also explain my motivation for refusing to leave a protest area on 17 April.

We are already living through a mass extinction of other species and it is now clear that this is due to human activities. If we do not change, our own species is likely to suffer the same fate.

In the very near term we are less at risk in the UK than in other parts of the world. However, many here *are* already feeling the impact, in particular the young and the old. The 2003 heat-wave, attributed by researchers to climate change, caused the loss of 70,000 lives across Europe, including in the UK.[289] Homes in parts of the UK, such as Carlisle and Manchester, are already uninsurable due to flood risk.[290] Tens of thousands of lives are lost every year in the UK due to air pollution attributable to fossil fuels, with children's lungs badly affected.[291]

Carbon dioxide, the main driver of climate change, stays in the atmosphere for hundreds of years, and much of the change we're experiencing is now already 'locked in'.[292]

There is mounting evidence that we are accelerating towards runaway climate change and a 'hothouse Earth', leading to conditions that will no longer support human life.

In October 1988, the World Meteorological Organisation, the International Council for Science (ICSU) and the United Nations Environment Programme Advisory Group on Greenhouse Gases (AGGG) issued a report based on their research project, co-ordinated by the Stockholm Environment Institute. It was to establish appropriate limits for global warming and concluded as follows:

Temperature increases beyond 1°C may elicit rapid, unpredictable, and **non-linear responses** that could lead to extensive ecosystem damage.[293]

By 2018 the 1°C limit had already been breached.

Let's clarify the concept of 'non-linear responses'. At a certain point feedback effects in the climate system will lead to a 'tipping point', beyond which the world will continue to warm rapidly, even if human emissions of greenhouse gases were to cease altogether. Ice, for example, reflects heat away from the Earth's surface. As the world warms, sea ice melts, to be replaced with dark water which, instead of reflecting heat away from the Earth's surface, absorbs it, speeding up the process of ice melt, in a vicious cycle of warming. With rising temperatures forest fires increase in frequency and severity. Trees which were absorbing CO_2 from the atmosphere, instead release it, further compounding the warming process.[294]

Lord Deben (the current Chair of the Committee on Climate Change) described the 'tipping point' in the following terms (in a 2007 report for the Shadow Cabinet):

Tipping point. This refers to the point at which these changes in the climate system lead to runaway global warming.

At this stage, what little influence we had on the climate system will no longer have any effect on the outcome. *Runaway global warming could lead to mass extinction.*[295] [emphasis added]

In 2008, when the UK's Climate Change Act became law, the 'absolute temperature limit' of 2°C was used as the goal for UK targets, as noted by the House of Commons Environmental Committee in its review of the Climate Change Bill:

The Secretary of State for Environment, Food and Rural Affairs confirmed to us that the government was still completely committed to limiting global warming to a rise of 2°C. By stressing the dangers even of this level of warming, he emphasised the reasons why the UK and EU were committed to holding a rise in temperature at no more than 2°C: 'Just to put that in perspective, I was told... that with a two-degree average change it will not be uncommon to have 50°C in Berlin by mid-century... and I think that is quite a sobering demonstration because 50°C is beyond our experience... Climate change is on a different scale from any other political challenge. Its potential effects could be both physically and economically devastating. It is not just the size but the timing of these effects that poses such a challenge.'[296]

From about 2010, however, there was increasing recognition that the 2°C limit was inadequate and dangerous.

In 2011, Christiana Figueres, Executive Secretary of the UN Framework Convention on Climate Change warned: 'Two degrees is not enough – we should be thinking of 1.5°C. If we are not headed for 1.5°C we are in big, big trouble.'[297]

In 2013, Lord Stern, whose 2007 Review informed the setting of the 2050 Target, gave a presentation to the World Economic Forum in Davos, in which he said:

Looking back, I underestimated the risks. The planet and the atmosphere seem to be absorbing less carbon than we expected, and emissions are rising pretty strongly. Some of the effects are coming through more quickly than we thought ... This is potentially so dangerous that we have to act strongly. Do we want to play Russian roulette with two bullets or one? These risks for many people are existential.[298]

In May 2015, the Structured Expert Dialogue, commissioned by the UN Framework Convention on Climate Change Conference of the Parties in 2012, issued its Final Report, which concluded:

The 'guardrail' concept, in which up to 2°C of warming is considered safe is inadequate... Experts emphasised the high likelihood of meaningful differences between 1.5°C and 2°C of warming regarding the level of risk from... extreme events or tipping points...[299]

In December 2015, the 197 governments which are parties to the UN Framework Convention on Climate Change united in rejecting the 2°C limit as dangerous and inadequate, by adopting the Paris Agreement on Climate Change, which reframes the limit as follows:

Holding the increase in the global average temperature to well below 2°C above pre-industrial levels and to pursue efforts to limit the temperature increase to 1.5°C above pre-industrial levels.[300]

Leading research concludes that beyond the Paris Agreement limit, a tipping point may be crossed leading to runaway climate change and a 'hothouse Earth':

This analysis implies that, even if the Paris Accord target of a 1.5°C to 2°C rise in temperature is met, we cannot exclude the risk that a cascade of feedbacks could push the Earth System irreversibly onto a 'Hothouse Earth' pathway... Hothouse Earth is likely to be uncontrollable and dangerous... it poses severe risks for health, economies, political stability... and ultimately, the habitability of the planet for humans... Where such a threshold might be is uncertain, but it could be only decades ahead...[301]

It is evident from numerous authoritative sources, including the UK government itself, that we are rapidly heading beyond the Paris Agreement temperature limit and into the zone of extreme danger for all humanity and the rest of life on Earth.

The Intergovernmental Panel on Climate Change, provides the definitive synthesis of all peer-reviewed science on climate change. Its last full report in 2014 concluded that: 'In most scenarios without additional mitigation efforts... warming is more likely than not to exceed 4°C above pre-industrial levels by 2100.'[302] [emphasis added]

In November 2016, the United Nations Environment Programme published its 'Emissions Gap Report' asserting that 'urgent action' was necessary to 'avert disaster':

This report estimates we are actually on track for global warming of up to 3.4 degrees Celsius. Current commitments will reduce emissions by no more than a third of the levels required by 2030 to avert disaster. So, we must take urgent action.[303]

In October 2017, the government published its Clean Growth Strategy:

Without significant reductions in emissions, the world is likely to be on course for average temperature rise in excess of 2°C above pre-industrial levels, and possibly as much as 5°C for the highest emissions scenarios, by the end of this century... Scientific evidence shows that increasing magnitudes of warming increase the likelihood of severe, pervasive and irreversible impacts on people and ecosystems. These climate change risks increase rapidly above 2°C but some risks are considerable below 2°C.[304]

The scientific evidence is clear and unequivocal: an urgent and radical change, of course, is required if the Paris Agreement temperature limits are to be respected and disaster averted.

In June 2017, a coalition of eminent scientists, diplomats and policy-makers, published a comment piece in the leading scientific journal Nature headed 'Three years to safeguard our climate'. This showed that in order to meet the Paris Agreement temperature limit, global carbon dioxide emissions would need to peak by 2020, and collapse to 'net zero' within 20 years, explaining:

The year 2020 is crucially important for another reason, one that has more to do with physics than politics. When it comes to climate, timing is everything... should emissions continue to rise beyond 2020, or even remain level, the temperature goals set in Paris become almost unattainable.[305]

In 2018 the Foreign & Commonwealth Office referred to climate change as an 'existential threat'.[306]

On 9 October 2018, the Intergovernmental Panel on Climate Change published its final report into the implications of crossing the 1.5°C temperature limit and concluded that:

the implications for humanity of exceeding the 1.5°C threshold were extremely severe at current rates of emissions that threshold was likely to be crossed at some point after 2030 avoiding such an outcome demanded urgent and radical action to reduce greenhouse gas emissions.[307]

The BBC reported the Intergovernmental Panel on Climate Change conclusions under the headline: 'Final Call to Save the World from "Climate Catastrophe"'.[308]

In the face of all these dire scientific warnings the UK government should immediately communicate to the public the danger and start building a democratic mandate for the urgent and radical action that is required, which is why these were, and still are, part of the Extinction Rebellion's demands.

The government is not only failing to inform the public about the exceptional risks of climate breakdown and a hothouse Earth but is in fact carrying on as usual. Rather than taking urgent action to reduce emissions it is, for example:

- expanding aviation, which is one of the most polluting forms of transport, with Chris Grayling MP, the Transport Minister, claiming that the Paris Agreement was 'irrelevant' to plans to expand Heathrow Airport;
- encouraging 'fracking' for shale gas, contrary to the advice of leading climate scientists;
- and providing the highest fossil fuel subsidies of any country in Europe.[309, 310]

Leading experts, including the government's own statutory advisers, the Committee on Climate Change, have noted the conflict between the government's climate obligations and its actions.

In October 2018 *The Guardian* newspaper wrote as follows:

One of the world's leading climate scientists has launched a scathing attack on the government's fracking programme, accusing ministers of aping Donald Trump and ignoring scientific evidence. James Hansen, who is known as the father of climate science, warned that future generations would judge the decision to back a UK fracking industry harshly... The science is crystal clear, we need to phase out fossil fuels starting with the most damaging, the 'unconventional' fossil fuels such as tar sands and 'fracking'.[311]

Belief leading to action

The information I have presented to you is a dry summary of only a minute fraction of the information that has come my way. It has left me feeling frustrated, depressed and, at times, hopeless. I cannot really understand why those 'in power' have refused to act. After all it is their world too. I know politicians are relentlessly lobbied by the fossil fuel and extractive industries, that there is a revolving door from politician, civil servant to CEOs of the oil and aviation industries etc. But when our society and ecosystem collapses around us, none of us will be able to eat, drink, or breathe money.

We collectively know what to do to halt climate change but it is not being done. But to be depressed and to lose all hope only makes the problem worse. I am fearful for the future for myself, for my family and for all living creatures on this fragile planet. I believe there is a real and substantial threat to all our lives, and that, in accordance with the science, urgent and systemic changes to our society must be taken now to mitigate the danger. That is why I took action on 17 April with Extinction Rebellion.

There had been countless scientific reports, letters from concerned scientists, marches, petitions, and promises. But the government was not acting responsibly and enacting the policies that are needed to address the climate emergency. I therefore took nonviolent direct action as a matter of last resort.

In December 2018, Sir David Attenborough told the United Nations:

Right now we are facing a man-made disaster of global scale, our greatest threat in thousands of years: climate change... If we don't take action, the collapse of our civilisations and the extinction of much of the natural world is on the horizon... The world's people have spoken. Time is running out. They want you, the decision-makers, to act now. Leaders of the world, you must lead.[312]

Following the wave of actions in London that commenced on 15 April, I believe that the necessity for the actions, and their success in raising the alarm, are now widely acknowledged. This was reflected in the following articles across the political spectrum in the mainstream media:

'Extinction Rebellion protests have WORKED as MPs succumb to calls for change' (*Daily Express*, 25 April 2019)[313]

'Jeremy Corbyn forces MPs to vote on declaring climate emergency after

Extinction Rebellion protests over political inaction' (*Daily Mail*, 28 April 2019)[314]

Like most people, I do not like being arrested. I did not want to spend three days in police cells refusing what I considered to be unreasonable bail conditions preventing me from returning to the protests. I do not enjoy spending time in courts nor do I wish to spend scarce resources travelling from Wales to London for the hearings.

If the government had done its job of acting in the public interest by providing the public with honest information about the scale and urgency of the threat, and had addressed the threat instead of compounding it, I would not have needed to engage in nonviolent direct action.

Finally, I want to assure the court that all my peace and environmental actions over the decades have been done in a considered, accountable and nonviolent manner and my latest Extinction Rebellion actions were carried out in a similar nonviolent and responsible manner.

The xr Rebel Code was and still is part of the nonviolence trainings given to participants and not only is it on their website but was repeated at all five resistance sites in London. They say:

> We show respect to everyone – to each other, the general public and to the government and police. We oppose systems, not persons.
> We engage in no violence, physical or verbal, and carry no weapons.
> We wear no masks – we hold ourselves accountable for our actions.
> We bring no alcohol or illegal drugs.
> We take responsibility for ourselves; we are all crew.

xr also engaged in extensive police liaison with the Metropolitan Police. I met Paolo Enock, of xr, in the xr office, before the week of rebellion and was told that xr held many meetings with leading Police Liaison Officers from the Met as well as with other senior officers in the run-up to 15 April. The sitings of the roadblocks, for instance, were made known to the police in advance in order for diversions and re-routing to take place to allow traffic to by-pass the blockades and to minimise hassle for road users. I was assured that not only were the nonviolence guidelines (the Rebel Code) made clear but that this included moving for ambulances and fire engines. For instance on 5 April 2019, at a meeting held with the Met (at their offices) with a senior 'Silver Commander' present, the outline of the nonviolent structuring of the planned protests was given and xr's presentation included features such as the presence of stewards, of nonviolent communication and de-escalation teams and that an agreement was given that police officers would be accepted and not hindered when circulating on the occupied sites. Concerns were shared about the possible co-opting of the xr protests by violent factions, and a written reassurance was given by xr that when any roadblock is approached by a vehicle with an activated blue light (including police vehicles to allow for the eventuality of a terrorist attack) the roadblock would let that vehicle through immediately.

I was later told by him that during the rebellion days xr had their own team of police liaisons working a shift system across all five occupied sites. These liaisons were in constant contact with police liaison teams during the day and with duty sergeants in the evenings and at night. Paolo himself was in constant telephone contact with the co-ordinating desk for police liaison during the rebellion days – often on a minute-by-minute basis.

Paolo told me that police vehicles were included in xr's bluelight policy. He witnessed two medical emergency incidents on Waterloo Bridge in both of which xr rebels were proactive in helping with getting the emergency services where they were needed. In the second of these incidents, which happened during a major police arrest operation, a 'fire lane' was formed and held open on the northbound carriageway of the bridge for approximately one hour so that ambulances could deal with a medical emergency – a passer-by had suffered a major heart attack on the pavement and required prolonged treatment by medical staff. Not only did xr stewards and police liaisons alert the police of the emergency, but they collaborated with the police in keeping the emergency lane clear for the full period of the emergency so that ambulances could come and go in both directions.

Paolo said he would be away for this trial date, which is why I have not called him as a witness.

I can testify that I witnessed a beautiful and compassionate atmosphere at all five sites that I visited over the first few days, before being arrested. Local shop keepers and business people walked through our focal blockade points to get to work and congratulated us on the people's assemblies, the music and carnival atmosphere, and said they wished traffic was stopped every day as there was less air pollution and it was quieter. Many local shops and cafes enjoyed good business and some offered free use of their facilities as a way of showing solidarity.

I am pleading not guilty, even though I did refuse to move when asked to by a policeman on 17 April. I am pleading not guilty because I believed I was justified in remaining at the protest in what I considered to be a reasonable and proportionate response to the climate chaos emergency. I believed that my action, along with many of the thousands gathered in London that week, would help avoid disaster and lead to change. And this has been proved to be true. It has opened up a space for real debate about climate change and what practical actions can be taken. Just days after the Extinction Rebellion actions in London on 29 April, Wales was the first country to formally declare a climate emergency.[315] This was followed a few days later on 1 May by the UK government declaring a climate and environmental emergency.[316]

I have been involved, as have many thousands of others around the UK, in persuading my own Town Council in Knighton to declare a climate emergency and to hold public meetings to decide what practical actions can be taken. I believe that this would not have happened without the creative disruption we caused in central London.

Given that our fragile planet is undergoing massive climate change that will soon, possibly within 11 years, culminate in catastrophic climate chaos that will lead to massive loss of life, I had to do all in my power to bring about the necessary changes to prevent this catastrophe. I hope you will agree that what I did was a reasonable, proportionate and necessary response to the emergency situation that we are in.

I urge the court to find me not guilty. Thank you.

Women, Peace, Security and International Solidarity
A short presentation by Angie Zelter, given at the FMH, Edinburgh
as part of the World Justice Festival on 9 October 2017

WOMEN ARE OFTEN the main resolvers of conflict, intimately involved in peace-making as they rear their children, look after the elderly and keep their families together. Conflict is a natural part of our human society and when handled constructively and peacefully enables us all to change, develop and grow in a healthy manner. Armed conflict, however, is the antithesis of healthy conflict resolution and has little to do with peace and security. And 'defence' is a word that has been terribly misused given that defence forces are so often involved in offensive attacks frequently in order to support exploitative resource extraction of oil, gas, and minerals, to the detriment of local people and their environment.

The 'Women and War' report by the Red Cross provides a useful summary that includes information about how many armed conflicts are now, not so often 'cross border' as, 'internal' between rival ethnic, religious or political groups over the control of resources, territories or populations.[317] And how, unfortunately, civilians, are all too often directly targeted or caught in the cross-fire. While men make up the vast majority of those killed, detained or made to disappear during war, women are increasingly targeted as civilians and exposed to sexual violence. They also generally bear all the responsibility for ensuring the day-to-day survival of their families.

With millions of people worldwide brutally uprooted from their homes and livelihoods they often find themselves living in difficult conditions with inadequate access to food, water, shelter and health care. Displaced women often have to manage alone and assume extra responsibilities, which takes its toll on their health and puts them at greater risk of sexual violence and abuse.

The world is becoming a more dangerous place and there are now only ten countries which can be considered at peace and completely free from conflict – in other words, not engaged in any armed conflicts either internally or externally.[318]

The UK bears a great deal of responsibility for the violence so prevalent in the world today. Not only was the colonial era one of terrible violence and disruption but it also contributes to many current conflicts. And, as the historian Marc Curtis explains:

> Britain's role **remains** an essentially imperial one: to act as junior partner to US global power; to help organise the global economy to benefit Western corporations; and to maximise Britain's… independent political standing in the world and thus remain a 'great power'.[319]

As women we must be concerned that Britain is the sixth largest arms dealer in the world and that Saudi Arabia, where women are still treated as second-class citizens, is the UK's biggest arms customer. It is one of

> the world's most authoritarian regimes, its repression at home and aggression abroad is propped up and supported by UK arms sales. Not only does it brutally repress its own population, it has used UK weapons to help crush democracy protests in Bahrain; now UK-made war-planes are playing a central role in Saudi Arabia's attacks in Yemen.[320]

Britain is heavily involved in many of the current conflicts providing weapons, training and intelligence, for instance, in Iraq, Syria, Afghanistan, Nigeria, Libya, Yemen and Somalia. And its heavy involvement in out of area NATO military exercises is also hugely provocative and disturbing to global peace and security.

Which brings us to here and now – ordinary women in the UK – what can we do to enhance international peace and security?

We clearly need to be involved in work against the arms trade and there are many other things that we can do. I will just highlight those that I myself have been involved in to give some context to the coming discussion.

Firstly, ongoing civil resistance in the UK against nuclear weapons.

I have been closely involved in Trident Ploughshares over the last 20 years, which trains and organises nonviolent resistance against Trident in the UK including Aldermaston, Burghfield, Devonport, Faslane and Coulport.

I also initiated the Faslane 365 year of blockades.[321] I believe these nonviolent actions not only effectively disrupted the 'business as usual' nuclear war preparations but also alerted and empowered many ordinary people to get involved and supported the current Scottish Government in its anti-nuclear stance. If many more people were involved then we might be able to get rid of Trident. When a thousand of us turn up at Faslane and stay in the roads and do not move then the base is closed down for the day as the police cannot deal with those kinds of numbers. If we stay for days at a time we will soon learn our power. But it needs all of us out there to bring our friends and families.

This coming year with the Nuclear Weapons Ban Treaty coming into force is vital, so I encourage you all to come and join in the blockades and resistance. And most importantly to keep the pressure on the Scottish Government to stop the nuclear convoys using Scottish roads and to sign a strong declaration in support of the Nuclear Weapon Ban Treaty.

Moving into the international arena, it is also important to provide solidarity for communities suffering from conflict, give a voice to people caught up in conflict zones and provide a physical international supportive presence. I chose to get involved with the solidarity network in Palestine and helped set up the International Women's Peace Service – Palestine based in villages in Salfit to support Palestinians suffering from the Israeli occupation in the West Bank.[322, 323]

We set up a group of women volunteers to provide accompaniment to Palestinians under threat and to support them with our international presence at their nonviolent demonstrations against the occupation and the building of the Apartheid Wall. We wrote human rights reports about the house demolitions, arrests of children and the Israeli army incursions into the peaceful rural villages where armed Israeli settlers were stealing land and water resources from the Palestinians.

Although we were not able to stop most of these human rights abuses nevertheless we could publicise them and make sure that the relevant international and UN agencies were informed of what was going on. We were also able to alleviate the sense of isolation and abandonment that so many villagers had when blocked into their villages by Israeli armed checkpoints that prevented their free movement.

We cannot do everything but if we want peace then we must work for it.

Further Reading

General

Diamond, Jared, *Collapse: How Societies Choose to Fail or Survive*, Penguin, 2006.

Earnshaw, Helena and Penrhyn Jones, Angharad (eds), *Here We Stand: Women Changing the World*, Honno Welsh Women's Press, 2014.

Goldsmith, Edward, et al., *A Blueprint for Survival*, Tom Stacey, 1972.

Seager, Joni, *Earth Follies: Feminism, Politics and the Environment*, Earthscan Publications, 1993.

Sharp, Gene, *The Politics of Nonviolent Action*, Porter Sargent, 1973.

Wilkinson, Richard and Pickett, Kate, *The Spirit Level: Why Equality is Better for Everyone*, Penguin Books, 2010.

Obedience

Arendt, Hannah, *Eichmann in Jerusalem: A Report on the Banality of Evil*, Penguin, 1994.

Milgram, Stanley, *Obedience to Authority: An Experimental View*, Harper and Row, 1974.

Corporations

Bakan, Joel, *The Corporation: The Pathological Pursuit of Profit and Power*, Constable and Robinson, 2004.

Feinstein, Andrew, *The Shadow World: Inside the Global Arms Trade*, Penguin, 2012.

Korten, David C, *When Corporations Rule the World*, Earthscan Publications, 1995.

Foreign Policy/Colonialism/History

Brody, Hugh, *The Other Side of Eden: Hunter-Gatherers, Farmers, and the Shaping of the World*, Faber and Faber, 2001.

Curtis, Mark, *Web of Deceit: Britain's Real Role in the World*, Vintage, 2003.

Davidson, Basil, *Black Mother: The Years of the African Slave Trade*, Little, Brown and Co, 1961.

Dunn, James, Timor: *A People Betrayed*, ABC Books for the Australian Broadcasting Corporation, 2001.

Easwaran, Eknath, *Nonviolent Soldier of Islam: Badshah Khan, A Man to Match His Mountains*, Nilgiri Press for the Blue Mountain Center of Meditation, 1984.

Galeano, Eduardo, *Mirrors: Stories of Almost Everyone*, Portobello Books, 2009.

Galeano, Eduardo, *Open Veins of Latin America: Five Centuries of the Pillage of a Continent*, Monthly Review Press, New York, 1973.

Hersey, John, *Hiroshima*, first published in *The New Yorker*, August 1946; reissued as a Penguin Modern Classic in 1983.

Lasse, Udtja, *Bury My Heart at Udtjajaure*, Emma Publishing, Sweden, 2007.

Lindqvist, Sven, *Exterminate All the Brutes, Granta*, 1998.

Lindqvist, Sven, *A History of Bombing*, Granta, 2001.

Morris, Donald R, *The Washing of the Spears*, Sphere, 1973.

Paik Sunoo, Brenda with Han, Youngsook, *Moon Tides: Jeju Island Grannies of the Sea*, Seoul Selection, 2011.

Sang Soo, Hur (ed), *For the Truth and Reparations: Cheju April 3rd of 1948 Massacre Not Forsaken*, Backsan Publisher Co, Seoul, 2001.

Werfel, Franz, *The Forty Days of Musa Dagh*, Penguin Classics, 2018.

Nuclear

Green, Commander Robert, Royal Navy (Ret'd), *Security without Nuclear Deterrence*, Spokesman, 2018.

Forsyth, Commander Robert, Royal Navy (Ret'd), *Why Trident?*, Spokesman, 2020.

Manson, Robert, *The Pax Legalis Papers: Nuclear Conspiracy and the Law*, Jon Carpenter Publishing in association with the Institute for Law and Peace, 1995.

Yaroshinskaya, Alla, *Chernobyl: The Forbidden Truth*, Jon Carpenter Publishing, 1994.

Zelter, Angie (ed), *Faslane 365: A Year of Anti-nuclear Blockades*, Luath Press, 2008.

Zelter, Angie and Bernard, Oliver (eds), *Snowball: The Story of a Nonviolent Civil Disobedience Campaign in Britain* compiled and edited by and published by Arya Bhushan Bhardwaj of GANDHI-IN-ACTION, New Delhi, India, 1990.

Zelter, Angie, *Trident on Trial: The Case for People's Disarmament*, Luath Press, 2001.

Zelter, Angie, *Tri-Denting It Handbook: An Open Guide to Trident Ploughshares*, third edition, 2001.

Economics

Mellor, Mary, *The Future of Money: From Financial Crisis to Public Resource*, Pluto Press, 2010.

Schumacher, EF, *Small is Beautiful: A Study of Economics as if People Mattered*, Sphere, 1974.

Agriculture

Balfour, EB, *The Living Soil*, Faber and Faber, 1943; later published as *The Living Soil and the Haughley Experiment*, Palgrave Macmillan, 1975.

Fukuoka, Mansanobu, *The One-Straw Revolution*, Emmaus, Pa, Rodale Press 1978.

Hills, Lawrence D, *Grow Your Own Fruit and Vegetables*, Faber and Faber, 1971.

Howard, Sir Albert, *An Agricultural Testament*, Oxford University Press, 1940.

King, FH, *Farmers of Forty Centuries, or Permanent Agriculture in China, Korea and Japan*, Democrat Printing Co, Madison, Wis, 1911.

Forests

Chin, SC, Devaraj, Jeykumr and Jin, Khoo Khay, *Logging Against the Natives of Sarawak*, INSAN, Malaysia, 1989.

Colchester, Marcus, *Pirates, Squatters and Poachers: The Political Ecology of Dispossession of the Native Peoples of Sarawak*, a report from Survival International published in association with INSAN, Malaysia, 1989.

Environmental Investigation Agency, *Corporate Power, Corruption and the Destruction of the World's Forests: The Case for a New Global Forest Agreement*, Environmental Investigation Agency, 1996.

Lang, Chris, *Genetically Modified Trees: The Ultimate Threat to Forests*, World Rainforest Movement and Friends of the Earth, 2004.

Mendes, Chico, *Fight for the Forest: Chico Mendes in his Own Words*, Latin America Bureau, 1989.

Pakenham, Thomas, *Meetings with Remarkable Trees*, Weidenfeld and Nicolson, 1996.

Sahabat Alam Malaysia, *Solving Sarawak's Forest and Native Problem: Proposals by Sahabat Alam Malaysia*, Sahabat Alam Malaysia, 1990.

Endnotes

1   www.disarmsecure.org

2   Edward Goldsmith, et al., *A Blueprint for Survival*, Tom Stacey, 1972.

3   Some of this is covered in an interview with me carried out by Angharad in Chapter 11, 'With my hammer' in Helena Earnshaw and Angharad Penrhyn Jones, *Here We Stand: Women Changing the World*, Honno, 2014.

4   My husband was also born in South Rhodesia and was known as a second-generation White African.

5   Now Harare.

6   Basil Davidson, *Black Mother: The Years of the African Slave Trade*, Little, Brown and Co, 1961.

7   EB Balfour, *The Living Soil*, Faber and Faber, 1943; later published as *The Living Soil and the Haughley Experiment*, Palgrave Macmillan, 1976.

8   www.gardenorganic.org.uk

9   www.soilassociation.org

10   FH King, *Farmers of Forty Centuries, or Permanent Agriculture in China, Korea and Japan* by Democrat Printing Co, Madison, Wis, 1911.

11   When I was 16 years old my dad got a job in Vienna and so my stepmother and half-brother all moved there while I stayed in the UK to complete my schooling. I stayed in the home of a friend of my parents and visited my parents once or twice a year.

12   EF Schumacher, *Small Is Beautiful: A Study of Economics as if People Mattered*, Sphere Books Ltd, 1973.

13   Mary Mellor, *The Future of Money: From Financial Crisis to Public Resource*, Pluto Press, 2010.

14   positivemoney.org

15   In 1981 a group of women, angered by the decision to site cruise missiles (guided nuclear-armed missiles) in the UK, organised a protest march from Cardiff, Wales to Greenham Common Air Base near Newbury in Berkshire. Here they set up what became known as the Greenham Common Women's Peace Camp. Thousands of women protested and helped gather and strengthen the European peace movement. This led to massive political pressure, eventually culminating in 1987 with US President Ronald Reagan and Soviet President Mikhail Gorbachev signing the Intermediate-Range Nuclear Forces (INF) Treaty which paved the way for the removal of cruise missiles from Greenham. Between 1989 and 1991 all the missiles sited at Greenham were removed. The United States Air Force left the base in 1992 and were soon followed by their British counterparts. The Peace Camp remained as a continuing protest against nuclear weapons, and the last of the Greenham women

left the base in September 2000, 19 years after they had first arrived. Greenham no longer belongs to the military: part is now a business park and the rest is common land.

16 My 'little' brother is ten years younger than me and we are quite close. He left the RAF when his time was up and did not renew.

17 There were at least nine different women's encampments around the perimeter fence and they were named after different colours.

18 I chose the name as it was during the anti-apartheid campaign and she was the public face of her husband Nelson Mandela while he was imprisoned. She had been tortured, detained, in solitary confinement and suffered a great deal. It was before it became known that she had endorsed human rights abuses herself with the 'Mandela United Football Club', her security detail.

19 Starting with three activists cutting the fence at USAF Sculthorpe in Norfolk, the Snowball campaign, in its 14 stages, lasted just over three years, with 2,796 people taking part at 42 different bases in the UK.

20 Liz is an old friend who over the years has been involved in making banners for and with us over many different campaigns. She helped us design and make the Seeds of Hope banner in my barn in East Runton and then made the original Trident Ploughshares banner, which we still use.

21 The 1987 Intermediate-Range Nuclear Forces (INF) Treaty required the United States and the Soviet Union to eliminate and permanently forswear all of their nuclear and conventional ground-launched ballistic and cruise missiles with ranges of 500 to 5,500 kilometres. The treaty marked the first time the superpowers had agreed to reduce their nuclear arsenals, eliminate an entire category of nuclear weapons, and employ extensive on-site inspections for verification. As a result of the INF Treaty, the United States and the Soviet Union destroyed a total of 2,692 short-, medium- and intermediate-range missiles by the treaty's implementation deadline of 1 June 1991.

22 By this time we had the support of the Greenhouse in Norwich, a wonderful central meeting and gathering place run by the amazing Tigger, Frankie and Sylvia, and supported by lots of volunteers there who campaigned on a multitude of issues. Steve Bell, then a cartoonist at *The Guardian*, had designed the logo of the snowball for us to use on our newsletters, packs and publicity materials. Using the Greenhouse as a base, the Snowball campaign went from strength to strength.

23 'Jail Threat For Woman Who Started "Snowball"', *Eastern Daily Press*, 18 February 1986.

24 These prison experiences are described in Chapter 9, 'Prison Records', of *Snowball: The Story of a Nonviolent Civil Disobedience Campaign in Britain* by Angie Zelter and Oliver Bernard (eds), published by Arya Bhushan Bhardwaj of GANDHI-IN-ACTION, New Delhi, India, 1990.

25 'The Snowball Marathon: Stiffer Fines for the Wire-cutting Protestors', *Lynn News*, 21 February 1986.

26   Granada TV investigative current affairs programme.

27   *Trident on Trial: The Case for People's Disarmament*, Luath Press, 2001 & *Faslane 365: A Year of Anti-Nuclear Blockades*, Luath Press, 2008.

28   The Shutdown Sizewell Campaign – www.shutdown-sizewell.org.uk – has been going for over 30 years and many of us in Norfolk and Suffolk took part in the demonstrations and actions to try to close down these polluting and dangerous places and prevent new ones going up, Maybe now that wind and solar power are able to produce the energy we need by their much cheaper and safer technologies, and can provide more jobs too, these nuclear power stations can start to close down. However, the problem is still the undue influence of the nuclear power industry and the close connection between the civil and military nuclear industries.

29   The Chipko movement originated in the foothills of the Himalayas of India to conserve the forests. Many women were involved in nonviolent protection of the trees and it had a worldwide impact. Chico Mendes was the charismatic founder of the Brazilian rubber tappers' union and was murdered by a hired assassin on 22 December 1988. He led a nonviolent campaign to protect the Amazon rainforest and was killed because he was a threat to the big landowners and business interests who profited from the destruction of the forest. I had read *Fight for the Forest: Chico Mendes in his Own Words* published by the Latin America Bureau, 1989. The Penan was the Dayak tribe in Sarawak that we were in solidarity with.

30   This was a lucky move as she got a day out of prison to collect her passport. It was like a holiday, she said. The rest of us told where our passports were stored and they were collected from various places in hotels in Miri.

31   Survival International, a superb organisation that highlights the plight of indigenous peoples all around the world, produced a report which was very illuminating: *Pirates, Squatters and Poachers: The Political Ecology of Dispossession of the Native Peoples of Sarawak*, Survival International in association with INSAN, 1989.

32   Iban are a Dayak people in Sarawak renowned for having headhunted in the past. When I eventually got out of prison with Anja, Antalai took us to his village where we planted mango, coconut and durian trees. He also took us to a special hut where some old, dried heads were hanging in baskets from the dusty roof. I had not realised how small they became when treated and dried.

33   The Indonesian part of the island of Borneo.

34   When I was talking to a military officer who came to interview us separately whilst we were in prison, it became very clear that the military thought the Penan were uncivilised savages who needed to be taught how to live in houses not in the forest; so the military felt justified in driving the Penan out of the forests and forcibly resettling them.

35   Bruno Manser Fonds is a Swiss organisation that continues the work of Bruno Manser and is committed to the Penan and saving the rainforest. See bmf.ch/en

36   Białowieża Forest is a last remaining part of the primeval forest that once stretched across the European Plain. The forest is home to 800 European bison, Europe's

heaviest land animal. It contains huge oak trees and reminds us of what the UK has lost.

37 *The UKFN Forests Memorandum* was written and edited by Nigel Dudly incorporating information from all of the groups in the UKFN and was published by the Greenhouse, Norwich. It covered the problems, causes, effects of and solutions for the Global Forest Crisis.

38 I helped co-found the North Norfolk Community Woodland near North Walsham which we later handed over to the Woodland Trust to manage – see www. woodlandtrust.org.uk/visiting-woods/woods/pigneys-wood and in Wales co-founded the Knighton Tree Allotment Trust, now called the Knighton Community Woodlands Group – see tveg.org.uk/wordpress/what-we-do/woodland-project

39 Nitya from the Sarawak action was living in my house at the time and she came along with me on this first action.

40 The *Evening Standard*, among many other papers, covered the protest with a headline saying 'Harrods Raided By Trees Protesters'. The paper said Harrods was the target 'for a carefully planned two-pronged attack by militant environmentalists'. *The Guardian* article on 11 December 1993 was titled 'Ethical Shoplifters Carve Out a Niche at Top Store'.

41 Article in *Time Out* magazine, 22–29 June 1994.

42 *Blue Peter* is the longest-running children's TV show in the world, having broadcast continuously since 1958. The Nuxalk chiefs at the police station were shown in the news section of their programme.

43 'Mahogany Means Murder', article in *Red Pepper*, March 1995, explaining why 'voluntary agreements are not worth the paper they are written on'.

44 'Eco-shoplifters Snatch Mahogany', article in *Timber Trades Journal*, 26 November 1994.

45 'Mahogany is Murder', article in *The Independent*, 25 November 1994.

46 'The Pros and Cons of Shoplifting' article in *Timber Trades Journal*, 6 May 1995.

47 'Angie Zelter Has the Last Word': article presenting 'an environmentalist's view of forestry in British Columbia', *Timber Trades Journal*, 26 April 1997.

48 We were a group of three women: Helena, Ricarda and myself.

49 The talk was given to the London Softwood Club, 9 October 1997.

50 'Meyer Tightens Up Mahogany Buying Policy After Brazil Trip' article in *Timber Trades Journal*, 18 March 1995.

51 www.fsc-uk.org/en-uk

52 Joel Bakan, *The Corporation: The Pathological Pursuit of Profit and Power*, Constable and Robinson Ltd, 2004.

53 www.opendemocracy.net/en/odr/corporate-courts-latest-threat-democracy-armenia

54   For background information on East Timor see James Dunn, *Timor: A People Betrayed*, ABC Books for the Australian Broadcasting Corporation, 2001.

55   For information on the Ploughshares movement, see the *Tri-Denting It Handbook*, 1.6 'Background History and Philosophy of the Ploughshares Movement to Date' at tridentploughsharesarchive.org/wp-content/uploads/2013/01/1.pdf

56   This included Zoe, who has been an amazingly supportive person and helped produce films free of charge for many of the campaigns I have been involved in.

57   The quote and film footage was taken from John Pilger's film *Death of a Nation: The Timor Conspiracy*. This film had influenced all ten of us involved in the Seeds of Hope Ploughshares action.

58   My hammer was lovingly carved by Rowan for me with a sword made into a ploughshare and acorn, seedling and oak leaf – beautiful. I still use it around the house; it was returned by the court after our acquittal along with our banners and other court 'exhibits'.

59   This was quite a fraught decision, as obviously we all four wanted to do the hammering.

60   We had all made the banner in my barn at Valley Farmhouse over several of our weekend meetings. I still have it; it was returned after we won the case, along with our hammers. It was made from an old purple sheet of mine and was designed with the help of my Norfolk artist friend Liz. All ten of us worked on the banner, which showed a Hawk jet with a massive hammer pounding on it, surrounded by seeds of hope and other meaningful symbols as well as our main message 'Women Disarming for Life and Justice'.

61   All ten of us were involved in this meaningful ceremony that focused us all and brought us together. We wrote on pieces of paper how we felt about the genocide happening and then lit them with a candle, collecting the ashes afterwards. We had collected seeds to symbolise our hope for freedom for East Timor, mixed these with the ashes and divided the mixture between all ten of us, to be sprinkled on the Hawk jets and to keep with us until the trial.

62   Just in time, as the police raided the house soon after I left.

63   This was to present a Declaration calling for an emergency parliamentary debate on the immediate cancellation of the Hawks to Indonesia, to approach the Attorney General to institute proceedings against the Department of Trade and Industry, and for an internal Parliamentary investigation into arms sales to Indonesia.

64   Gareth is an amazingly humble and wonderfully compassionate and brilliant solicitor who is well known for her successful defence of the 'Guildford Four' amongst many other human rights cases. We were so very fortunate to have her represent Jo and help all of us.

65   Angie Zelter, *Civil Society and Global Responsibility: The Arms Trade and East Timor*, International Relations 18(1), SAGE Publications 2004.

66   I was lucky to be invited to attend this occasion, which was astonishingly

sumptuous. Frederik, a Norwegian international lawyer I knew, invited me to stay at his home in Oslo and accompany him to the prizegiving and celebrations.

67   2–6 December 1996.

68   'CAAT Lays Siege to DTI', *Campaign Against Arms Trade News*, February 1997.

69   'Eleven Protesters Held By Police After Factory Break-in', *The Independent*, 6 May 1997.

70   caat.org.uk/news/uk-has-given-1-billion-in-aid-to-yemen-but-has-licensed-6-5-billion-worth-of-arms-to-countries-bombing-it

71   John Vidal, 'Industry Terrified at Outbreak of Ethics', *The Guardian*, 7 May 1997.

72   The most recent was in September 2019 when Trident Ploughshares worked with Extinction Rebellion on the No Nuclear Day, blockading all the ExCeL Centre's entrances with two cars and a boat. See tridentploughshares.org/nine-arrests-as-anti-nuclear-activists-block-entrances-to-london-arms-fair

73   Andrew Feinstein, *The Shadow World: Inside the Global Arms Trade*, Penguin, 2012.

74   17 January 1961, outgoing address, at www.ourdocuments.gov/doc.php?flash=false&doc=90&page=transcript

75   Keith Mothersson, Robbie Manson, Fred Starkey, Colin Archer, David Head, Edward Stanton and I were the co-founders.

76   lcnp.org/wcourt – I remember whilst in Ecuador (working for the Rio Mazan Cloud Forest project) lobbying the Ecuadorian government to vote in the UN General Assembly to enable the ICJ to take on the Advisory Opinion on the Legality of Nuclear Weapons. Kate Dewes has also written about the World Court Project at www.disarmsecure.org/text-resources/the-world-court-project-the-evolution-and-impact-of-an-effective-citizens-movement

77   This followed on from the original Snowball campaign, integrating some of what we were doing in INLAP at the time.

78   For a chronology of Trident Ploughshares see tridentploughshares.org/trident-ploughshares-chronology

79   tridentploughshares.org/trident-ploughshares-handbook-tridenting-it

80   In later months and years many of the Helensburgh CND group joined TP and Jane became a driving force, especially in giving legal support. She witnessed and reported on hundreds of court cases held in Helensburgh and gave essential support and advice to everyone turning up for their cases, often providing a place to sleep and food too! She has now moved to Edinburgh and continues to be active co-ordinating TP.

81   She was one of the Greenham women who fought for our right to camp and protest outside the Greenham base and took legal action to defend our right to protest. The judgement on the Greenham Bylaws case in the Lords came in May 1990 and they won. Eventually the whole peace movement also won when the cruise missiles were

removed in 1991, due to thousands of us who had protested at Greenham for over ten years.

82   We now manage it with the help of a skilled forester, Julie, who is one of the trustees.

83   Peaton Wood Peace Trust was set up in 2002 and is administered by seven women trustees.

84   We have slowly cleaned up the woodland that locals had been dumping on for years, the bracken is being reduced, the ponticum rhododendrons cut back to allow the ancient oaks to breathe, and a woodland management plan is being implemented during regular work sessions and overseen by our forester trustee, Julie.

85   Open Letter to Tony Blair, 18 March 1998: see p. 20 of TP Handbook at tridentploughshares.org/wp-content/uploads/2013/01/2_3.pdf – the letter was drafted by Rebecca to make it consistent with the demands being made internationally. Many more letters were to follow over the years and each one was signed by the current list of those who had signed the Pledge to Prevent Nuclear Crime.

86   See 'A Women's Guide to Smashing Up Trident', *Sunday Telegraph*, 15 March 1998 & 'Faslane Activists Make Trident Sabotage Threat', *The Herald*, 2 April 1998.

87   An admonition is basically a judicial warning. A conviction is recorded, but there is no substantive penalty and one can walk free.

88   tridentploughshares.org/newsletter-number-1-speed-the-plough

89   Angie Zelter, *Trident on Trial: The Case for People's Disarmament*, Luath Press, 2001.

90   13 March 1998.

91   13 November 1998.

92   The bandit alarm is a very loud siren and announcement alerting all in the base that there are intruders. Everyone has to stop what they are doing and clear the outside areas so the police and their dogs can discover and arrest the intruders. Peace campaigners have entered the base and set off the alarm on numerous occasions.

93   For instance, on 30 January 1999 Rachel and Rosie of the 'Aldermaston Trash Trident' affinity group swam into the dockyard of Barrow-in-Furness, and climbed aboard the fourth Trident submarine HMS *Vengeance* which was undergoing final tests before launch. They got onto the conning tower and opened and hammered on the electronic control box. Their action delayed the launch of the sub by several months. You can read their story along with many others in *Trident on Trial: The Case for People's Disarmament*, Luath Press, 2001.

94   Living in Norfolk at the time, I was part of the longer-term 'Woodwoses' affinity group but for special one-off actions it is often necessary to form a special affinity group. The one for Loch Goil was called 'The Pheasants Union'.

95   Ellen wrote a description of our action: see tridentploughsharesarchive.org/loch-goil-action-pheasants-union-outing

96   HMP Cornton Vale Prison.

97   tridentploughsharesarchive.org/greenock-1999-case-summary

98   *The Independent*, 22 October 1999.

99   *Morning Star*, 22 October 1999.

100   *The Mirror*, 22 October 1999.

101   *Daily Record*, 22 October 1999.

102   See Lord Advocate's Reference No. 1 of 2,000 [30 March 2001] Misc 11/00 H.C.J. (Scot.)

103   The trial and LAR documents can all be found at tridentploughsharesarchive.org/loch-goil-action-and-greenock-1999-trial and at tridentploughsharesarchive.org/lord-advocates-reference

104   Charles Moxley wrote a refutation of the LAR in *Disarmament Diplomacy*, Issue No. 58, June 2001, Opinion and Analysis section: see tridentploughshares.org/larthe-unlawfulness-of-the-united-kingdoms-policy-of-nuclear-deterrence-the-invalidity-of-the-scottish-high-courts-decision – Charles J Moxley Jr. is author of *Nuclear Weapons and International Law in the Post-Cold War World*, Austin & Winfield, Lanham, Maryland, 2000. Moxley is a member of the board of the Lawyers' Committee for Nuclear Policy (LCNP) and a former board member of the Lawyers' Alliance for World Security (LAWS).

105   Angie Zelter, 'People's Disarmament', in *Disarmament Diplomacy*, Issue No. 58, June 2001, Opinion and Analysis section.

106   Rebecca Johnson and Angie Zelter (eds), *Trident and International Law: Scotland's Obligations*, Luath Press, 2011.

107   www.icanw.org/the_treaty

108   The TPNW was adopted at the UN in July 2017 with the support of 122 member states. On 24 October 2020, the TPNW reached the required 50 states parties for its entry into force. On 22 January 2021 this treaty became binding on those 50 states that ratified it, cementing a categorical ban on nuclear weapons, 75 years after their first use. Trident Ploughshares wrote an open letter to Prime Minister Boris Johnson on 30 November 2020 entitled 'RESPECT THE LAW: DISMANTLE THE UK'S NUCLEAR WEAPONS', which urges the UK to join the treaty. Full text at tridentploughshares.org/open-letter-to-the-right-honourable-boris-johnson-mp

109   Such as those banning chemical weapons, landmines and cluster munitions.

110   www.washingtonpost.com/world/the_americas/us-urges-countries-to-withdraw-from-un-nuke-ban-treaty/2020/10/21/21918918-13ce-11eb-a258-614acf2b906d_story.html and apnews.com/article/nuclear-weapons-disarmament-latin-america-united-nations-gun-politics-4f109626a1cdd6db10560550aa1bb491

111 My stepmother Sheila, my half-brother Ian and me.

112 Bursa had been a home to Armenians for over 500 years when the genocide took place.

113 The Armenian genocide, carried out in Turkey and neighbouring areas by the Ottoman government, was considered the first genocide to have taken place, on account of its organised implementation. One of the most interesting and horrendous accounts is Franz Werfel's *The Forty Days of Musa Dagh*, 1933, available as a Penguin Classic, 2018.

114 *Eichmann in Jerusalem: A Report on the Banality of Evil* was written by Hannah Arendt for *The New Yorker* and later enlarged and published as a book in 1964.

115 Stanley Milgram, *Obedience to Authority: An Experimental View*, Harper and Row, 1974. For a recent article on the experiment see www.simplypsychology.org/milgram.html

116 Nathan's other sister and cousins had moved to Israel after WWII. Nathan did not believe that it was right to settle in Israel, as he did not believe in Zionism nor in forming a religious Jewish state. He was an internationalist and a secularist and liked to define himself as a non-Jewish Jew.

117 Women in Black is a worldwide network of women committed to peace with justice and actively opposed to injustice, war, militarism and other forms of violence: womeninblack.org

118 The conference was entitled 'Women's Coalition for a Just Peace'.

119 See icahd.org – more than 100,000 Palestinian homes have been demolished in Israel and the Occupied Palestine Territory OPT) since 1948.

120 icahd.org/2020/03/15/end-home-demolitions-an-introduction

121 Uri Avnery and Gush Shalom received the Right Livelihood Award – www.rightlivelihoodaward.org/laureates/uri-and-rachel-avnery-gush-shalom – at the same time as Trident Ploughshares – www.rightlivelihoodaward.org/?s=trident+ploughshares – so I met him on several occasions. He was a truly remarkable and compassionate man.

122 www.theguardian.com/commentisfree/2017/nov/01/arthur-balfour-declaration-100-years-of-suffering-britain-palestine-israel

123 Rina, a Jewish woman originally from Aleppo, has lived in the UK for many decades but still spoke a little Arabic which was a great help. Then there was Liz, Sue, Camilla and myself. I had first met Sue and Liz at the WiB conference in Jerusalem the previous year.

124 Twenty-seven refugee camps are situated in the West Bank and Gaza. The Palestinian refugee crisis was created as a result of the An-Naqba of 1948 and An-Naqsa of 1967, massacres and other aggressions perpetrated by the Jewish underground and terror groups such as Haganah, Irgun and Stern. After the 1948 war the UN estimated that 726,000 Palestinians had fled outside and 32,000 within the armistice lines. Of the 800,000 Palestinians originally situated in the area that

became Israel, only some 100,000 remained in their homes, becoming a minority in the Jewish state. 531 villages and towns were destroyed or resettled with Jews.

125   The unspeakable things were screamed at us in Hebrew and translated by accompanying Israeli colleagues, and included violent, aggressive, sexual threats.

126   I wrote up these incidents in *Report of Israeli Police Violence in Jerusalem on 10th and 11th August 2001* and sent it to the British Consul in Jerusalem, and also to the Israeli lawyer dealing with the repercussions of the violence.

127   Al Khalil is the largest Palestinian city in the West Bank.

128   Hebron is the city where Baruch Kopel Goldstein, an American-Israeli and a Jewish religious extremist, perpetrated a mass killing of 30 and wounding of 125 Palestinian Muslim worshippers in the sacred Cave of the Patriarchs.

129   For instance, Beit Hadassah is a Jewish settlement only one block long that overlooks the Palestinian market, and Palestinians are not allowed to walk in front of it. Tel Rumeida is built on top of Palestinian property over archaeological remains, despite a High Court Stop Order.

130   Some of the IDF soldiers, after having to serve in places like Hebron and seeing the inhumanity they were perpetuating, decide to become conscientious objectors, or refuseniks. In Hebrew they are known as *sarvanim*. An interesting article in *New Internationalist* interviews some of these brave refuseniks: newint.org/columns/makingwaves/2005/07/01/refuseniks

131   Angie Zelter, *Report of Assault on Angie Zelter, UK Citizen*, 29 August 2001.

132   I was held in Ben Gurion Airport cells on 29 December 2002 for four days.

133   Some of this was written about in a mini-profile of me in *The Big Issue*, 23–29 January 2003.

134   Angie Zelter, *Dispossession and Terror: A Report of 6 Weeks in Palestine/Israel Aug/Sept 2001*, 1 October 2001.

135   Angie Zelter, 'Taking the Initiative', *Peace News*, March–May 2002. An account of the two weeks of nonviolent direct action against the illegal military occupation of Palestine ISM organised by ISM and the Rapprochement Centre in December 2001.

136   www.btselem.org/settlements/20100830_facts_on_the_settlement_of_ariel

137   iwps.info

138   The training took over two weeks at my home in North Norfolk, which had plenty of space for the 20 women who attended. It was a chance for us to get to know each other and solidify the project as well as learning about nonviolent resistance, human rights monitoring, basic history of the Middle East, some Arabic phrases and how to deal with traumatised people. A psychologist friend from the UK military who helped soldiers suffering from post-traumatic stress gave some useful sessions on this.

139   Our card said 'IWPS provides a constant presence of international women to serve the people of the Salfit region of Palestine. They witness, document and publicise

human rights abuses; peacefully intervene to try to prevent the abuses from occurring and support the growth of the nonviolent resistance to the illegal and brutal Military Occupation of Palestinian lands. They live in Hares Village and can be contacted in the following ways...'

140   Hares, being so near to the illegal settlement of Ariel, was particularly targeted by the IDF. Children are often taken from their homes in the middle of the night, at demonstrations or at checkpoints. They are held in military bases or detention centres for interrogation, are frequently coerced into admitting things they did not do, and forced to sign statements in Hebrew that they do not understand. Israel is the only country in the world that systematically prosecutes children in military courts – around 600 each year.

141   OCHA is the UN Office for the Coordination of Humanitarian Affairs – www.ochaopt.org

142   See Gideon Levy, 'Bitter Harvest', a report for *Haaretz*: www.haaretz.com/1.5121621

143   Many of the more fanatical settlers are from the USA.

144   He told me he had been born and brought up in Chicago and it was much worse there.

145   'Statement concerning incident at Yasouf on 17th October 2002 made by Angie Zelter to Ariel Police Station on Monday 28th October' was presented to the police chief along with photographs of the settlers who had carried out the violence – they were from Tapuach settlement and Tapuach Chadasch. Signed witness statements from IWPS, ISM, Ta'ayush and from the mayor of the village of Yasouf were also included.

146   The 760km Apartheid Wall, so named by human rights activists, including those from South Africa as well as Palestinians, is known in Israel as the West Bank wall or fence. It separates Palestinians from their land and cuts them off from their neighbours and families. Although the Israeli state claims it separates the West Bank along the 1967 Green Line, in fact it deviates from the Green Line into Palestinian territory. Israel calls it a security barrier against terrorism, while Palestinians call it a racial segregation wall. Fifteen years ago the International Court of Justice found that the wall was illegal: see www.un.org/unispal/document/auto-insert-188884

147   'Israel is the only country in the world that systematically prosecutes children in military courts – between 500 and 700 each year. The Israel Prison Service revealed that an average of 204 Palestinian children have been held in custody every month since 2012.' From www.palestinecampaign.org/campaigns/childprisoners

148   See iwps.info

149   Whilst in the cells at Ben Gurion Airport for eight days – an experience in itself, hearing the stories of others being held there – I was surprised one day to be hauled out to speak to an airport official who told me that my grand-daughter, Laura, had been born. It was 24 October 2004. It was only then that I learnt that my daughter-

in-law's stepmother worked at the airport and had managed to get this message to me. Small world indeed.

150   David, Anna-Linnea and Adam.

151   Angie Zelter (ed), *Faslane 365: A Year of Anti-Nuclear Blockades*, Luath Press, 2008.

152   At Büchel Air Base, Germany.

153   At Kleine Brogel Air Base, Holland.

154   At Les Landes, Biscarosse military testing site, France.

155   At NATO HQ in Brussels, Belgium.

156   At the NEAT site near Luleå, Sweden.

157   See ofog.org/english

158   See www.youtube.com/watch?v=K7SolYq5vIQ

159   'Why I am going to Luleå in July': presentation by Angie Zelter to Swedish Feminist groups, 13 February 2011. 'Militarisation and NATO': presentation I gave to Swedish groups on 18 February 2011.

160   For the OFOG video of some of the pink anti-militarist actions see www.youtube.com/watch?v=AGizHwZoagY

161   Udtja Lasse, *Bury My Heart at Udtjajaure*, Emma Publishing, Sweden.

162   Menwith Hill in Yorkshire is nominally an RAF base but is operated and controlled by the National Security Agency and is one of the US's most important overseas bases, playing an integral role in the broader strategy of US global power projection, and is at the heart of US targeted killings. See yorkshirecnd.org.uk/campaigns/menwith-hill and theintercept.com/2016/09/06/nsa-menwith-hill-targeted-killing-surveillance

163   I was arrested on 19 June 2000 after cutting into Menwith Hill with two other women and attempting to get to one of the huge white domes. I was given a two-month sentence, spent in Low Newton prison in Durham.

164   space4peace.org

165   Jeju International Peace Conference was held in Jeju, 24–26 February 2012.

166   Hur Sang Soo (ed), *For the Truth and Reparations: Cheju April 3rd of 1948 Massacre Not Forsaken*, Backsan Publisher Co, Seoul, 2001.

167   For up-to-date news on the ongoing campaign see savejejunow.org/newsletter

168   Catherine Lutz (ed), *The Bases of Empire: The Global Struggle Against US Military Posts*, Pluto Press, 2009.

169   The seas around there are the traditional fishing ground of the Haenyeo women, who are free divers (without any breathing equipment at all) and live by harvesting seaweeds, crabs, fish and all kinds of sea life. I became very friendly with the

daughter of a Haenyeo, who gave me a present of the book written about her mother, *Moon Tides: Jeju Island Grannies of the Sea* by Brenda Paik Sunoo with Youngsook Han, Seoul Selection, 2011.

170　wri-irg.org/en/story/2012/angie-zelters-first-report-gangjeong-24th-february-2012 and wri-irg.org/en/story/2012/nonviolent-resistance-us-war-plans-gangjeong-jeju

171　UNESCO – United Nations Educational, Scientific and Cultural Organization.

172　IUCN – International Union for the Conservation of Nature.

173　savejejunow.org/wp-content/uploads/2013/03/Gangjeong-Village-Story_ March-2013.pdf

174　Angie Zelter, 'Eighth Report from Gangjeong 16 March 2012', at tridentploughshares.org/wp-content/uploads/2013/03/News_index_2012.pdf

175　'Activist is Defiant in Korean Protest', *The Journal*, 16 March 2012 & 'Peace Campaigner Faces Deportation to UK', *The Journal*, 23 March 2012 from www. shropshirestar.com

176　savejejunow.org/wp-content/uploads/2020/11/SepOct2020-2.pdf

177　'The Jeju Naval Base and US War Plans in the Asia-Pacific Region', talk by Angie Zelter, CND Cymru AGM, 2 June 2012.

178　There were tragic evictions of large numbers of Scottish tenants in the Scottish Highlands and Islands, mostly in the period 1750–1860.

179　The Dyke is a large earthwork on the border between Wales and England. It is named after the Anglo-Saxon King of Mercia (757–96) who ordered its construction.

180　Of course, we do not call it defence, as so often our 'defence' forces are used for offence and illegal 'interventions' on behalf of corporate interests, not for defending the UK from invasion.

181　In 2004 the Aldermaston Women's Peace Camp (AWPC) helped set up Block the Builders: see peacenews.info/node/5899/campaign-profile-aldermaston-womens-peace-camp-awpc & peacenews.info/node/3942/laser-has-landed

182　Nukewatch – www.nukewatch.org.uk – is a group of dedicated peace campaigners who monitor and track the movement of UK weapons of mass destruction from Aldermaston and Burghfield to Coulport and Faslane, active ever since 1984. Their recent report, *Unready Scotland* – www.nukewatch.org.uk/wp-content/ uploads/2017/08/UnreadyScotland-Report.pdf – highlights the dangers of the traffic and poor level of readiness at local authority level. They also research the number of accidents there have been on the nuclear convoys as they travel through town centres and on motorways up and down the country.

183　For instance, there is a 19-minute film of a round-up of the June 2016 month of action at Burghfield by Action AWE.

184　picat.online/reporting-a-crimetrident-at-uk-police-stations-2

185   picat.online/wp-content/uploads/2016/09/AngieZelter-Letter.pdf

186   For details of this project and collections of all the evidence sent to the Attorney
       General see http://picat.online/ – an article I wrote in 2015 can be found at
       peacenews.info/blog/8174/citizens-prosecutions-british-secretary-state-defence-
       conspiring-commit-war-crime

187   The five PICAT groups were based in Powys, Pembrokeshire, West Wales, Norwich
       and Sevenoaks.

188   Robert Manson did most of the legal work for PICAT and is well-known for previous
       attempts to get the courts to adjudicate on the UK's nuclear weapons. See his book
       The Pax Legalis Papers: Nuclear Conspiracy and the Law, Jon Carpenter Publishing
       in association with the Institute for Law and Peace, 1995.

189   For a full record of our communications see picat.online/project-updates/
       communications-with-a-g-govt-legal-office

190   I had helped organise the No New Nukes action at Hinkley Point on 10–11 March
       2012 where over 1,000 of us marked a year after the Fukushima accident in Japan.
       We had formed the Stop New Nuclear Alliance, which included the Stop New
       Nuclear Network, Stop Hinkley, CND Cymru, CND, Kick Nuclear, South West
       Against Nuclear, Trident Ploughshares, Shut Down Sizewell, Sizewell Blockaders
       and Rising Tide. We organised a rally and did a 24-hour blockade of the nuclear
       power station site, which was right by the sea and had in the past been inundated
       with seawater. This was probably the first time that there had been a total blockade
       of a nuclear power station in the UK.

191   www.bbc.co.uk/news/uk-wales-mid-wales-28175308 – and the video of it can be
       found at www.youtube.com/watch?v=8fmJ9soJWVk&feature=youtu.be

192   creativeresistance.org/peace-activists-roll-out-enormous-pink-scarves-in-uk-seven-
       miles-long-and-us

193   A 70-second romp down the pink scarf: www.youtube.com/watch?v=2bKt_dIhS_o

194   indyrikki.wordpress.com/2015/01/27/trident-protest-wraps-ministry-of-defence-in-
       peace-scarf

195   tridentploughshares.org/trident-a-british-war-crime-an-oratorio

196   tridentploughshares.org/house-of-commons-lobby-filled-with-singers-objecting-to-
       trident-with-video

197   The Black Rod (officially known as the Lady Usher of the Black Rod or, if male,
       the Gentleman Usher of the Black Rod) is an official in the UK Parliament (and in
       that of several Commonwealth countries). The Black Rod is responsible for and
       participates in the major ceremonial events in the Palace of Westminster, including
       the State Opening of Parliament, royal and state visits, and other ceremonial events.
       I am not sure what he was doing when he confronted us, but he looked very fine in
       his black gear!

198   You can see various videos of the MPs being interviewed and also of the singers and
       protesters at tridentploughshares.org/interesting-useful-films and reports like this

one at tridentploughshares.org/protesters-chained-to-houses-of-parliament-railings-call-for-uk-to-sign-nuclear-weapons-ban-treaty

199 A black bear joined us on one of the blockades we had set up on the logging roads. It seemed to know we were trying to protect its habitat, and after a while wandered off to give us more room to deal with the loggers who were advancing towards us rather menacingly.

200 Quote is from the Prison Records chapter in Angie Zelter and Oliver Bernard (eds), *Snowball: The Story of a Nonviolent Civil-Disobedience Campaign in Britain* published by Arya Bhushan Bhardwaj of GANDHI-IN-ACTION, New Delhi, India, 1990.

201 Angie Zelter, 'Taking action in prison', *Peace News*, Dec 2001–Feb 2002.

202 Writing this reminds me of Benedikt Erlingsson's *Woman at War*, an amazing Icelandic film about a woman's campaign to save Iceland's environment. It includes the twin sister of the major character swapping with her sister to do her time in prison as she is a Buddhist practitioner and was in any case going to do a long silent retreat. It is a great film and very funny.

203 See Chapter 4 for more details of the action itself.

204 *The Guardian*, p. 7 'Women' section, 30 December 1996.

205 Angie Zelter, 'Woman Speaks Out About Inhumane Prison Conditions and the Need for Reform', November 1996.

206 Letter dated 3 December 1996 from CJ Allen, HM Deputy Chief Inspector, HM Inspectorate of Prisons, 50 Queen Anne's Gate, London SW1H 9AT.

207 1998: Helen and I from England, Krista from Holland, and Katri and Hanna from Finland.

208 Letter of 18 November 1998 from RA Hastings, Prisoner Casework Manager, Scottish Prison Service to Mr Williams.

209 A term used in prison for when you are taken out of your cell while prison officers remove everything from cupboard and rip anything off the walls, strip the bed and make a horrible mess. It is done quite often, usually at random and often to search for drugs. It is quite an aggressive action and not done in any respectful way.

210 19 September 1998.

211 'Procurator Fiscal to Decide on Activists' Complaints', *The Herald*, 15 October 1998.

212 The Loch Goil action is described in Chapter 5.

213 Angie Zelter, *Cornton Vale Prison Report*, from 9 June–21 October 1999.

214 'Free the Trident 2 – Fresh Call to Release Pensioners JAILED for Peaceful Anti-nuke Protest' and 'Comic Book Hero Offers to Pay Costs of Trident Protest Pensioners', *The National*, 20 July 2017. 'Roadblock Lands Protester in Jail', *Shropshire Star*, 22 July 2017.

215   The TP camp was held at Peaton Glen next to Coulport, 8–18 July 2017.

216   You can see the treaty at treaties.un.org/doc/Treaties/2017/07/20170707%20
03-42%20PM/Ch_XXVI_9.pdf

The preamble to the Ban Treaty stated the following:

Reaffirming the need for all States at all times to comply with applicable
international law, including international humanitarian law and international
human rights law,

Basing themselves on the principles and rules of international humanitarian
law, in particular the principle that the right of parties to an armed conflict to
choose methods or means of warfare is not unlimited, the rule of distinction,
the prohibition against indiscriminate attacks, the rules on proportionality and
precautions in attack, the prohibition on the use of weapons of a nature to cause
superfluous injury or unnecessary suffering, and the rules for the protection of the
natural environment,

Considering that any use of nuclear weapons would be contrary to the rules of
international law applicable in armed conflict, in particular the principles and rules
of international humanitarian law,

Reaffirming that any use of nuclear weapons would also be abhorrent to the
principles of humanity and the dictates of public conscience.

217   Honduras was the 50th state to ratify, on 24 October 2020. See www.icanw.org/
historic_milestone_un_treaty_on_the_prohibition_of_nuclear_weapons_reaches_50_
ratifications_needed_for_entry_into_force

218   Time spent out of individual cells when one could associate with other prisoners.

219   Letter to Angie Zelter from David Strang, HM Chief Inspector of Prisons for
Scotland, 5 September 2017.

220   www.amnesty.org.uk/how-support-our-campaigns-writing-letters

221   The North Norfolk Woodland Trust that I and my husband helped set up, which
is now owned by the Norfolk Wildlife Trust – see www.norfolkwildlifetrust.org.
uk/wildlife-in-norfolk/nature-reserves/reserves/pigneys-wood – and the If Not
Now When Wood that I helped set up with others on the wishes of David Hood, a
dear friend who made me one of the two executors of his will, which bequeathed
enough money to set up the Trust that now owns and manages the woodland:
ifnotnowwhen.org

222   Peaton Wood Peace Trust, which I helped set up as a trust with a group of women.

223   Knighton Tree Allotments Trust which I helped set up with others and is now called
Knighton Community Woodland: tveg.org.uk/wordpress/what-we-do/woodland-
project

224   From 1995 to 1998 I was a member of the standards sub-committee of the UK
section of the FSC, which was setting the standards for forest certification in
the UK and trying to merge government standards with FSC standards. We were

especially concerned that genetically-modified trees should not be cloned and used in plantations, but there were other issues too. See Chris Lang, *Genetically Modified Trees: The Ultimate Threat to Forests*, World Rainforest Movement and Friends of the Earth, 2004.

225   When I wrote an article for a local church magazine about what it was like to live in a small rural town in Palestine, taking examples that I had seen with my own eyes and just transferring them to a similar small Norfolk rural town, the editor received letters from all around the world accusing him of anti-Semitism.

226   freedomflotilla.org

227   See www.facebook.com/KnightonandDistrictRefugeeSupportGroup

228   See www.countytimes.co.uk/news/18697659.almost-70-000-people-sign-save-river-wye-petition and www.theguardian.com/environment/2020/apr/07/life-in-the-poultry-capital-of-wales-enough-is-enough-say-overwhelmed-residents

229   I was in Seattle with my son and his family when Greta started her school strike. She was the same age as my granddaughter so we naturally talked about it: Mount Rainier, which was nearby was an example of climate change as it was losing its mantle of ice, and the loss of the glaciers globally that will have a big impact on water sources. It was a daily reminder of climate change. See fridaysforfuture.org/what-we-do/who-we-are

230   See the article in *The Independent*, 19 April 2020, where he talks about human beings over-running the world. See www.independent.co.uk/environment/climate-change/david-attenborough-life-planet-new-documentary-bbc-climate-crisis-coronavirus-a9472946.html

231   rebellion.global

232   An amazing place in the very centre of Norwich, Norfolk which was owned and run by the Abel family. It supported hundreds of volunteers over the years providing a safe space, laughter and love.

233   This was started by Tigger and others of us at the Greenhouse and we used to meet regularly, sharing a meal and then discussing what we would do. Lots of publications, projects and actions arose out of these productive meetings.

234   www.theguardian.com/world/2019/jun/25/extinction-rebellion-first-protester-convicted-public-order-offence

235   Matthew Taylor, 'Climate Activist, 68, is Found Guilty of Public Order Offence', *The Guardian*, 26 June 2019. Also see www.theguardian.com/commentisfree/2019/jun/26/climate-activism-extinction-rebellion-protest-guilty and extinctionrebellion.uk/2019/06/25/witness-box-statement-angie-zelter-hendon-magistrates-court-25th-june-2019

236   For a chronology of XR Peace see xrpeace.org/chronology

237   xrpeace.org/xr-peace-key-message

238   xrpeace.org

239   peacenews.info/node/9515/xr-peace-forms-%E2%80%93-57-arrests-october

240   tridentploughshares.org/xr-peace-at-the-october-rebellion

241   xrpeace.org/media

242   www.countytimes.co.uk/news/17951870.knighton-campaigner-angie-zelter-arrested-extinction-rebellion-protest

243   The corporations involved include all the seed, feedstock, breeding, fertiliser- and pesticide-producing corporations, like Cargill, Charoen Pokphand, Genus, Hendrix Genetics, Nutreco, Syngenta, Yara. See *Agropoly: A Handful of Corporations Control Food Production*, EcoNexus, 2013.

244   xrpeace.org/leaflets-and-posters

245   You can see it on the website at tridentploughsharesarchive.org/from-trident-ploughshares-core-group and also find other dialogue and negotiation letters there.

246   xrpeace.org/police-liaison

247   Cutting teams are trained people who know how to cut you out of lock-on tubes, remove superglue or get activists down off their tripods. They are usually very professional and really careful to protect themselves and the activists.

248   Disability groups had been working for months within XR to ensure that the demonstrations would be accessible and inclusive. See www.disabilitynewsservice.com/anger-as-police-confiscate-extinction-rebellion-accessible-toilets-ramps-and-wheelchairs

249   Dwight D *Eisenhower* exit speech on 17 January 1961 warning of the military industrial complex.

250   Catherine Lutz (ed), *The Bases of Empire: The Global Struggle against U.S. Military Posts*, Pluto Press, 2009.

251   www.independent.co.uk/news/uk/politics/dsei-2017-london-arms-fair-weapons-saudi-arabia-excel-centre-sadiq-khan-cancel-a7853286.html

252   This is according to authors of the tenth annual Global Peace Index see www.independent.co.uk/news-19-8/global-peace-index-syria-named-worlds-most-dangerous-country-in-latest-research-on-international-10408410.html

253   Mark Curtis, *Web of Deceit: Britain's Real Role in the World*, Vintage, 2003.

254   www.caat.org.uk/campaigns/stop-arming-saudi

255   UNICEF – The United Nations International Children's Emergency Fund – www.caat.org.uk/campaigns/stop-arming-saudi/yemen

256   'Women and War' – ICRC. See www.icrc.org/en/publication/0944-women-and-war

257   popstats.unhcr.org/en/overview#_ga=1.1490737.1410439585.1452783218

258   www.dsei.co.uk/visiting/exhibitor-list#/

259   tridentploughshares.org/well-stop-worlds-biggest-arms-fair/

260   www.theguardian.com/business/2011/feb/18/envoy-saudi-bae-systems

261   www.telegraph.co.uk/news/uknews/defence/4268661/Trident-nuclear-deterrent-completely-useless-say-retired-military-officers.html

262   Human Rights & Democracy – The 2016 Foreign & Commonwealth Office Report. Presented to Parliament by the Secretary of State for Foreign and Commonwealth Affairs by Command of Her Majesty, July 2017.

263   www.transparency.org.uk/our-work/defence-security-corruption/#.We9NpZ_txN

264   Andrew Feinstein, *The Shadow World: Inside the Global Arms Trade*, Hamish Hamilton, 2011.

265   www.sipri.org/publications/2016/other-publications/special-treatment-uk-government-support-arms-industry-and-trade

266   www.gov.uk/government/news/arms-trade-treaty-enters-into-force & treaties.un.org/pages/ViewDetails.aspx?src=TREATY&mtdsg_no=XXVI-8&chapter=26&clang=_en (States parties: 92; Ratifications: 89; Accessions: 3; Signatories: 130).

267   www.theguardian.com/world/2017/oct/25/michael-fallon-urges-mps-prioritise-arms-sales-human-rights & www.independent.co.uk/news/uk/politics/michael-fallon-saudi-arabia-defece-secretary-tory-arms-deals-conservative-parliament-criticism-a8019641.html

268   Estonia sang its way out of the rule under the Soviet Union. In 1988, more than 100,000 Estonians gathered for five nights to protest Soviet rule. This was known as the Singing Revolution.

269   As of 10 March 2004 out of a total of 655 civilians killed, 392 were killed by suicide bombers. The total number of Israelis killed from 29 September 2000 to 10 March 2004 is 931 (276 security forces and 655 civilians). For statistics on killed and wounded on both sides of this conflict you can search the Israeli Defence Forces website and also the website of the Palestinian Red Crescent Society. Up to 10 March 2004 they are as follows – number of Israelis killed is 931 and number of Palestinians killed is 2,739; number of Israelis wounded is 6,237 and number of Palestinians wounded is 25,107.

270   Bags are searched at the entrances to certain shops and malls, theatres and cinemas.

271   Most villages are now unable to sell the bulk of their oil due to the closures and restrictions on transport and business.

272   I have changed the names of all my friends – on both sides of the conflict – to respect and protect them.

273   Salfit is known by Palestinians as the green gold area – it is the centre of Palestinian olive oil production. It is also the area known by the Israelis as Samaria. A recent brochure produced by Ariel Settlement describes the area as being in the centre of Israel, the capital of Samaria, and the map on the brochure shows an Israel from the Mediterranean Sea right to the Jordan Valley without any indication of the West Bank and Gaza and the contents do not mention the Palestinian villages or that the settlement was built on the land of these villages that can be seen from the

settlement. The pictures show a swimming pool and gardens, well-resourced schools and clinics and a university with quick and easy access into Tel Aviv and Jerusalem. A stark contrast to the lives of the Palestinian villagers all around which are not mentioned – it is as if the Palestinians have 'disappeared' and do not exist – in this publication at least. The original Hebrew brochure and an alternative one being produced at the moment by the villagers will soon be up on our website at www. womenspeacepalestine.org

274   According to IDF statistics two Israeli citizens have been killed through rock throwing, and 62 from shootings at an ambush.

275   All the settlements in the West Bank and Gaza are illegal under international law. The fourth Geneva Convention [Article 49 (6)] expressly prohibits an Occupying Power from deporting or transferring parts of its own population into the territory it occupies. In addition, Israeli settlements violate United Nations Security Council Resolutions, including UNSCR 452 (1979) calling upon 'the Government and people of Israel to cease, on an urgent basis, the establishment, construction and planning of settlements in the Arab territories occupied since 1967, including Jerusalem'. According to references quoted in Passia 2004 there are between 145 and 250 non-military settlements in the West Bank (figures differ because of different definitions and the varying number of the illegal settlements) plus 108 outposts in the West Bank. Jewish settlers comprise around 8 per cent of the total Israeli-Jewish population and around 10 per cent of the total West Bank population.

276   The occupation of the West Bank began in June 1967, since when over 50 per cent of the total land area is effectively under the control of settlements. B'Tselem, *Land Grab Report*, May 2002.

277   The Israelis control all movement in and out of the territories and there is no reliable and safe postal service in rural areas.

278   See IWPS Incident Report No 84 – Soldiers in Marda, 2 March 2004. Amnesty International has estimated that around 3,000 houses have been destroyed by the Israeli army during the current intifada. A further 600 plus houses have been demolished for lack of building licenses.

279   IWPS Incident Report No 59 – Two shot in Qarawat Bani Zeid, 16 October 2003; IWPS Incident Report No 45 – One boy aged 11 years old killed in Qarawat Bani Zeid, 26 May 2003; IWPS Incident Report No 44 – Two People Killed in Qarawat Bani Zeid, one injured, 21 May 2003; IWPS Incident Report No 40 – Killing and injuring of students in schoolyard, 24 April 2003; Qarawat Bani Zeid village under attack.

280   Israel has the fourth largest army in the world and most of the soldiers are in the occupied territories, a tiny area in global terms.

281   IWPS Incident Report No 89 – Soldiers open fire on schoolboys wounding two, 9 March 2004.

282   Biddu, Beit Souriq, Qattana, Al Qubeiba, Beit Anan, Beit Lekiya, Beit Duqqu and Beit Ijza villages are situated very close to each other, north of Jerusalem. Altogether, they stand to lose 51,650 dunums of land. They will also be enclosed in their own

enclave, or prison, locked in on all sides by the 'settler's only' Apartheid Road 443 and totally disconnected from Jerusalem. The villages have been constantly losing land for the past three years, due to settlement expansion. They will also lose all eight water wells which will fall on the other side of the wall. The villages have been demonstrating with support from Israeli and international activists since 19 February 2004 when the bulldozers first arrived. Three villagers from Beit Duqqu and Beit Ijza were shot dead by Israeli army snipers on 25 February and a 70-year-old villager died from a heart attack after being heavily gassed – the first people to be killed for resisting the Apartheid Wall. A child was seriously wounded by a rubber coated bullet in his chest on the same day. At some of the demonstrations, the people have been able to stop the bulldozers totally, even capturing one in Beit Duqqu for a few hours on 8 March 2004. The residents also filed a petition to the Israeli High Court to stop the Wall and bulldozing was stopped for several days in all but one section of Beit Duqqu which lies in the Ramallah area. Israelis from settlements close by also signed the petition, fearing the barrier will only serve to incite violence from what they describe as their peaceful neighbours.

283   IWPS Incident Report No 90 – Soldiers open fire on village, wounding one man and damaging much property, 9 March 2004.

284   The risks referred to here are: to be caught in areas that settlers consider to be theirs and thus to risk being beaten, tear-gassed or shot, to be caught by soldiers who may take your ID and put you on a security list and thus you may be harassed again in the future, or to be delayed at a checkpoint so long that you are unable to get home before dark when it is then so unsafe to travel that you will not be able to find transport, or to be caught in a lock-down or curfew and again maybe stranded for days before being able to get home.

285   The books had to be air-freighted into Israel to a safe Israeli contact who then kindly brought them in by Israeli number-plated car on the settler road. We then carried the boxes of books up the hill through the olive trees to the house from which we will distribute the books. There are many Jewish Israelis who are part of the peace movement who support Palestinians in ways such as these. They are honoured and respected by the Palestinians who know and care for them.

286   See IWPS Incident Report No 91 – A private unit of soldiers kill one man and injure four, 8 March 2004.

287   See IWPS Incident Report No 87 – Woman on the way to see the doctor detained by soldiers at Huwara, 10 March 2004.

288   IWPS Report No 32 – One month of 24 hour nonviolent resistance to Apartheid Wall, 2 May 2003; IWPS Report No 43 – Palestinian Women Organise against the Apartheid Wall; IWPS Report No 45 – The Rise of the Wall.

289   Daniel Mitchell et al., 'Attributing human mortality during extreme heat waves to anthropogenic climate change' July 2016, iopscience.iop.org/article/10.1088/1748-9326/11/7/074006

290   'Rise in flood risk could make one million homes uninsurable', *The Independent*, 9 January 2011, www.independent.co.uk/environment/climate-change/rise-in-flood-

risk-could-make-one-million-homes-uninsurable-2179746.html

291   'UK air pollution "linked to 40,000 early deaths a year"', BBC, 23 February 2016, www.bbc.co.uk/news/health-35629034

292   'Climate change impacts already locked in, but the worst can still be avoided', November 2017, University of Exeter, www.sciencedaily.com/releases/2017/11/171116105020.htm

293   *Targets and Indicators of Climatic Change*, report co-ordinated by the Stockholm Environment Institute (SEI), 1990: mediamanager.sei.org/documents/Publications/SEI-Report-TargetsAndIndicatorsOfClimaticChange-1990.pdf

294   'What is "Hothouse Earth", and how bad would such a climate catastrophe be?', *The Independent*, 7 August 2018 https://www.independent.co.uk/environment/hothouse-earth-climate-change-global-warming-greenhouse-gas-sea-level-arctic-ice-a8481086.html

295   *Blueprint for a Green Economy*, Submission to the Shadow Cabinet, Chair John Gummer, September 2007, p. 375:conservativehome.blogs.com/torydiary/files/blueprint_for_a_green_economy110907b.pdf

296   Environmental Audit Committee, July 2007 report, *Beyond Stern: From the Climate Change Programme Review to the Draft Climate Change Bill*, Seventh Report of Session 2006–07, pp. 31, 65: publications.parliament.uk/pa/cm200607/cmselect/cmenvaud/460/46002.htm

297   'UN Chief Challenges World to Agree Tougher Targets on Climate Change', *The Guardian*, 1 June 2011,www.theguardian.com/environment/2011/jun/01/climate-change-target-christiana-figueres

298   Lord Stern, 'I got it wrong on climate change – it's far, far worse', *The Guardian*, 26 January 2013,www.theguardian.com/environment/2013/jan/27/nicholas-stern-climate-change-davos

299   Report of the Structured Expert Dialogue (2015), p. 18: unfccc.int/resource/docs/2015/sb/eng/inf01.pdf

300   Paris Agreement on Climate Change, 2015: web.archive.org/web/20171202230958/http://unfccc.int/resource/docs/2015/cop21/eng/l09r01.pdf

301   Hans Joachim Schellnhuber et al., *Trajectories of the Earth System in the Anthropocene*, August 2018, www.pnas.org/content/115/33/8252

302   IPCC, AR5, Synthesis Report 2014, www.ipcc.ch/site/assets/uploads/2018/02/SYR_AR5_FINAL_full.pdf

303   UNEP, Emissions Gap Report, 2016, wedocs.unep.org/bitstream/handle/20.500.11822/10016/emission_gap_report_2016.pdf?sequence=1&isAllowed=y

304   UK Government Clean Growth Strategy, 2017, assets.publishing.service.gov.uk/government/uploads/system/uploads/attachment_data/file/700496/clean-growth-strategy-correction-april-2018.pdf

305   'Three Years to Safeguard Our Climate', *Nature*, June 2017,
www.nature.com/news/three-years-to-safeguard-our-climate-1.22201

306   www.parliament.uk/business/publications/written-questions-answers-statements/
written-question/Commons/2018-03-27/904604/

307   IPCC, SR1.5, www.ipcc.ch/site/assets/uploads/sites/2/2018/07/SR15_SPM_version_
stand_alone_LR.pdf

308   'Final call to save the world from "climate catastrophe"', BBC, 8 October 2018,
www.bbc.co.uk/news/science-environment-45775309

309   planb.earth/wp-content/uploads/2019/02/Skeleton-Plan-B-Trial-FINAL.pdf

310   'UK Has Biggest Fossil Fuel Subsidies in the EU, Finds Commission', *The Guardian*,
23 January 2019, www.theguardian.com/environment/2019/jan/23/uk-has-biggest-
fossil-fuel-subsidies-in-the-eu-finds-commission

311   'Top Climate Scientist Blasts UK's Fracking Plans as "Aping Trump"', *The Guardian*,
13 October 2018, www.theguardian.com/environment/2018/oct/13/top-climate-
scientist-james-hansen-attacks-uk-fracking-plans

312   'Sir David Attenborough Tells UN Climate Change Summit "Collapse of Civilisation
is on the Horizon"', *Evening Standard*, 3 December 2018,
www.standard.co.uk/news/world/david-attenborough-says-collapse-of-civilisation-
is-on-the-horizon-a4006976.html

313   www.express.co.uk/news/uk/1117913/extinction-rebellion-news-latest-london-
protests-climate-change-mps-succumb-demands

314   www.dailymail.co.uk/news/article-6967851/Jeremy-Corbyn-forces-Mps-vote-
declaring-climate-emergency-Extinction-Rebellion-protests.html

315   www.bbc.co.uk/news/uk-wales-politics-48093720

316   'UK Parliament declares climate change emergency', BBC, 1 May 2019,
www.bbc.co.uk/news/uk-politics-48126677

317   'Women and War' – ICRC. See www.icrc.org/en/publication/0944-women-and-war

318   This is according to authors of the 10th annual Global Peace Index see
www.independent.co.uk/news-19-8/global-peace-index-syria-named-worlds-most-
dangerous-country-in-latest-research-on-international-10408410.html

319   Mark Curtis, *Web of Deceit: Britain's Real Role in the World*, Vintage 2003.

320   www.caat.org.uk/campaigns/stop-arming-saudi

321   Angie Zelter (ed), *Faslane 365: A Year of Anti-nuclear Blockades*, Luath Press 2008.
Blockades took place from October 2006 to October 2007 with over 1,200 arrests
taking place.

322   iwps.info/

323   Hares and then Deir Istiya in the Governate of Salfit, which the Israelis refer to as
Judea and Samaria.

Acknowledgements

A very big 'thank you' to all the following people:

Gavin MacDougall of Luath Press, who has been generous and supportive throughout.

Stig, who has contributed many banners and graphics for several of the campaigns discussed in this book and kindly designed the book cover.

Val Stein and Rob Green for their editing advice and help as well as Carrie Hutchison at Luath Press who was a great help in the final stages.

Liz McGowan for all the banners she made or helped us make for ourselves over many decades.

Zoe Broughton, amazing film-maker and activist, who so generously recorded many of the actions described in this book.

The brilliant lawyers who have helped with advice and support through numerous trials – Connor Gearty, Gareth Pierce, Mike Schwartz, Nick Grief, Robbie Manson and many, many others.

Jane Tallents and David Mackenzie, who have been colleagues and friends over so many years.

The thousands of fellow activists who joined and supported the campaigns. They are too numerous to mention by name, but nonetheless appreciated so much.

Special thanks to Charlie Beresford who has helped keep my computer updated and in working condition as well as taking the picture of me used on the back cover.

Thanks to Kate Holcombe, an amazing campaigner with great techie skills, who designed and kept updated many of the websites used in various campaigns over long years and to Mark Leach who continues this essential work.

The many activists in Norfolk who took part in the first actions and campaigns and especially all those at The Greenhouse in Norwich where so many of us were based in those first heady days of the Snowball Campaign and Trident Ploughshares.

Thanks and solidarity to all those who have continued to work and campaign over long decades concentrating on their particular subject while acknowledging the many other issues that face us. Their in-depth work enabled me to join with them for shorter periods of time to act in solidarity and on the back of all their work.

Love and gratefulness to my family who accepted and supported me in my campaigning, especially my thoughtful daughter Zina, a determined and hard-working campaigner in her own right, who encourages me to practise the personal changes I advocate when I seem to be slipping!

And last but not least, Camilla, my partner, who has put up with the stresses and strains of dealing with me when I was totally focused on a current campaign or when I was burnt out. She says I was awful to live with during those times! She has helped me immensely – a constant companion.